Junkers Airplanes of W

Volume 2: J.5–J.11

A Centennial Perspective on Great War Airplanes

Colin A. Owers

Great War Aviation Centennial Series #31

This book is dedicated to Colin Huston whose friendship and dedication to the recording of WWI aviation history helped me, and many others, over many years, to reach a better outcome than we would have otherwise achieved.

Acknowledgements
This work would be much poorer were it not for the generous help provided over many years from friends, old and new, some sadly no longer with us. Any errors are mine alone.

Thanks to Gregory Alegi; Richard Alexander, Lennart Andersson; Garry Barling; Klas Bask; Carl Bobrow, Amy Brennan; the late Jack Bruce; Moshe Bu, Jean-Luc Claessens; Christophe Cony; Matt Dravitzki; Juanita Franzi; Roberto Gentilli; the late Peter M Grosz; Jack and Nicol Herris; Colin and Barbara Huston; Sir Peter Jackson; Roland Jahne; Stuart Leslie; Piotr Mrozowski; David Ostrowsky; Gennady Petrov; Charles Schaedel; Bruno Schmäling; the late Ian Stair; Gennady Sloutskiy; Chuck Thomas, William Bill Toohey; John Weatherseed, The Vintage Aviation Team; Aaron Weaver; Greg VanWyngarden; Reinhard Zankl; the staff of the RAF Museum; the British and US National Archives; the Deutsches Technikmuseum, Berlin; the Technikmuseum "Hugo Junkers", Dessau; and the Aviation Heritage Trust (AHT). Especial thanks to my wife, Julie, who accompanied me to the various archives and copied many of the documents used to develop this history. The colour scheme drawings by Piotr Mrozowski are based on his research.

Cover painting by Steve Anderson. Please see Steve's website at: **www.anderson-art.com**

Color aircraft profiles © Juanita Franzi. Scale drawings by Marty Digmayer.

For our aviation books in print and electronic format, please see our website at: **www.aeronautbooks.com**. You may contact the publisher at **jherris@me.com**.

ISBN: 978-1-935881-66-7

Design and layout: Jack Herris
Cover design: Aaron Weaver
Cover painting: Steve Anderson
Color profiles: Juanita Franzi
Scale drawings: Marty Digmayer
Digital photo editing: Aaron Weaver & Jack Herris

Aeronaut Books

Books for Enthusiasts by Enthusiasts
www.aeronautbooks.com

Table of Contents

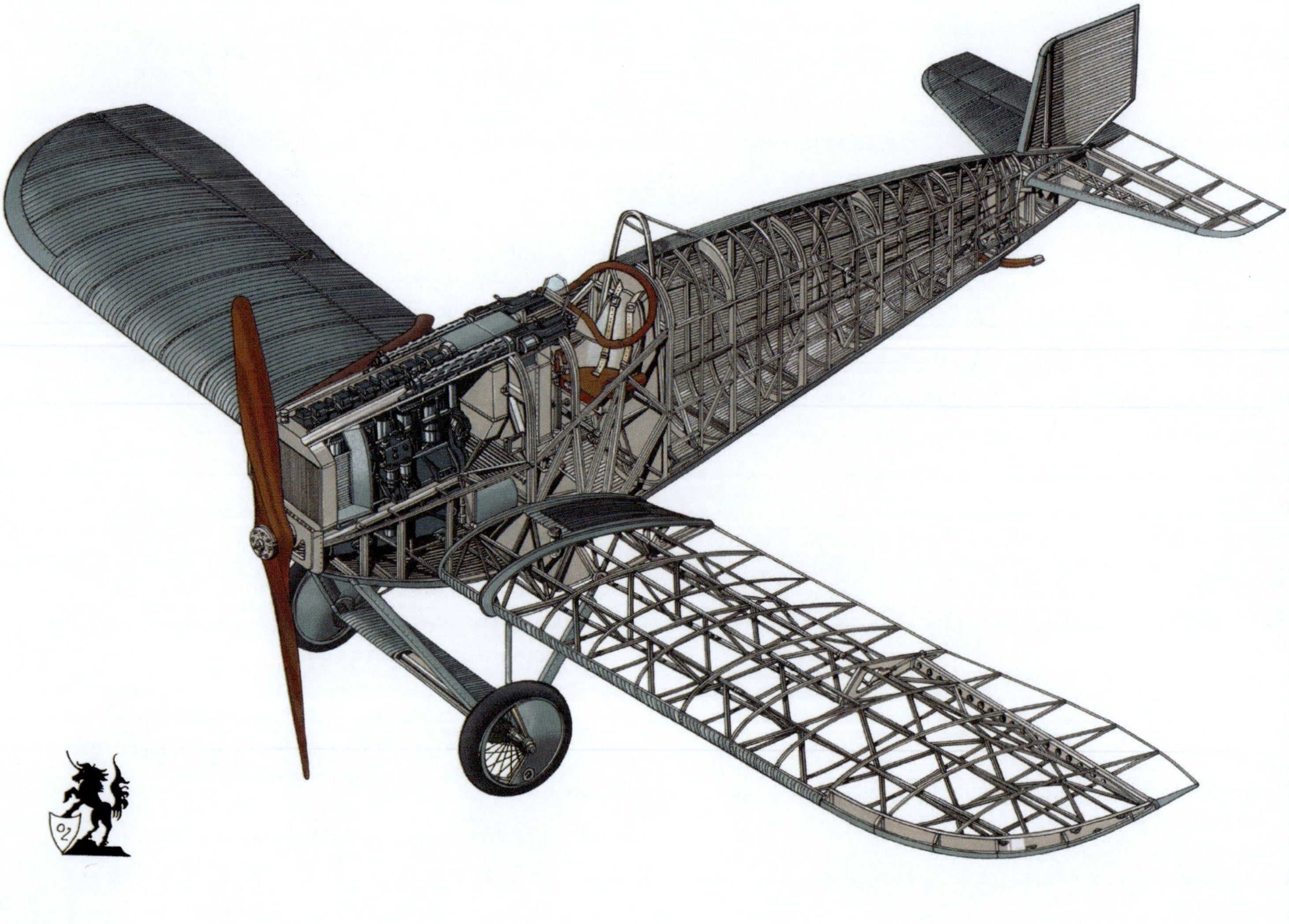

6. Junkers Fighter Projects J 5 and J 6

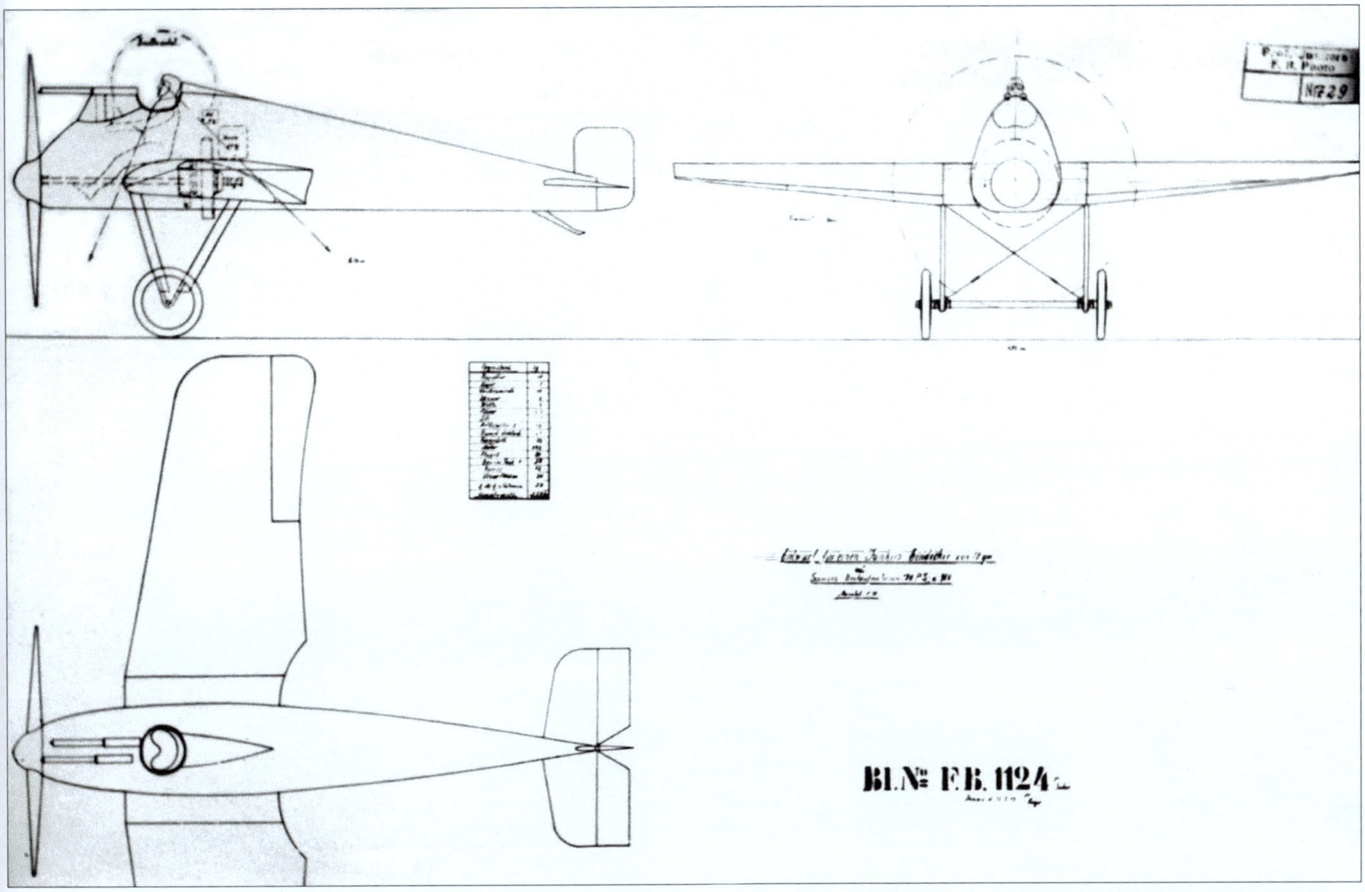

The J 5

As noted above the forced marriage between Junkers and Fokker led to the formation of a new company, *Junker-Fokker Werke AG* (*Jfa*). It was hoped that Fokker's experience in mass production would counter balance Junkers tendency to experiment and for his lack of experience in mass production. The two were of temperaments that differed so much that there was little likelihood that they would cooperate. Fokker left the association with knowledge of the thick wing while Junkers seems to have utilised the financial input of Fokker to his advantage.[2] Fokker was able to test fly the new Junkers aircraft and would have been able to contribute his skilled test pilot experience towards the progress of Junkers aircraft. However, his interference in the day to day running of the company was resented by the other directors.

While the military authorities were interested in the armoured J 4, Professor Junkers continued independently working towards his ideal of a monoplane constructed entirely of metal. Three generic J 5 projects of January to March 1917, were for a low wing fighter monoplane with two fixed synchronised machine guns with an endurance of 1½ hours. Structurally the aircraft followed the unfinished J 3 with a load-bearing internal framework, with the low wing centre section built integral with the fuselage. The wing tapered in chord and thickness towards the tips. The aircraft was to have a corrugated Dural skin. The machine had an unusually high undercarriage. The machine was to be powered by a rotary engine. The use of a rotary was proposed in order to give less weight per horse-power, an important consideration given the weight of all metal construction. The other remarkable idea other than all-metal construction was that the proposed rotary engine was to be mounted totally enclosed within the fuselage. While the use of a rotary engine removed the weight of the radiator and coolant, cooling of the engine buried within the fuselage would have been a problem.

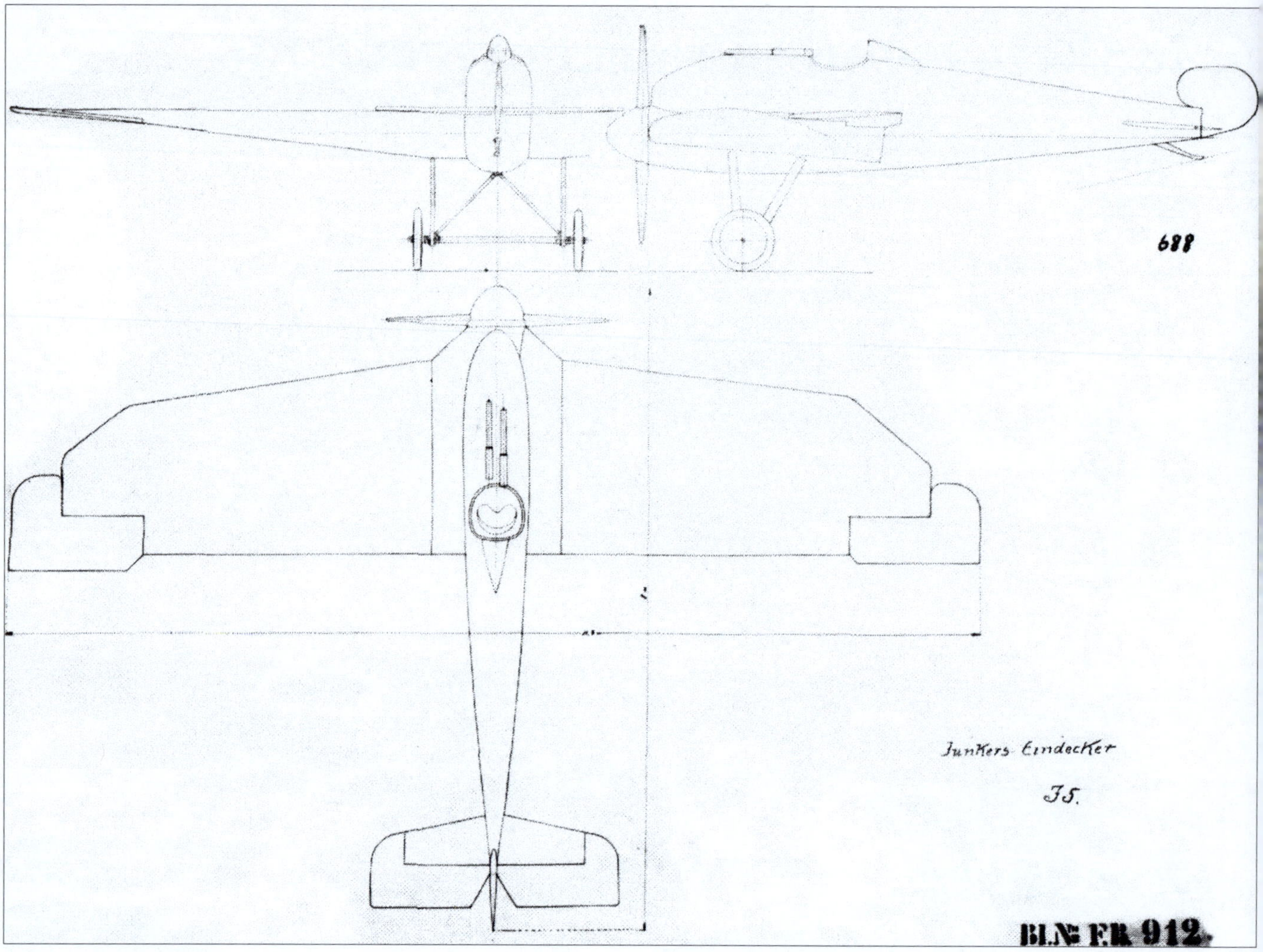

The J 5 Project I had the pilot seated high up in front of the engine, either a 120-hp Siemens and Halske Sh II nine cylinder or 110-hp Oberursel UR.II rotary engine with an extension shaft to the airscrew passing between the pilot's legs.[3]

J 5 Project II spanned only 8.60 m and weighed 100 kg less when empty than the earlier version of the J 5. The positioning of the totally enclosed engine in front of and below the pilot and on the Centre of Gravity was hoped to improve manoeuvrability, a criticism of the earlier Junkers aircraft. The same two engines were the proposed powerplants. A large spinner was fitted to the slab-sided fuselage and no provision for cooling was evident on the drawings. The wing contours were simplified to straight lines to make production easier. All control surfaces were aerodynamically balanced. Armament was to be the usual two forward firing synchronised machine guns for the pilot who had a good field of vision from his elevated perch but would have almost certainly been killed in the event of a roll over.

A third version of 22 May 1917, envisaged the use of a 169-hp water-cooled Mercedes D.IIIa inline engine, mounted behind the pilot with an extension shaft passing under the pilot. No further data is available on this project.

The J 6

The J 6 was another late 1917 project. This time the monoplane was of parasol configuration with a droppable fuel tank below the fuselage. The engine was again a rotary, this time the more powerful 160-hp Siemens and Halske Sh. The span was shown as 8 m, with a length of 5.600 m, on one three-view drawing.

Although the J 6 was never built the wing design was utilised on the final form of the J 9 (D.I). The J 6 in its various forms remained a viable proposition until the war's end. *Idflieg* reported in July 1918 that a 195-hp Benz Bz.IIIb V-eight powered parasol fighter was under construction.[4] This machine was probably the J 12 parasol fighter.[5] Pilots who saw the machine were said to be enthusiastic about it. *Ltn* Gotthard Sachsenberg asked Junkers in August when this

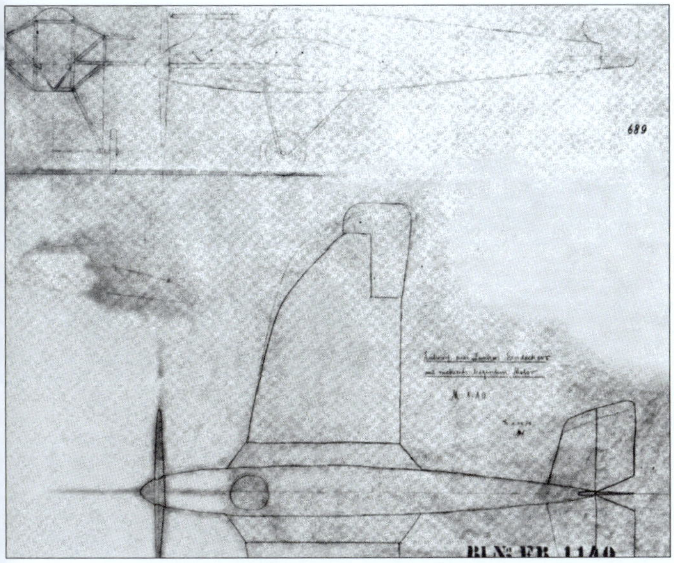

machine would be ready. When *Idflieg* refused to give Junkers an order, work on the J 6 was halted as Junkers could not afford to risk building it without an order. Apparently, the prototype was nearly 50% complete in November 1918, but the end of the war saw no future for the aircraft and it was scrapped.[6] Junkers returned to the parasol fighter post-war when he built the K.16 for the Soviet air force.

Specifications Proposed J 5 Fighter		
Model	**Project 1 I03.01.1917**	**Project II II13.01.1917**
Dimensions in m		
Span	11.80	8.60
Length	8.00	6.75
Height	2.80	2.70
Wing Area, m²	20.00	12.00
Weights, kg		
Empty	465	355
Fuel	58	58
Oil	10	10
Pilot	80	80
Payload	47	47
Load	195	195
Loaded	660	550
Endurance, hrs	1.5	1.5
Climb to		
Source: Wagner, W. *Hugo Junkers. Pionier der Luftfahrt – seine Flugzeuge*, Bernhard & Graefe, Germany, 1996. P.98.		

Specifications Junkers Parasol Monoplane	
Dimensions in m	
Span	8.000
Length	5.600
Span tailplane	2.400
Wing Area, m²	12
Weight Empty	420 kg
Engine	Sh.III
Source: Junkers drawing of Parasol monoplane.	

Endnotes Chapter 6

1. Leaman, P. *Op Cit*, notes that the J.5 was a proposed R-plane – a multi-engine bomber.
2. In his autobiography Fokker stated that he had lost his investment in the company when Junkers regained control after the war.
3. For the story of these most interesting engines see Bennett, R.L. "The Siemens-Halske Counter-Rotary Engines", *Over the Front*, Vol.30, No.3, 2015.
4. According to Wagner, W. *Ltn* Gotthard Sachsenberg wrote in August 1918 asking Junkers when the machine would be ready.
5. The proposed Junkers parasol fighter's story is confusing. Wagner describes it as having a Siemens Sh.III, that is the J 6, whereas Grosz does not mention a J 12, thinking that the Benz powered parasol was a continuation of the J 6. Wagner notes that parasol appears first in a document dated 8 August 1918, and is designated J 12 in letters thereafter. Wagner refers to an *Idflieg* report of September where in the cantilevered monoplane with high position wing and Bz.IIIb engine is mentioned. Wagner states that *Idflieg* was interested in the parasol but considered that a rotary engine was necessary for manoeuvrability. At this period of the war castor oil was in short supply and this may be why the Benz was chosen. From the comments of pilot's who visited the Junkers' works, the half-completed parasol was to be powered by an inline engine. To further confuse the issue, the designation J 12 was used post-Armistice for a further development of the J 10 that led to the F 13.
6. "The Junkers Aircraft Type Pages: Part 1: Junkers Aircraft of WWI (1915-1918). http://ourworld.compuserve.com.\/homepages/hzoe/ju_airc2.htm.

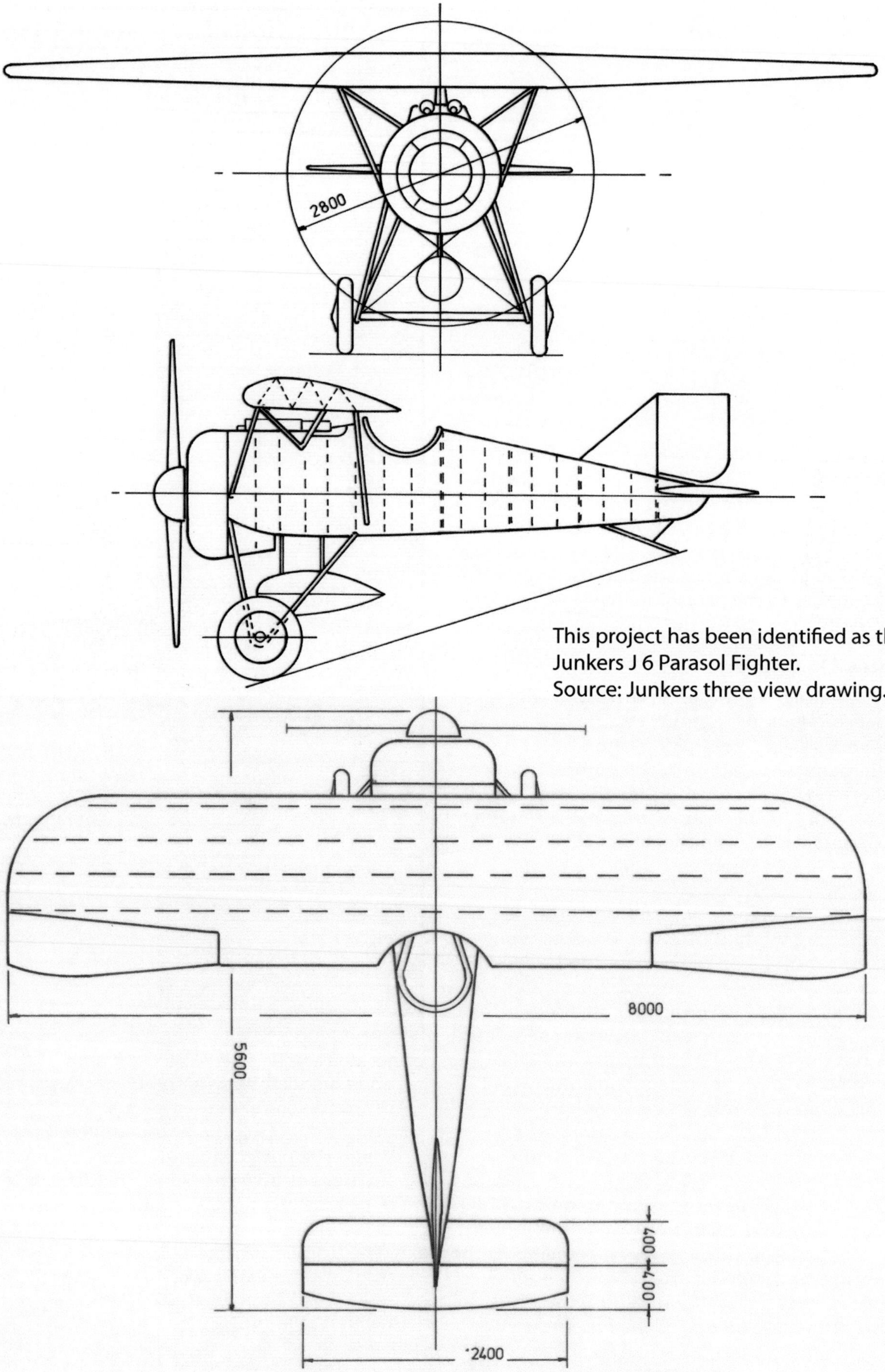

This project has been identified as the Junkers J 6 Parasol Fighter.
Source: Junkers three view drawing.

7. Junkers J 7 – The Way to the First All-Metal Fighter

Above: The engine frame for the 160-hp Mercedes D.III and cockpit section of the J 7 monoplane. The pilot's seat is made from corrugated material with a leather covering.

Idflieg ordered three experimental all-metal monoplanes from Junkers in December 1916.[1] The J 7 was a low-wing monoplane with corrugated metal covering. Junkers had discovered that the low position of the wing below the engine generated additional lift and the wing would absorb the forces in the event of a crash protecting the pilot. Junkers gained a patent for the fuselage to wing juncture in March 1918. It has to be appreciated that the low wing monoplane format was not favoured in military circles. It was considered that this layout limited the downward vision that was considered essential for the fighting tactics then in use. Combat pilots favouring the dive from altitude – hit and run tactics. Future developments were to justify Junkers, but at the time prejudice had to be overcome.

The J 7 was designed by *Dipl Ing* Reuter to Junkers' requirements. When first flown in September 1917 by Junkers test pilot *Fwbl* Arved Schmidt the J 7 had swivelling wingtips rather than ailerons. The entire tip of each wing was hinged on a torque tube. According to some reports these proved vicious and were prone to flutter and were soon replaced by conventional ailerons. In his report Schmidt noted that they were somewhat overbalanced. The engine was completely enclosed but the sleek looking monoplane's lines were spoiled by the box radiator suspended on top of the engine cowling blocking the pilot's forward vision.[2] Junkers' engineers had already designed an automobile type radiator and this was later installed in front of the engine. Powered by a 160-hp Mercedes D.III engine, the performance of the J 7 was promising with a speed of 124 km/h while climbing. The J 7 matched that of the Fokker V.11 (later D.VII). The machine was given a new wing with conventional ailerons of large chord but short span to overcome the flutter problems. They were replaced by ailerons with horn balances but these also proved prone to flutter. They were finally replaced with ailerons that conformed to the wing outline and these proved satisfactory.

Ltns Gotthard Sachsenberg and Theo Osterkamp of the German Naval air service flew the J 7. "On the 22nd "October, wrote Sachsenberg, "I had the opportunity to fly the new Junkers single-seater aircraft." The weather was fine with a wind force about 5 m/sec. Temperature + 1°. Load 60 litres of fuel.

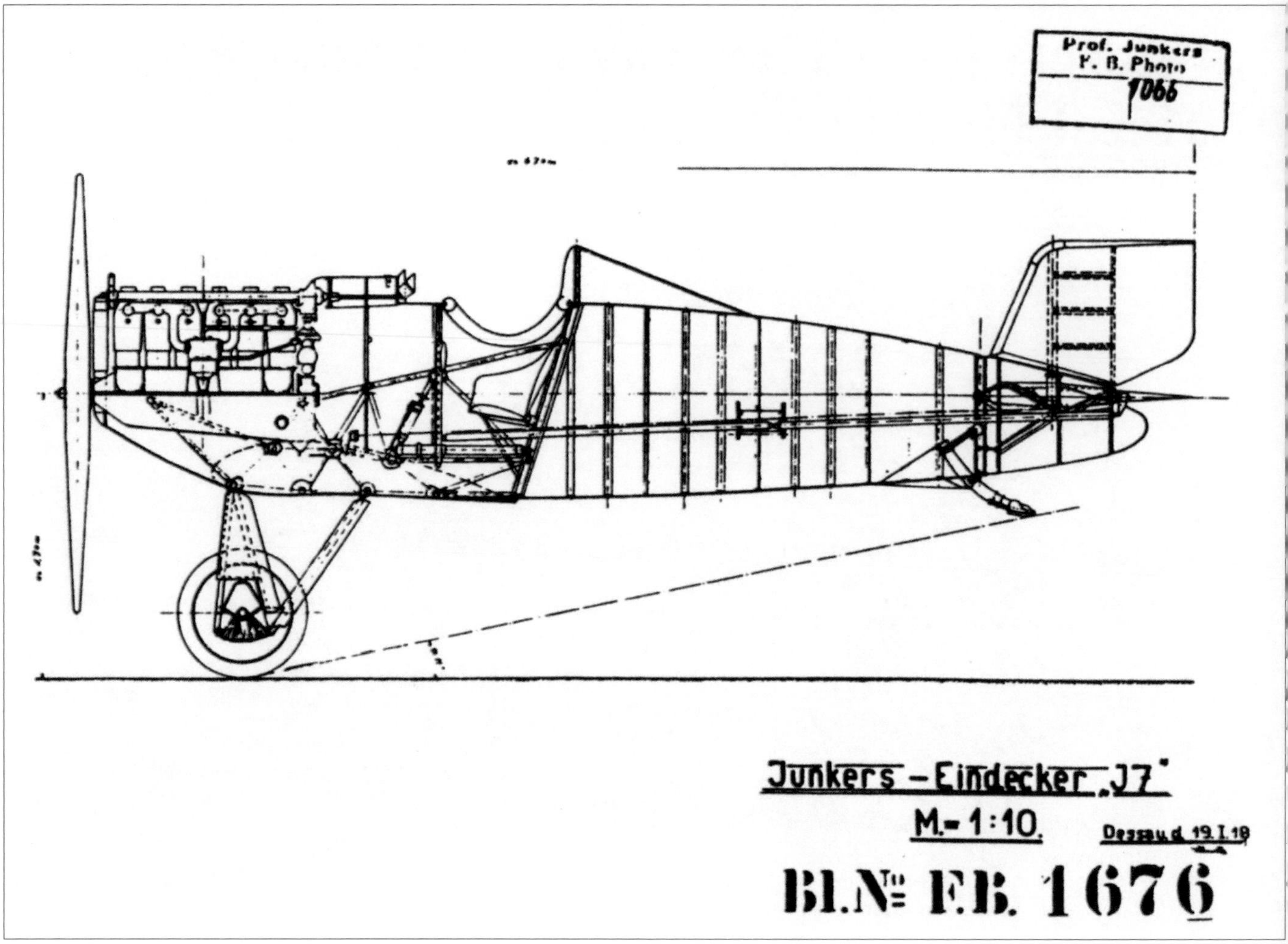
Prof. Junkers
F. B. Photo
1066
Junkers - Eindecker „J7"
M.= 1:10.
Dessau d. 19.I.19
Bl.№ F.B. 1676

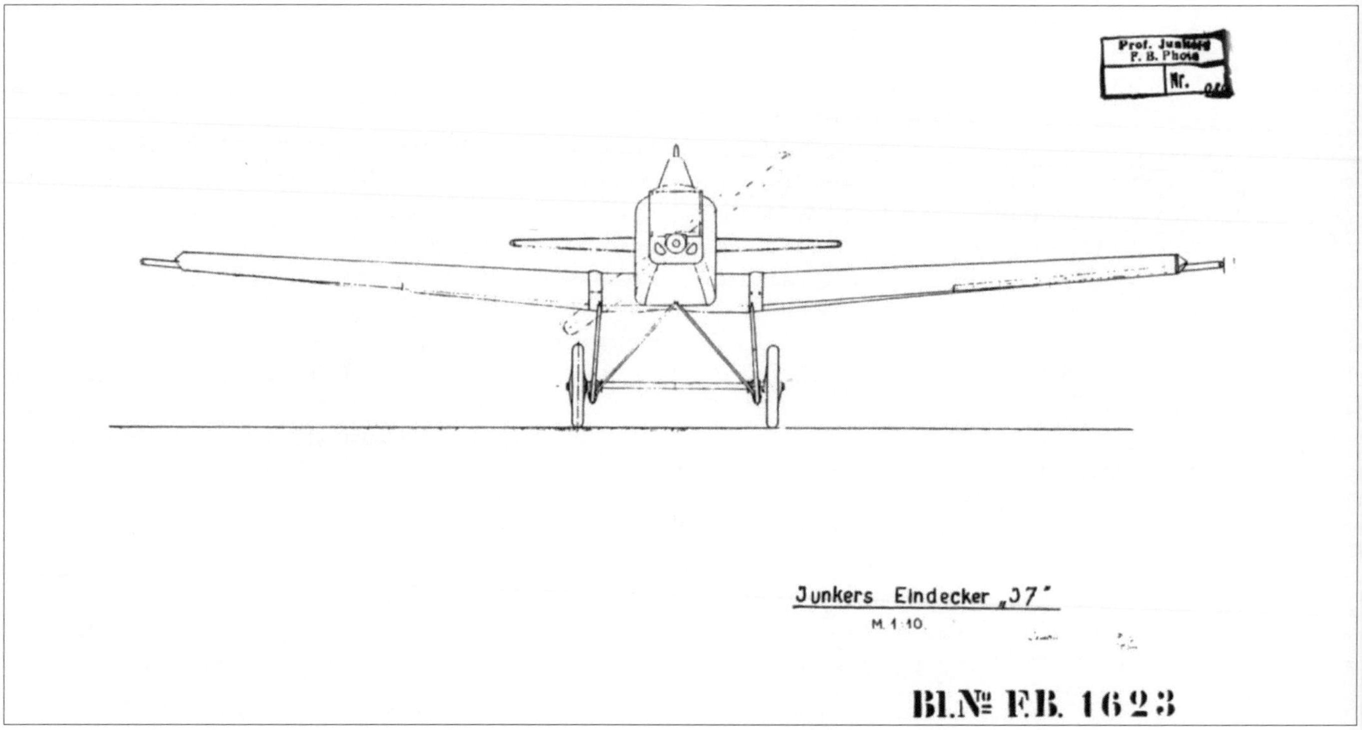
Prof. Junkers
F. B. Photo
Nr.
Junkers Eindecker „J7"
M. 1:10.
Bl.№ F.B. 1623

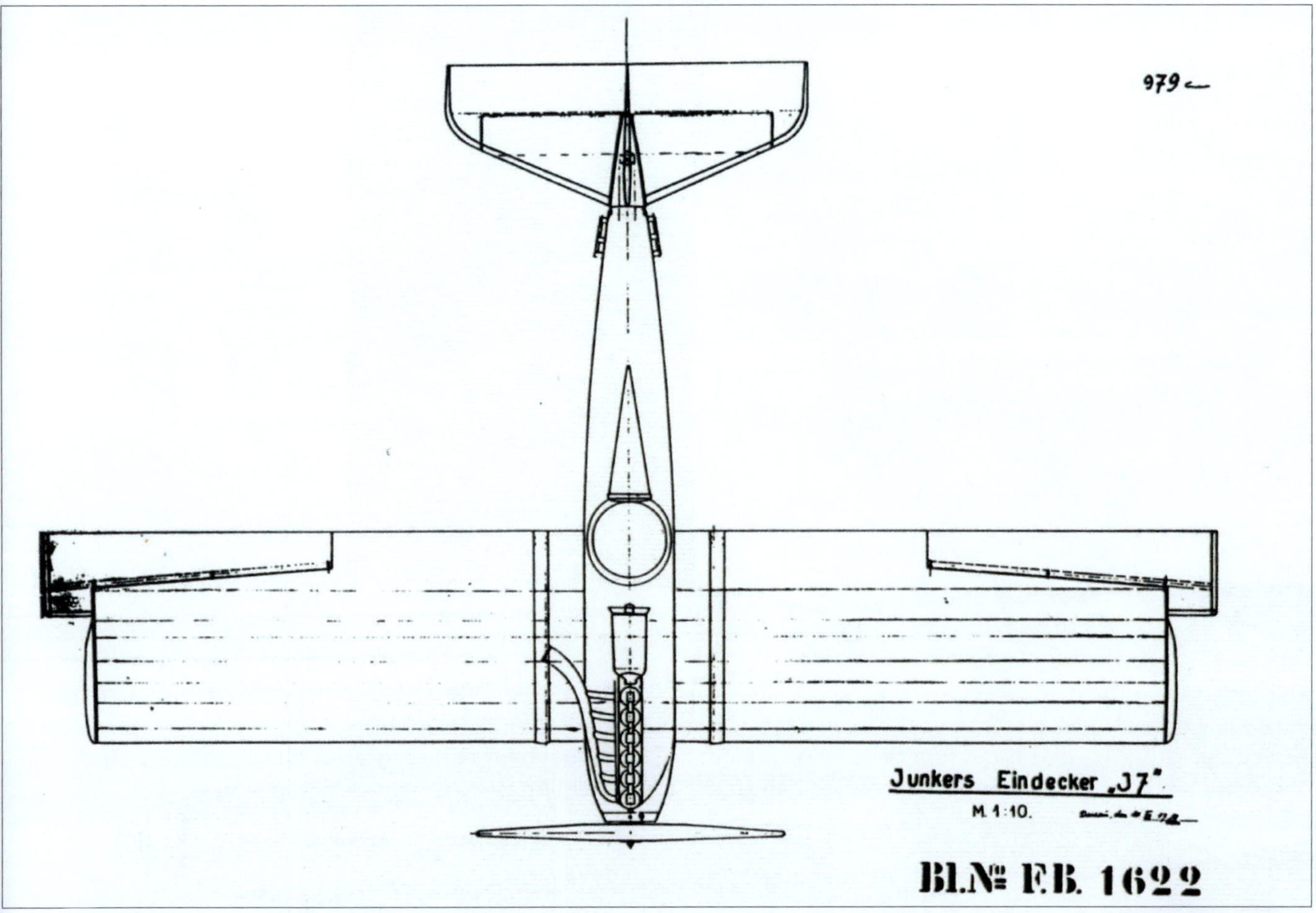
979
Junkers Eindecker „J7"
M. 1:10.
Bl.№ F.B. 1622

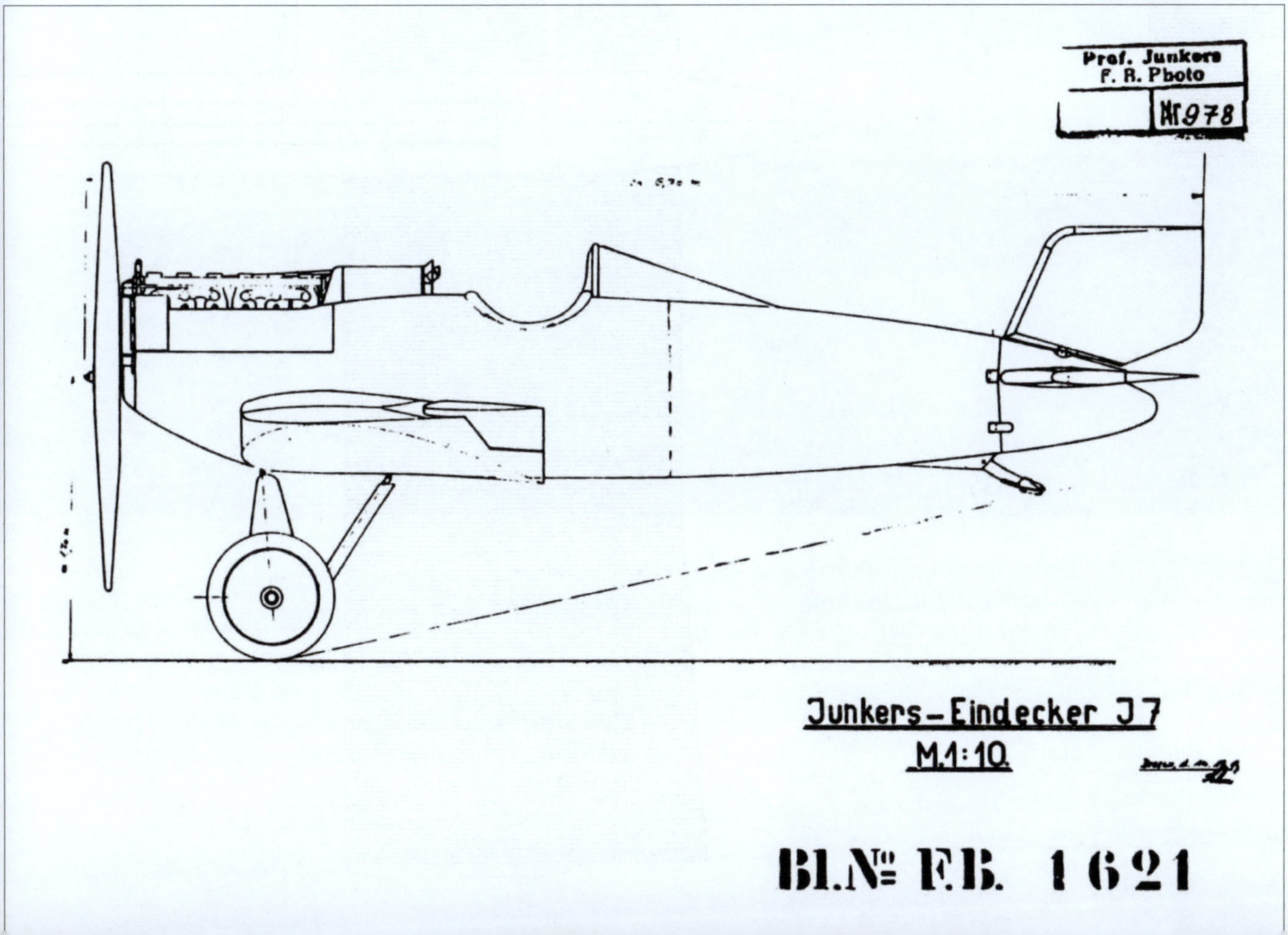
Prof. Junkers
F. R. Photo
Nr 978
Junkers-Eindecker J 7
M.1:10.
Bl.№ F.B. 1621

Above & Below: The original form of the J 7 with swivelling wing tip ailerons. The radiator is temporarily mounted on the engine cover. Note the stencil on the front edges of the wings and to the wheel covers. Junkers' photograph dated 12 October 1917. This date is thought to be incorrect and 13 September has been suggested, that recorded on the photograph of the machine outside the canvas hangar at Halle airfield.

The take-off run was unusually short. The machine displayed an excellent climbing performance, and an Albatros D.III, that had started without a MG and carrying only 60 l Benzin (flown by Ltn d.Res Osterkamp), accompanied me for a comparison flight. Accurate climbing performance could not be ascertained.

It is estimated that the speed of the Albatros D.III is 25 km/hr less than the J 7. The aircraft was stable in a power turn, however the machine is not yet manoeuvrable enough, which was chiefly due to the only moderately modified ailerons. The machine lands easily and has very short run. The visibility from the machine was excellent. It appears

Above & Below: The J 7 after fitting with conventional ailerons after the September trials. Junkers' photograph dated 12 October 1917. This date appears correct for the machine at this stage.

almost inviolable, especially when the conversion of the Bezin tank from the seat into the wing area is carried out. The machine promises to be an excellent Jagdflugzeug zu warden (*hunting aircraft) if the manoeuvrability is improved by fitting the new wing and ailerons.*[3]

Although the manoeuvrability was not good they found the fighter to have a good performance, outflying the Albatros D.III and became champions of the Junkers aeroplanes.[5]

The J 7 was seriously damaged when overturned on landing when being flown by Anthony Fokker on 4 December 1917, but Fokker escaped unscathed.[6] The monoplane was to be rebuilt yet again, this time with a nose radiator and balanced ailerons and was ready to take part in the first *D Flugzeug Wetthewerb* (Fighter Competition) in January 1918.[7] Fokker flew the fighter against the Albatros D.Va flown by *Hauptmann* Schwarzenberger, the head and chief test pilot of the *Flz*. (*Flugzeug,* a department of *Idflieg*). The J 7 was not as fast as the D.Va to everyone's surprise; however, Fokker claimed that the airscrew had too fine a pitch. There was definitely something wrong with the airscrew as it

Above: The J 7 in its final elegant form after the fitting of a frontal radiator and longer ailerons. Junkers' photograph dated 23 March 1918. The instrument mounted on the starboard wing is a Morel airspeed indicator.

Above: The J 7 on 2 February 1918, in the final wing aileron configuration adopted for the production J 9, the D.I. Note the wheel covers.

Gotthard Sachsenberg (06.12.1892 – 23.08.1961) was born in Rosslau, a part of Dessau. He entered the Navy in 1913 and transferred to the Voluntary Naval Flying Corps as an observer, then as a pilot. He was ordered in May 1917 to form the first naval fighter unit. It was here that he met with Osterkamp and the two were to become friends, a friendship that survive two World Wars. He was the commander of MLFI from 1 February 1917, to 2 September 1918, when he was promoted to lead Marine Jagdgruppe I, Flanders.

A promoter of Junkers aircraft he appears to have had a regular corresponded with the Professor. The following is a letter Sachsenberg wrote to Junkers on 17 November 1917:

Many thanks for your letter of 09.11.17. My brother has most likely arrived with you in the meantime and hopefully can assist to smooth the way for your advanced designs. (Constructions literally). The many difficulties which have been caused you everywhere, should, now that your J aircraft has had such an impact, disappear more and more. The order for 100 Infantry aircraft is probably the best evidence of how the airplane is thought of at the front and the service these few machines have given to the flying troops in Flanders.

Now that the Marine G-aircraft have been ordered and the Inspektorate is much closer to accepting the delivery conditions of the R-aircraft is proof that the main resistance seems to have been overcome. I was in the Reichsmarineamt the day before my departure where I had the opportunity to discuss your new type of construction with the relevant officers. It was obvious that the Navy were absolutely positive about your design and would like to work with you. My conclusions about the single seater I will add to this letter. A report as to the status of the single seater and the results of the two seater and if you have received a 200-hp light motor would be of great interest to me.

Once again thanks for your letter and best wishes for your continued success

I am
your devoted
Gotthard Sachsenberg

Sachsenberg joined Junkers after returning from leading his unit in the post-war activities in the Baltic against Soviet forces. He was instrumental in the founding and operation of a number of airlines with support from Junkers. He became director of the new Junkers Luftverkerkehrs AG (Department of Air Traffic) at Dessau in 1921. He was forced to leave his position in October 1925 by the RVM who blamed him for the German air traffic situation. In 1926 he was a manager of the Junkers sales department. He served as a member of the Reichstag from 1928 to 1932, adopting a pacifist stance. During this time he left Junkers. He returned later as a managing director but finally left after a new dispute with Junkers. (Some sources give 1931, others 1933). He was apparently tried by the Nazis for his defeatist opinions, but due to his involvement in the family shipyard was allowed his freedom. He was associated with the hydrofoil pioneer Hanns von Schertel and built some prototype hydrofoils before and during the war. As Dessau fell under the Communists control after WWII he moved to Switzerland where he continued developing the hydrofoil. He was credited with 31 victories in WWI.

His older brother, Hans Sachsenberg, ("our Sachsenberg") was an inspector of aircraft at Junkers works in WWI and it was through him that Gotthard became aware of the wonderful work being carried out at the Junkers factory. Hans also worked for Junkers after the war.

disintegrated in flight on the 22nd and Fokker had to make an emergency landing that, fortunately, caused only slight damage to the aircraft. The J 7 and J 8 prototypes attended the first Fighter Competition, but were there only to give demonstration flights and did not take part in the final performance evaluations as monoplanes were excluded from the competition.

Suggestions that Fokker deliberately crashed the J 7, as he would then be in a better position to obtain fresh Army orders for his proposed new fighter aircraft that was to emerge as the D.VII, appear to be unsubstantiated.[8] The J 7 was at the First Fighter Competition, not as a competitor to Fokker, but as a demonstration of future aircraft in the process of development. Besides, Fokker needed orders for the *Jfa* in order to make a return on his investment. *Jfa* was to receive the orders for the production version of the J 7, the J 9 (D.I), and as will be related, Junkers had to fight to get orders for *Jco* to be able to build the J 9.

After the trials, the J 7 was again modified at the beginning of February as pilots at the competition reported strong vibrations and these were considered to have been caused by the balanced ailerons. Rounded wingtips were fitted to the outer wing

Theodor Osterkamp was studying forestry when the war broke out and had just celebrated his 22nd birthday the previous April. He joined the Naval Flying Corps first as an observer and later as a pilot. He underwent his fighter pilot training in March 1917. On completing his training he was posted to *Marine Feld Jasta* I on 14 April, the day after his birthday, and stayed with this unit for the remainder of his service. On 15 October 1917, he became the commanding officer of *MFJ*I. He was credited with 32 victories. He also had the distinction of flying the Fokker E.V monoplane in combat but was shot down while doing so and managed to bail out. He took part in the post-war fighting in the Baltic. He joined the *Luftwaffe* in 1935 and was credited with a further six victories in WWII. He served until December 1944 when he was forced to retire with the rank of *Generalleutenant*, due to his criticism of the High Command. He died on 2 January 1975, in Baden-Baden.

Osterkamp wrote the following letter to Professor Junkers from the field on 14 November 1917.

Highly admired Herr Professor

Firstly, thank you for your letter. Now once again I take up your precious time which I would have liked to avoid knowing how overworked you are.

There is little good weather here at this time so there is not much on. Last Sunday I managed to down another Englishman, sadly over enemy territory and without confirmation, as our infantry was in the trenches under barrage fire and saw nothing.

The enemy is noticeably not flying much at this time, as it seems he is saving his strength for a major offensive. If only your monoplane would reach us in time.

Time is moving on in huge strides and unfortunately I have not heard news from you that the monoplane has advanced at all in the 14 days since I have flown it. By spring we absolutely require a machine which due to its qualitative superiority will balance, to some degree, the quantitative superiority of the enemy. The only machine that has that superiority and can be put in the field by spring in large numbers, because *it only requires a 160hp Mercedes, is your monoplane. The more I think about it the more I become convinced that the critical factor for us to have air superiority next spring is whether your monoplane is ready in time. We do not have a light 200hp motor yet. Even though a few good test engines exist it will take far too long to test them in a machine and have them ready for mass delivery. Single machines at the front with these engines do us more harm than good. A new type should not be flown for months at the front in single examples allowing the other side to work up a defence, so that when the type finally arrives in large numbers the enemy have already had time to prepare a counter type. We saw when the Albatros entered service everything went beautifully. Within a very short time nearly all* Jagdstaffeln *were equipped with the Albatros and it took a long, long time before a surprised enemy managed to recover. It is wrong for example, that the Fokker Triplanes are at the front in such small numbers, one or two would not hurt, but as now with 20-25 examples the enemy has time to slowly deal with them and has time work up countermeasures. At this time there is no aeroplane with struts and bracing wires and a 160hp motor that is any better than our Albatros and as we have to rely on this engine for the time being, so actually even if speed and climb of your monoplane are not that much better, as test flights showed, your monoplane without bracing remains our only hope. I say deliberately, even if performance is not greatly better, then its other advantages are notable. Its durability: there is no warping or distortion of the wings which is a huge problem here in damp Flanders. Notoriously, even after a few days, the climb rate in our single seat Albatros declines so much that it requires a minimum of 40 minutes to reach 5000m and enemy two seaters just climb away in front of our noses. Besides the view from the monoplane with its low wing is first class, almost like the Albatros without the obstructing upper wing.*

How much better speed and climb were than the Albatros we saw during the comparison tests where the monoplane climbed better and was considerably faster even though the motor was down a 100 rpm in the evening. Manoeuvrability, despite the rectangular wings, which are to be replaced, is at least as good as the Albatros, and after what I could feel from flying the machine, I am of the opinion that with new wings it will be markedly better than the Albatros. The safety from fire by housing the petrol tanks in the wings also weighs very, very heavily in its favour.

All these points, and in particular that this machine is the only one that, with so little drag due to the missing bracing, that the 160hp Mercedes on which we must rely on for a while yet, can achieve the marked performance improvements we need, force me again and again to plead and push that no day or minute passes without having been used to develop and build this type.

I urge you to use these words anytime the opportunity presents to further interest in the military to build this monoplane.

I must close for now as it has become quite late. Again many thanks for your letter. With a request to be remembered to your admired daughter

I am
With best wishes
Theo Osterkamp

He followed this with a letter of 14 February 1918:

Highly admired Herr Professor!

I am urged now that I have returned to the Front to write to you again to emphasise that, despite all obstacles that envy and bad luck put in your path, I will remain steadfastly by your side, as I am convinced then as now that the Junkers single-seater is the aircraft of the future.

And I strongly hope, come what may, that at some stage that good will prevail and then people's eyes will be opened and they will bang their heads and say: "God, why did we not see this sooner." I know you are not the kind of person to be discouraged by a few failures but despite that I beg you, ignore all advice that would impede the single-seater and tackle the second machine with full vigour so it cannot happen again that thru damage, as has occurred now to the single-seater at a most inopportune time, the project is stalled. Sadly I was unable to fly the machine again after the last modifications so am unable, as I had hoped, to give you an accurate view of its flying characteristics, but this much can be gleaned from Schmidt's report that they had markedly improved which I have no reason to doubt. It would be good if the results learned from flying the first machine could be incorporated in the second. I repeat once again my proposal that I have already given you orally. Let me be advised when repairs to the old machine have been completed and it is airworthy again, maybe I can then manage to go there for a few days or if I cannot come myself send you a good Flying Officer from my Staffel.
I would be ashamed of myself if I did not do everything possible to promote something whose undoubted advantages I have recognised to help our victory.

Signed
Theo Osterkamp

Osterkamp's championing of Junkers was the result of his flying the J 7 and the problems that conventional aircraft experienced in Flanders. These letters also show that he thought of more than just achieving aerial victories for himself.

panels. Handling was good except for some lateral stability problems that were appeared to have finally solved by a longer fuselage. Such were the modifications that the machine was redesignated J 9.

Ltn Krohn was assigned to the Junkers research institute as a test pilot and filed a report on his flight in the J 7 on 23 March 1918. This aircraft had the final modifications to the aileron control.

On 23.3.18 I made a flight with the Junkers single-seater J 7 to determine if the modification in the aileron control had the desired result. I noted that the aircraft responds completely normal to the controls.

The aileron control is now slightly light in the case of large deflections and somewhat heavier than the elevator. This is also desirable, since you must have some pressure in the aileron when entering and leaving a turn. On the whole, the controls can be described as well balanced.

Besides, I have tried; to pull the plane up and out in a turn and I succeeded very well. But I still stand today on the point of being able to get a whole lot more out of the plane when I am more familiar with it. I have placed the aircraft perfectly perpendicular, and I have even been able to tilt it over 90°, but I did not feel as if it would not return instantly from every position.[9]

On 30 March, Wagenführ recorded that the J 7 was not yet ready for the Front, the machine gun had not been installed and flight tests were planned for 2 April.[10]

A letter from the Junkers management dated 21 March 1918, was headed "Start on the mass production of the D.I" and referred to the meeting that had occurred that day between Major Seitz, Dr. Mader, and Lurken, on the one hand, Major Wagenführ, and *Oberstltn* Siegert, the commander of *Idflieg*, on the other. Junkers had renewed serious doubts concerning the program due to the erroneous views of *Idflieg* and he considered that failure of the production program was inherent from the outset, as *Idflieg* only wanted to build six test airframes, these to be built as soon as possible, and then to wait until these were tested and proven at the Front before placing a large order.

While agreeing that a number of test machines

Above Below: The J 7 at the 2nd Fighter Competition, Aldershof, May/June 1918. The interim style of straight sided cross national markings are applied and the aileron shape has been finalised. (SDTB)

should be built as quickly as possible, the Junkers management was concerned that to delay series production until the experiences from the Front could be received, would ensure failure. If the D.I did not fulfil expectations, then the question was answered, but if the machine fulfilled expectations, and the probability was extraordinarily high that it would, then the Front would scream for more such aeroplanes but they would not be available. This failure would be worse than if the machine had

Right: Barograph recording of the J 7, 3 October 1917.

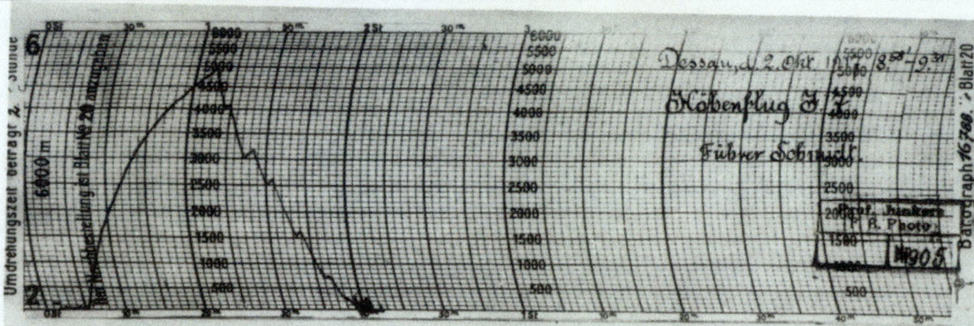

Höhenflug d. Eindeckers "J.7".

Führer: Schmidt.

Fluggewicht 713 Kg

ohne Ballast.

0 - 1000 m	in	2,2	Min.
1000 - 2000 m	in	2,6	"
2000 - 3000 m	in	3,0	"
3000 - 4000 m	in	4,0	"
4000 - 5000 m	in	5,2	"
0 - 5000 m	in	17,0	Min.

Dessau, den 2.10.1917.

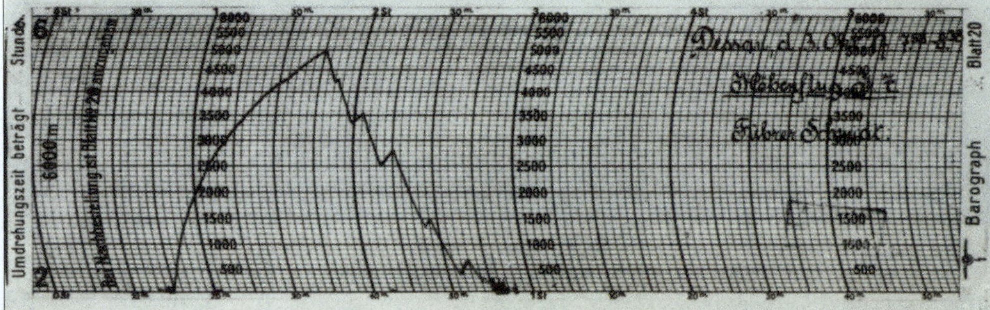

Höhenflug d. Eindeckers "J.7".

Führer: Schmidt.

Fluggewicht 765 Kg

ca. 50 kg Ballast

0 - 1000 m	in	2,4	Min.
1000 - 2000 m	in	3,0	"
2000 - 3000 m	in	3,7	"
3000 - 4000 m	in	4,5	"
4000 - 5000 m	in	6,2	"
0 - 5000 m	in	20,3	Min.

Dessau, den 3.10.1917.

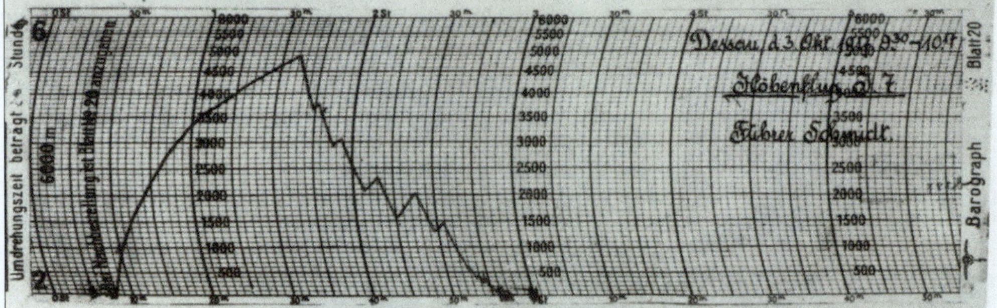

Höhenflug d. Eindeckers "J.7".

Führer: Schmidt.

Fluggewicht 805 Kg

ca. 100 kg Ballast.

0 - 1000 m	in	2,4	Min.
1000 - 2000 m	in	3,6	"
2000 - 3000 m	in	4,2	"
3000 - 4000 m	in	6,7	"
4000 - 5000 m	in	7,2	"
0 - 5000 m	in	24,1	Min.

Dessau, den 3.10.1917.

Specifications J 7

Source	**1**	**2**	**3**
Dimensions, m			
Span		9.20	9.00
Length	6.70	6.70	6.70
Height		2.60	2.60
Wing Area, m^2		11.70	11.70
Weights, kg			
Empty		656	656
Crew			80
Fuel			39
Oil			4
Military load			57
Gross		805	836
Speed, km/h			
Max at G.L.		205 (max)	205
Cruising at G.L.			185
Landing			80
Range in km			180
Climb in minutes			
1,000 m			2.30
5,000 m		24	23.70

Source:
1. Junkers Drawing F.B. 1676, 19.01.1918. Only the one dimension is shown.
2. Green, W and Swanborough G.
3. Wagner, W.

failed at all.

Junkers pressed that all measures must be taken now for serial production but this could not take place without *Idflieg's* support for timely access to materials and skilled workers. Even if everything went well, and the supply of materials and workers was assured, the company could not take over the whole financial risk associated with such a preparation.

Idflieg seemed to be quite incapable of understanding what a complicated mechanism a large-scale factory was and how much preparatory work and time was necessary for this mechanism to run. Conventional aircraft factories took several months before they could introduce a new design into mass production. The serial construction of metal aircraft required absolutely carefully designed manufacturing devices.

Junkers stressed that *Idflieg* must recognize that metal aircraft construction was the creation of a whole new industry. This would be a serious task in the pre-war days, so the difficulties were multiplied in the war.

"We only need to look at the progress of the infantry machine, and it was also said, 'first we must have the results from the Front, then we can issue more orders.'" It was August 1917 before the results were reported from the Front. In the interim the production line had been abandoned due to the financial pressure the company was under due to having initiated large scale mass production without the promise of a production order for success.

"These experiences have at least served us to go a different way, and *Idflieg* must be an important part of this, and it must now provide us with everything necessary for serial production. It must support us in terms of material, personnel and, to a certain extent, also financially."

The same was true with regard to workers' recruitment. If *Idflieg* did not immediately and without delay provide the people requested by Junkers, the realization of the construction program would not proceed. "We must above all have a large number of competent skilled laborers, we have asked for them by name."

Crucial to the whole attitude of *Idflieg* was, of course, how it valued the new aircraft. If, according to the communications of Herr Lürken, Major Wagenführ had expressed his opinion that our plane was no better than the those presently in construction, or at least not much better, support from *Idflieg* was therefore necessary. The men at the Front, above all, were the most important ones in the assessment of a new type, and it was very important to allow them to assess the aircraft.

"Since we cannot wait for the new Type J9 to be finished, the J7 type has to be placed" for assessment to bring the matter forward. However, the verdict should not be limited to the technical features of the aircraft, but it is above all necessary to try to show the advantages of the use of metal."

It appears that Junkers were concerned that Major Wagenführ was against the high price of metal aircraft which Junkers took as "remarkable sign" of the whole level from which the gentlemen in *Idflieg* form their judgment of the metal airplane. The letter was signed by Spaleck for Junkers & Co.[11]

The J 7 had been accepted by the *Fliegertruppe* during the week of 25 March 1918. It remained at Dessau for continuing testing and evaluation by military pilots. Brandenburg wrote to Dessau on 3 April 1918, reporting on the flight of the J 7 the previous day for representatives from Linke-Hofmann which firm was considering manufacturing

Above: The cockpit interior of the Junkers J 7. Photograph dated 27 April 1918. (SDTB)

the type. The flight was witnessed by Brandenburg, Major Carl Seitz[12], Steudel[13], Reuter[14], for *Jco* and *Ing* Becker for *Jfa.* Herr Stumpf and Dr Essig were the representatives of Linke-Hofmann. *Ltn* Sachsenberg and *Vize-Feldwebel* Schulz were there as observers.

Ltn Krohn first flew the J 7, starting at 23 minutes past 4 pm. He flew the J 7 to about 1,400 m taking about 2.5 minutes to reach the first 1,000 m. He made several sharp turns with the plane's wing perpendicular to the ground. He did this on the glide as well. The machine's gross weight was about 740 kg. While he was gliding one full turn took 15 seconds.

Vize-Flugmeister Bertram Heinrich of 1 *Marine Feld-Jagdstaffel* who was on leave, and had not flown the aircraft before, then took it up. He was the first Naval pilot to fly the machine. Henrich started smoothly and then pulled the aircraft up to 1,000 m in approximately the same time as Krohn. At about 2,000 m there was a thin, but still transparent, cloud cover which he pierced in a steep glide downwards. Heinrich began to perform loops, executing 18 consecutive loops, as was recorded on the barogram chart, the last between 1,000 and 800 m altitude! The loops were partly executed in the vertical plane and also partly laterally. He lost about 50 m height for a loop.

Before landing he made a steep spiral flight with a loss of height of 1,0000 m in about one minute.

Heinrich said that he was very satisfied with the aircraft. The controls were faultless. He could move the control stick all the way to his body. He recorded the following figures off the Anemometer speedometer:

Horizontally at 200 m – 135 km/hr.
During the looping flight – 65 km/hr.[15]

The J 7, J 9 and D.I took part in the Second *D Flugzeug Wetthewerb* in June 1918. Fokker again flew the J 7. The aircraft climbed to 5,000 m in 23.7 minutes at a loaded weight of 836 kg. The J 7 was primary a demonstration machine as the D.I had been accepted by the *Fliegertruppe* during the week of 25 March.

End Notes Chapter 7

1. Wagner records that Junkers had to absorb the costs of developing the J 7 as he did not have an *Idflieg* order for the machine. Wagner, W. *Op Cit.*
2. *Idflieg* had banned ear-type radiators on 10

Weighing of J 7 at Adlershof

Weight of aircraft with oil in engine and oil tank,
With coolant water but no fuel or pilot.
Calculated with three scales.

Weighed at right hand wheel	266.4
Weighed at left hand wheel	262.5
Weighed at the tail	81.8
Total	**610.7 kg**
For MG mountings	
Added	15.0
Deduct oil in tank	10.0
Empty weight including MG mounts	
Total	**615.7 kg**

For Flight:

Full fuel and oil tanks, pilot & ballast	
(Useful Military Load)	235
Total	850.7
Weighed again after flight	841.6 kg

(This weight in noted on 19 January 1918, as the All Up Weight (AWU) of the "Front ready" machine.

The flight of 19 January (1918) had to be aborted due to a leakage of a radiator conduit.

On 22 January the aircraft was again weighed with the following result:

At the tail	115
At the right-hand wheel	410
At the left-hand wheel	322
Add for instruments	2
Total	**849 kg**

With this AWU 5000 m was attained in 22 minutes and 24 minutes (barograph difference).

After the flight the aircraft was again weighed with the following result:

At the tail	109
At the right-hand wheel	312
At the left-hand wheel	402.5
Total	**823.5 kg**

The substantial difference between the right-hand and left-hand wheel is explained by the fact that the pilot was standing on the scale at the right-hand wheel.

Source: Report from Brandenburg, 29.01.1918. Via B Schmäling.

November 1916, as they drained much more quickly if there was a leak. One source contends that Junker's belly radiators came under the same ban.

3. Letter to Professor Junkers from *Lt zur See* Sachsenberg *"Im Felde"*, 17.11.1917. Copy via Bruno Schmäling.
4. Gotthard Sachsenberg to Junkers, 17.11.1917. Copy via Bruno Schmäling.
5. Sachsenberg and Osterkamp were natives of Dessau and Sachsenberg's brother was the *Idflieg* inspector at Junkers, while Osterkamp's father was a personal friend of Junkers. Both had written to the two aces about the developments that Junkers was trying to achieve.
6. According to A.R. Weyl and Peter M Grosz, Fokker flew a D.I/J 7 at the first *D Flugzeug Wettbewerb* in January 1918, although the J 7 is not listed by Gray and Thetford in their list of aircraft at the first competition.
7. For the full story of the Fighter Competitions see Herris, J. *Germany's Fighter Competitions of 1918*, Aeronaut Books, USA, 2013.
8. For example Byers, R.E.W. P.40.
9. *"Bericht von Herrn Leutnant Krohn über den Flug mit J 7 am 23.3.1918"* Copy via Bruno Schmäling.
10. Notes from Junkers internal notes and correspondence via L Andersson.
11. *Ober-Ing* Paul Spaleck was the assistant business manager and also involved with technical liaison. *"Aufnahme der Massenfabrikation des D-Flugzeuges."* 21.03.1918. Copy via Bruno Schmäling.
12. Carl Seitz. Junkers asked Seitz to assist him against Anthony Fokker. At the end of WWI Seitz was the head of the Junkers Head Office. He worked for Junkers until 1924 when he left after disputes with Sachsenberg.
13. Hans Stuedel joined Junkers in 1913 as a leading engineer in the office of ship engines. He was technical director of *Jco* at Dessau during WWI. In 1916 he was working on the design of the J 7. From 1933 to 1945 he managed the material research department of Junkers. After WWII he was forced to work for the Russians until 1953. He died in 1963.
14. Otto Reuter joined Jco in November 1915 as a technical design engineer. He was involved in the designs of the J 3 and J 7. After the war he was the first technical managing director and chief engineer of *Junkers Flugzeugwerke AG*. He was responsible for the design of the F.13. He died in 1922.
15. *"Erprobung* J 7." Report signed by Brandenburg. 3.04.1918. Copy via Bruno Schmäling.

J 7 First Version
Rotating Wingtip Ailerons
(Oct. 1917)

J 7 Second Version
Revised Cowling, Conventional
Ailerons (March 1918)

J 7 Final Version
Final Markings, Conventional
Ailerons (May/June 1918)

8. Junkers J 9 (Military D.I) – Serial Production of the All-Metal Fighter

Above: A brand-new Junkers/Fokker Co constructed D.I as shown by its wheel cover logos – *Jfa*. This is possibly the first D.I that was delivered in June 1918. (AHT AL0459-214)

Spaleck wrote to Professor Junkers on 20 March 1918, giving "a short description of the present situation" with introducing the J 9 into production:

Manufacturing J 9

The company is intensely occupied with the manufacture of the new type. The complete set of drawings will be delivered from the Forschungsanstalt (Research institute at Dessau, established 1 July 1915) *not later than 1 April. The completion of the aircraft is planned for 15 April. We hope to be able to keep this date or not very much later.*

At the same time a second machine J 9 will be built in order to have a replacement. A prerequisite for the completion at the right time is that certain materials, which are still lacking at Düren, will be delivered at the right moment.

Series production

1. Production documents, drawings etc

Preparation of the drawings for the series production, that have been delivered by the Forschungsanstalt, will be started one of these days. That is the first and most important work for the series production preparations.

2. Colleagues, engineers, assistants:
It is still difficult above all to quickly find suitable clerks, a few employments have already been made, but so far only minor assistants have been found. We hope, however, during April to obtain a greater number of first class and skilled assistants and colleagues. We are constantly endeavouring in this direction, Mj Seitz also gives us strong support in this.

3. General manufacturing devices, premises, etc
The prototype J 9 will be completed in (the shop at) *Fischergasse where it will also be assembled in specially prepared premises. In the workshops*

Above: The production prototype D.I (J 9). The undercarriage was to be simplified on later examples, the inverted V-strut was omitted. When displayed at the 2nd Fighter Competition it was flown by *Ltn* Krohn on 6th, 10th, and 14th June 1918. The join behind the cockpit where the fuselage metal covering was broken is visible. On later aircraft a single sheet of corrugated metal was used. Photographs dated 8 July 1918.

Above: Note how the camouflage fades in these photographs of the D.I powered by the experimental Benz Bz. IIIbo V-8 engine. Junkers' photographs dated 20 June 1918. Problems with the engine prevented this machine participating in the 2nd Fighter Competition. There is no nose radiator, it is slung under the fuselage.

Above: *Junker's Kampf-Eindecker (aus Metal)*. This version of the D.I was powered by the 185 hp BMW IIIa engine. It had a longer fuselage and a wider wingspan. The fuselage vibrated and the increase in span reduced manoeuvrability. This machine participated in the 3rd Fighter Competition held from 10 to 28 October 1918. (For the story of the German Fighter Competitions see Herris, J. *Germany's Fighter Competitions of 1918*, Aeronaut Books).

at Fischergasse and Mauerstrasse manufacture of wings and parts etc., could take place, also to greater extent. The new assembly shed on the new grounds will be completed at the end of the month.

Construction of the new building is progressing swiftly in spite of considerable difficulties with the carpenters but these difficulties have been remedied. It can be counted upon, if no particular difficulties are experienced, that the new building will be completed according to plan. We hope definitely that a part will already be used in May and the entire building in early June. At the present time more than 200 workers are engaged in the new building.

4. Special manufacturing devices
Preparation of jigs and fixtures etc., will begin as soon as the first drawings arrive; during April, in any case, these preparations for series production must be mostly completed.

5. Material
This gives us the greatest troubles; we have, as you know, made inquiries at Düren about material for 100 aeroplanes and informed Düren that they should always have these quantities in stock. We have demanded delivery of 1/3 on 1 April, 1/3 on 1 May and 1/3 on 1 June, but today we still have not been informed about when the delivery can be made. In spite of Mr Otto Junkers', Cologne, permanent contacts with Düren, they could not give any information due to the scarcity of Duralumin. We should, however, receive final information very shortly. As you know, there are particular difficulties with the delivery of tubes, once more we have to recommend consideration of use of profiles instead of tubes.

6. Workers
The search for workers is done energetically. Having studied the list of supported families with called up persons in cities and villages in Anhalt, we have succeeded in gathering more than 1000 addresses. When asking the families we could find out the field address and send a questionnaire in order to learn about the qualifications. After that the suitable persons were reclaimed at the Generalkommando where until now 200 reclaims have been deposited.

Above: A D.I in poor condition in US hands at Romorantin after the Armistice.

Below: Judging from the cuts in the fuselage metal panels, this D.I, photographed at Romorantin, is the same machine as above. (Note the number "5" on the hangar.) (AHT AL0613-019)

Above & Below: Probably the same aircraft as that shown on the facing page with its wings removed showing the tubular structure of the wing and the central tank. (AHT AL1164-068)

Above: Photographed in the new Junkers assembly building on 8 August 1918. There are four production D.I fighters, two long-fuselage examples with the elevator touching the floor, and two short-fuselage examples. The rudder at the extreme right belongs to the J 9/1 prototype. (SDASM)

Below: A view of *Kampfgeschwader Sachsenberg* at Swinemünde (now Świnoujście in Poland), 1919. A Halberstadt C.V and a Fokker D.VII are also on the field.

Above: A D.I of *Kampfgeschwader Sachsenberg* on the field at the Zeppelin sheds at Wainoden on the Kurland Peninsula. A LVG C.VI, Junkers CL.I "K", and another Junkers are in the background. The airship handling rail made a good chock for starting the machines.

Below: Junkers D.I and CL.I monoplanes *Kampfgeschwader Sachsenberg* at Peterfeld on 9 October 1919. The D.I fighters are in a different colour scheme that included the rudder.

Above: View inside the Wainoden Zeppelin shed showing at least eight Junkers monoplanes and a Halberstadt C.V on the right. Junkers D.I (Jco) D.9166/18 first in line on left. Wainoden is now Vainode in Latvia. (AHT AL0752-007)

Specifications J 9 (Military D.I)

Source	**1**	**2**	**3**	**4**
Type	**D.I**	**D.I**	**J 9/ D.I**	**D.I**
Dimensions, m				
Span	9 m	29 ft 2 in (8.890 m)		9.0 m
Length	7.25 m	22 ft 0 in (6.706 m)	7.25 m	7.25
Height	2.60 m	9 ft 5in* (2.870 m)	2.25 m	2.6 m
Chord	1.8 m			
Span tailplane	3 m			
Wing Area		158.8 ft^2 (14.753 m^2)	14.8 m^2	
Weights, kg				
Empty			654	654
Gross			834	834
Speed, km/h			185	
Climb in minutes				
1,000 m			2.3	
6,500 m				

Notes: * Estimated

Source:

1. Junkers three-view drawings.
2. British Report on the "Junker Single-Seat All-Metal Monoplane, Type D.I."
3. Gray, P & Thetford, O.
4. *Jllustrierte Flug-Welt*, Vol.1, 1919, P.376.

Facing Page: Three D.I monoplanes inside the airship hangars at Wainoden, 1919. (AHT AL0752-010)

Above: Abandoned D.I fuselage, possibly one of those found in Belgium. This photograph was included in the British report on the D.I The tailplane was reported to be over-painted white. (AHT AL0459-217)

It is most important that the Generalkommando is being informed about the importance of our company and that we actually receive the people.

Mj Seitz has visited the War office at Magdeburg and the determining central War office in Berlin. We have not heard anything yet about his results as he is still away.

We must take into account that we will have difficulties with other big companies here as the persons reclaimed by us often have previously been employed by them. They will of course protest at our reclaiming of these people. Yesterday the Polysius firm[1] already asked us on this question, but we will not refrain from attracting and reclaiming persons who appear to be useful to us even if we naturally want to retain good relationships with other companies. The other companies, after all, are not in a position to free the persons for themselves.

Sub-contractors:

By advertising we have obtained a great number of addresses to sub-contractors; there will present no difficulties to place extensive sub-contracting work. The most important thing now is to plan the manufacturing division of the aeroplane; we will energetically put all our power to this task.

Junkers & Co
Signed: Spaleck

The situation of the German aeronautical industry in early 1918 can be gauged in part from this letter. Supply of material was always a problem with the British blockade. Of more importance was the lack of manpower and the need to call back troops from the Front who had the necessary skills to build the metal aeroplanes. The British intelligence services would comb German newspaper advertisements for information as to where workers were wanted in order to ascertain where a future threat could lie.

The first J 9 (D.I) pre-production fighters appeared in April 1918 powered by the 185-hp BMW III engine. The problem with lateral stability was still evident and led to the late production D.I having the fuselage lengthened again. A pylon replaced the headrest of the J 7. *Idflieg* wished to repeat the J 4 experience by ordering six pre-production fighters for evaluation.

A meeting was held with Junkers management

Above: Note the serial application to this long fuselage D.I : Junk. D.I (Jco) D.5180/18. The Jco indicates that it was built by the Junkers factory and not the Junkers-Fokker concern. It was the first machine from *Jco* and was ready for static testing in August 1918. (SDASM)

and *Idflieg* on 21 March 1918, as related above. Junkers management pointed out the problems that had caused J 4 production to be delayed for months and it was agreed that Junkers would have an order for 100 aircraft in order to allow for serial production to commence. The first 20 machines were to be J 9 (D.I) fighters.[2] In order to increase competition and bring other firms into the new method of manufacturing aircraft *Idflieg* insisted that the aircraft be sub-contracted to Linke-Hoffman and Hansa-Brandenburg, both firms that had no experience of working with metal. There is no documentation to suggest that either of these firms started work on the Junkers Fighter.

A J 9 and D.I flew in the Second *D Flugzeug Wettbewerb* held at Adlershof in May and June. The J 9 was fitted with a Mercedes D.IIIaü (high compression) engine. Combat pilots did not appreciate the low wing and pressed for a parasol metal aircraft with good downward view. The D.I was suggested as a balloon attack machine where the downward view would not be of such importance. Another modification saw the J 9 fitted with the 200-hp Benz Bz.IIIb V-eight engine. On this machine the radiators were located under the wings.

According to Peter M. Grosz the J 9 differed little from the final J 7 with modifications to enable a high volume of production. Unlike wooden aeroplanes the Junkers metal aeroplanes required extensive factory preparations to set up the machinery and jigs necessary to turn out the finished airframes. To this end Junkers required financial support from the military. Professor Junkers was successful in obtaining an order in May 1918 for 100 all-metal aeroplanes. The production D.I was to have the lengthened fuselage.

The first flight of the D.I prototype (known as the J 9/I) occurred in early May under the hands of Junkers test pilot *Ltn* Krohn.[3] At the Second Fighter Competition only the Rumpler D.I surpassed the performance of the D.I with the 160-hp Mercedes D.IIIaü high compression engine. The 160-hp Mercedes D.III powered Fokker V.23, mid-wing monoplane at the competition was heavier than the Junkers D.I even though it was of conventional Fokker welded steel tube fuselage construction, with wooden, ply covered, cantilevered wing. Unfortunately, problems with the 195-hp Benz

Above: D.I in the Peterfelde hangar, Kurland, with an assortment of late German aircraft including a Siemens-Schuckert fighter and LVG C.V biplane. The Junkers appears to be in good condition.

Above: Junkers D.I 3112/18. (via G Ott)

Above & Right: Two views of the only surviving Junkers D.I when in the Musee de l'Air's store. It has been restored and is now on display.

Bz.IIIbo V-eight engine meant that the second Junkers D.I prototype did not reach the Fighter Competition.[4]

A J 9 powered by a Mercedes D.III took part in the Fighter Evaluation Flights by front line pilots held at Adlershof from 7 to 10 July 1918. According to Wagner, the J 7 was praised, but the judgement of the fighter pilots was that the D.I was a total failure. Why this was stated when the machine had demonstrated a superior performance is hard to understand without an understanding of the practices of the fighter pilots of that time. As noted above, the attack from above to pounce on an unaware adversary then disengage from the numerically superior Allied formations was the preferred tactic. Good downward vision was required and this was one aspect where the D.I fell down compared against contemporary biplanes. The Army pilots reported that the J 9 was less manoeuvrable than the J 7, while the Navy pilots liked the high speed of the J 9.

The other metal fighter at the demonstration, the Zeppelin (Dornier) D.I, suffered top wing failure during a flight by *Ltn* Reinhard on 3 July.

Above: Eric Schäfer posing with ground crew against short fuselage D.3188/18 on 9 October 1919. Note that the rudder is not the usual white colour and the Fokker D.VII in the background. This photograph was taken at Peterfelde.

Reinhardt was killed in the subsequent crash.

The D.I was recommended by Goering and Loerzer as an ideal machine to attack balloons, a situation where its all-metal construction would be of value. Late in July Junkers reflected that the D.I was not ready for the Front because it lacked a downward view. The ten aircraft on order "must be sent to the Front as quickly as possible to get a final judgement.... We are worried over the Inspection's unfavourable judgement."[5] *Idflieg* however placed a second order for 100 all-metal fighters in late August.

At the Third *D Flugzeug Wettbewerb* from 15 to 31 October 1918, the D.I entered was powered by a BMW.IIIa as were all the fighters at the competition, although some rotary powered fighters such as the Kondor E.III and Fokker D.VIII, as well as Allied fighters, were included for comparison purposes. This D.I had a longer fuselage and wider wingspan. It appears that this configuration had unpleasant fuselage vibration characteristics and poorer manoeuvrability.[6] From an examination of photographs Peter M. Grosz concluded that the first D.I to go to the front had the shorter fuselage and wingspan.

Idflieg gave the following results for the competition:

Climb:
1. Junkers D.I
2. Rumpler D.I
3. Pfalz D.XVI

Speed:
1. Junkers D.I (Faster than V 29 up to 4,000 m).
2. Fokker D.VIIF (Faster at higher altitudes).
3. Rumpler D.I.

Flight Characteristics:
Junkers D.I: Reacts too late to the ailerons and does not climb well in a turn. Vibrations in the rear fuselage are unpleasant. Field of vision is bad for dogfights and formation flying. Manoeuvrable only at low speeds.

Fokker V 29: Manoeuvrability good, better than Fokker D.VIII.

Rumpler D.I: Good flight characteristics but not useful for dogfighting as slides in tight turns and enters a spin. The vertical tail surfaces are inadequate due to the short fuselage.

The D.I in Detail

A 1919 USAS Report on the "Junkers All-Metal

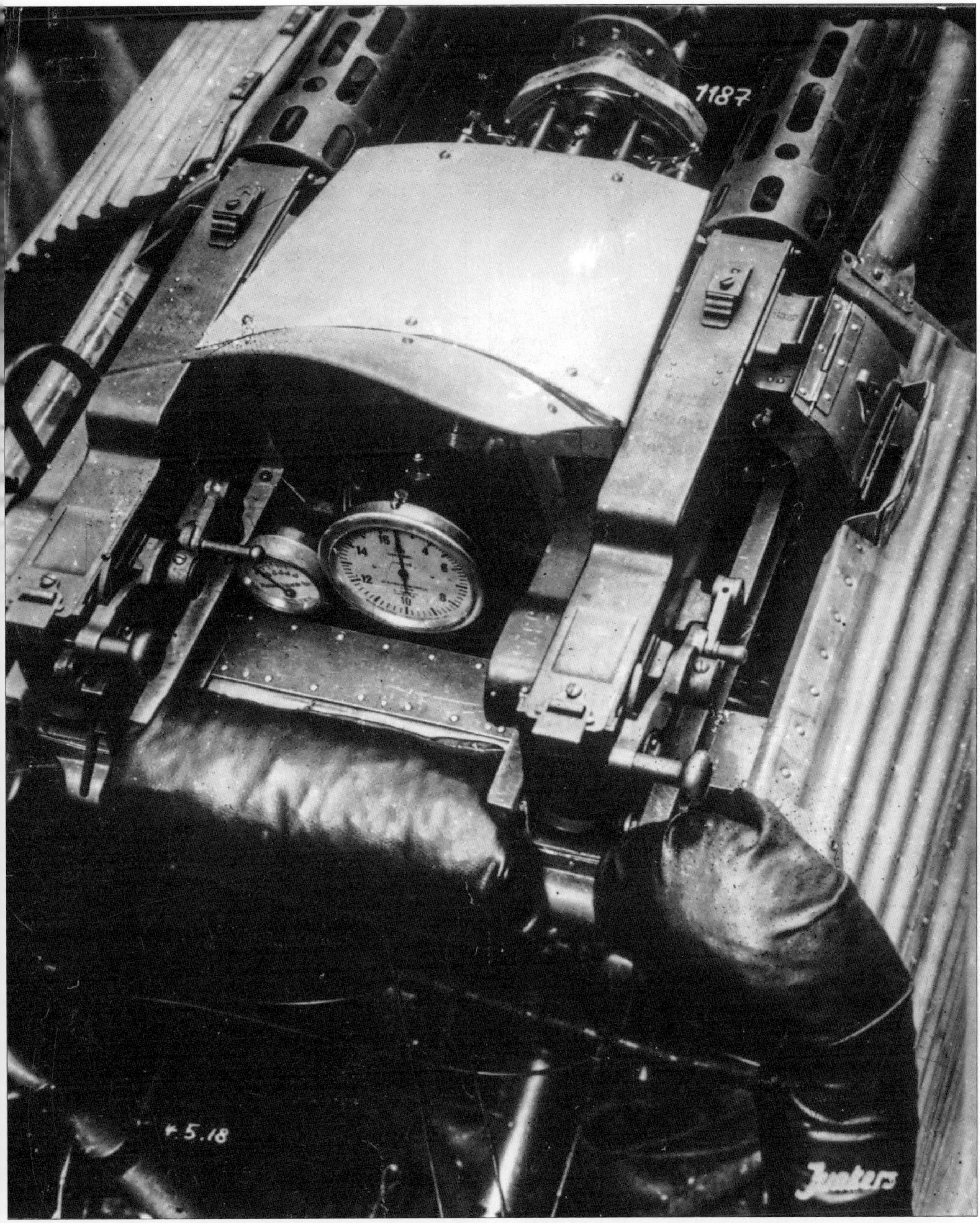

Above: The cockpit end of the twin LMG 08/15 machine guns with the cocking handles within easy reach of the pilot. (SDTB)

Above & Facing Page: Dated 3 October 1918, this trio of photographs show the reason why the pylon was necessary behind the cockpit. (SDTB)

Monoplane, Type R.E.-5" noted that while its frame was made entirely out of metal and its wing covering was thin sheet aluminium instead of cloth "It is however, not armoured." The underlining had been added to the typed copy of the Report.

It is a single-seater, with a pair of fixed, synchronised guns, and was evidently intended for pursuit work. Among the allied pilots who were interviewed at points where the surrendered German airplanes were being collected and listed, no one was found who had ever seen one of these airplanes in flight, or who could give any reliable information concerning its performance. Some of the R.A.F. pilots, however were sure it had been used in service, and had heard that it was successful.

The Report was based on the four machines abandoned at Hombeek, Belgium. One of the four was in good condition and could probably be made ready for flight. Another was good enough to study or measure up. The other two were complete wrecks. These planes were built by "Junkers & Co of Dessau. The inspection tag on one of the radiators is dated Aug. 6, 1918."

The unique features of the D.I were listed as:

(a). Its monoplane form with the fuselage, the line of the propeller thrust and nearly all the weight high above the lane, giving remarkable visibility, but seemingly bad stability.

(b). Entire absence of wing-bracing struts or wires.

(c). Quick assembly of the wings and fuselage on the field. The wings can be coupled and made ready to fly within a very few minutes after taking off the car or truck on which the plane is transported.

(d). All metal construction, making the airplane absolutely weather-proof, and also less liable to destruction by fire.

(e). The great thickness of the wing.

The assessment of "remarkable visibility" should be compared with that of the German fighter pilots referred to above. As no machine had been flown by Allied pilots the remarks as to stability seem out of place and based on hear-say.

The balance of the report describes the D.I fighter in detail. The Report was published in printed format under "Resumé of Foreign Data – German." The US publication that the printed Report was included in has not been identified.[7]

The following description is based on the British Air Ministry report on the "Junker Single-Seater All-Metal Monoplane Type DI" and the USAS report.[8] "The aeroplane forming the subject of the report was examined at Evere aerodrome, near Brussels. Its

earlier history is unknown, but the *fuselage* showed clearly that it had been struck by several bursts of machine-gun bullets."

The aerodynamic design was considered "interesting" but the method of construction was considered of greater importance. The point was made that the Junkers had been dumped with several conventionally constructed machines and been in the open for several months. While the others had shown considerable deterioration, the Junkers had hardly suffered but the duralumin had acquired a coating of white crystals and appeared to have become brittle. This example was fitted with a 180-hp Mercedes engine.

The machine was described as "a biplane with the upper plane removed." The wings were constructed

Above: Crash photographs often show details available nowhere else. Junkers' photograph No. 1394 shows the dark upper surface colours contrasted with the lower surface that is not white. (SDTB)

by a series of tubular duralumin spars strongly braces by means of riveted tubular duralumin cross-pieces. To this frame work is riveted the corrugated sheet covering. The corrugations flattened out at their extremities where they were riveted to the spars.

The tubular spars were spliced where they decreased in diameter but "owing to the fact that the outside diameter of the inner tube is not very much less than the internal diameter of the outer one, it has not been found necessary to press the outside tube into a square section" as was done on the J 4 (J.I). The separate wingtip was a substantial duralumin sheet riveted to a channel strip and between these two the corrugated covering is firmly held.

"The wing covering consists of corrugated sheet duralumin 0.14 in. thick (about 24 S.W.G). The pitch of corrugation is 1¼ ins, and the depth 3/16 in., of which there are seven strips lap-riveted together. Each strip forms a belt, commencing at the trailing edge, where the two edges are riveted together. Spars and coverings are joined together by iron rivets spaced in the hollows of the waves."

The centre section was the same as that of the Junkers biplane; that is the spars were connected by duralumin tubes, that were flattened at their extremities and riveted to lugs welded to steel collars, that were in turn riveted to the spars. The centre-section of the wing was integral with the fuselage and projected about 16 inches on each side. This made the unit suitable for conventional transportation. The wings could be altered for dihedral within "certain wide limits" due to the junction of the upper spar to upper spar having an internal sleeve that carried a threaded partly spherical head that is screwed into the spar. The junction of the four lower spars was not adjustable. After the wings were coupled up the narrow gaps in their surfaces were closed by bands of sheet duralumin about 5 inches wide that were put around the wing section and secured by clamps.

At the outer corners of the leading edges of the wings where the surface is curved in two directions, the corrugated sheet is replaced by plain sheet metal.

Strips of wood were riveted to the top surface of the centre-section for the mechanics to step on. The USAS report noted that while there was no knowledge of the weight of the wing, the photographer had no difficulty in lifting it for photographic purposes.

Ailerons were built up around a duralumin spar to the front of which a D-shaped smooth duralumin sheet was riveted. Two riveted corrugated sheets then made up the top and bottom surface of the

Above: Junkers D.I monoplanes on KPEV (Königliche Preußische Eisenbahn Verwaltung) twin axle rail flat cars Rm (Rungenwagen) type.

aileron. No ribs or formers are present in the aileron.

The USAS report found the thickness of the wing section "remarkable," being much thicker than the wings of the Fokker D.VII, the wing of which was considered to be unusually thick and "decided innovations in wing design at the time the plane first appeared."[9]

The British Report noted that the construction of the fuselage was "only one step further than the usual German metal tube construction." The usual wire bracing of A.E.G. and Fokker types was replaced by rigid tubular bracing in the D.I. No wire bracing was used in the fuselage, the construction being similar to the three-ply wood bulkhead principle found in German aeroplanes but translated into metal. The body consisted of a framework of duralumin tubes covered with the corrugated sheet lengthwise. A continuous channel section strip that ran longitudinally along the top and bottom of the fuselage allowed the internal built-up bulkheads to be held in place. "This strip is so frail, however, that its obvious function is to assist in the assembly of the body by holding the formers in place while the covering is riveted on." The engine section was braced from the centre section wing spars. A system of tubular bracing supported the engine bearers. Adjustable shutters of corrugated metal were positioned behind the radiator, and could be swung in or out, to control the water temperature.

Five sheets of corrugated sheet were employed to cover the body:-

One sheet covering the bottom of the fuselage.

Two symmetrical side sheets.

Two symmetrical top sheets.

In addition, two smaller sheets served as port and starboard engine cowls.

A wing-walk strip was placed only on the port side wing root of the machine under examination. A welded steel tube crash pylon was mounted behind the pilot. In typical British fashion, the Report noted that: - "Its function cannot be named with certainty, but it is highly probable that a certain amount of reluctance to fly all-metal machines was evinced by the pilots, and this is probably a concession to them."

The elevators and ailerons were operated by steel tubes. The aileron was actuated by the tube that was connected to the control stick in the cockpit. This tube was moved endwise, parallel to the tubes in the wing structure, and at its further end it transmitted angular motion to the aileron by means of bell-crank levers. The elevator was actuated by a tube running back through the fuselage, from the control yoke, and moving back and forth. The rudder bar was of conventional type, the rudder being worked by cables contained wholly within the fuselage. These were the only cables used on the plane. The rudder and elevators were balanced.

The tailplane was built up with the rear fuselage section. The fixed tailplane has a strong leading edge to which the corrugated sheets are riveted.

The landing gear was of the ordinary V-type with round tubular faired struts.

A sturdy roll-over pylon replaced the fairing of the J 7.

A postscript to the USAS Report, dated 8 February 1919, noted that a photograph was published in *Aeronautical Engineering* showing "what appears to be a two-place machine of the same general type and construction as the single-place machine." This would be the first that the USAS knew of the CL.I monoplane.

Junkers had to fight to get orders for *Jco* to build the D.I. According to a Junkers letter, *Idflieg* gave *Jco* a tentative order for 20 D.I fighters in March, six were to be delivered in June and 14 in July. Material for only three aircraft was in hand, however. Major Wagenführ then gave *Jfa* a letter of contract for 20 D.I fighters to be built at *Jfa*, not *Jco*! In order to get around this it was agreed by the end of the month, that in accepting the order *Jfa* "state their agreement with the choice of the firm Junkers & Co as sub-contractor and that the already complete machine by the firm Junkers & Co be used as the model machine and be transferred to Adlershof for strength testing." Thus the machines would be purchased from *Jfa*, but with *Jco* also building them as a subcontractor.[10]

The following Memorandum of a telephone call to *Idflieg* sets out the situation as the Junkers management saw things on the morning of 17 April 1918:

I demanded to talk with Hptm Mühlig-Hoffman; he was not available, Ltn Kersten answered and asked what it concerned. I informed (him) *that it concerned the order for D-machines. Ltn Kersten said that it had been decided to give orders to Jfa* (Junkers-Fokker AG) *only. I asked when this decision had been made. That was perhaps on last Sunday, he said. I said that the order had already been definitely promised by Major Wagenführ. Kersten thought that Major Wagenführ could not place the order in the absence of the inspector. I objected that Hptm Mühlig-Hoffmann the head of the department, had been present during the discussion and had raised no objections. I asked if not any of the other officers were there, perhaps Hptm Schwarzenberger. I was connected to him. He expressed the same information as that given by Ltn Kersten. I asked, since when had this decision been made. He said that it had always been like that. I expressed my astonishment at the acts of Idflieg and referred to the fact that we had repeatedly been promised a test order, latest on 5 April, by Mj Wagenführ and a certificate as well that we were authorized to obtain materials. Hptm Schwarzenberger said that Jfa had been formed for the purpose of taking over the aircraft production. He was, moreover, only able to say anything off the record.*

I referred to the fact that in the establishment agreement with Fokker it was strictly agreed upon, that as future licence holders first of all beside the Fokker Works at Schwerin Junkers & Co were specified. When the Jfa was established it was in advance reckoned with that Junkers & Co later would build aircraft. Schwarzenberger considered that a private matter. I re-joined that the establishment of Jfa with the aim to manufacture metal aircraft also was a private matter, but when Idflieg considered all the facts as directing its attitude, then the fact that Junkers & Co originally had been considered as additional licence holders this had to be heeded by Idflieg. I asked Hptm Schwarzenberger to use the given statements and inform the other officers of Idflieg. He promised me to do this. I agreed with him that on the following day at 10h AM I would come and see Idflieg in order to deliberate on the order matters with Hptm Mühlig-Hoffmann. Hptm Schwarzenberger then thought again, that Hptm Mühlig-Hoffmann perhaps was not in a position to independently authorize over the order matters.

Signed by Spaleck for the Junkers & Co Board of Directors.

The following note was added to the Memorandum: *It is well worth to observe that one of the officers says that Mj Wagenführ alone cannot decide, when the other says that Hptm Mühlig-Hoffmann is not authorized to do anything alone. There seems to be "passing the buck." with one hiding behind the other.*[11]

The following month things had not improved. Junkers (*Jco*) had been told to act to reserve material for another 100 aeroplanes and expected to receive the order for these shortly. The company had managed to gather material from earlier stock piles to enable the completion of three D.I fighters from the order for 20 but lacked almost every sort of material for the other 17. In order to work to the timetable for delivery then the material had to be supplied by the end of June. "For the additional 100 aircraft we ask to have them spaced, so that half be

Above: A D.I with windscreen, rollover pylon and non-white rudder. (AHT AL1139-006)

delivered in July and August."

The company noted that they had been able to hire several hundred workers for the proposed program that had been agreed upon but that it would not be able to employ them unless the delivery times set out by the company were adhered to.[12]

Not many D.I fighters reached the Front for operational assessment before the Armistice and no combat records are known for the type in World War I. *Jco* expressed concerns in July that 10 D.I fighters would be placed in storage rather than flown at the Front. The company asked for an order for 50 as "balloon machines." On 1 August, a *Jco* report on D-aircraft production noted that three of the fighters with long fuselages were complete, but the experimental shop still wanted to make a few changes before releasing them. They would be ready for shipment in one to two days. The next three were being put into "assembly today and should be ready at the latest on 15 August." The remaining five aircraft were stated to be completed by the beginning of September, at least three but probably all five. The static test machine (5180/18) was ready to be shipped when required.[13] These fighters had the longer fuselage and increased span wings. This modification affected manoeuvrability and they were given short fuselages before they left the factory. Despite it being stated that the short fuselage became standard photographs of the aircraft in action in the Baltic post-Armistice show both short and long fuselage D.I fighters.

Ltn Gotthard Sachsenberg[14], a proponent of Junkers, asked for 12 Junkers D.I fighters for his *Marine Jagdgeschwader* in Flanders. Four were found abandoned in Flanders after the war. Another in good condition was found at the Ev re airfield near Brussels. It appears that at least one was given personal markings as this machine, found at Hombeek, had a two-colour band around the rear fuselage. The US Air Service reported that the RAF officers thought that the aircraft had been flown and there is little doubt that at least some preliminary sorties would have been flown by the Marine fighter pilots in Flanders. Most of the

fighters were completed after the Armistice. The treaty of Brest-Litovsk had given the Germans control over the Baltic countries. In the unrest after the Armistice the Allies had the problem of what to do with the German troops in the Baltic. If they were removed then the Soviets would take control and so the German troops remained. The J 9 was used operationally on Germany's Eastern border in late 1918 and 1919 against Poland and Russia in the Baltic States. Operations were carried out from Wainoden and Swinemunde.

Facing Page: Constructing D.I wings.

Junkers D.I Contracts

The below tables give the sequence of the placing of orders for the D.I. Junkers was continually trying to get orders for *Jco*.

It appears that 40 D.I fighters were ordered from *Jco* and 27 were delivered, and that 20 D.I fighters were eventually ordered from *Jfa* and 13 were delivered.

The surviving D.I had the serial 5998/18 applied after its 1973 restoration. This machine came from Evere in Belgium and was obtained by the French in 1919.

Junkers D.I Contracts	
Spaleck report 17 April 1918. A contract for test aircraft verbally given by Wagenführ on 5 April.	Numbers not stated.
***Jco* to *Idflieg* letter 8 March 1918.** *Idflieg* has given *Jco* a verbal contract for 20 D aircraft. 6 to be delivered in June, 14 in July.	20 D.I (*Jco*)
Wagenführ to *Jfa* 28 May 1918.Letter giving contract to *Jfa* for 20 D.I fighters. *Jfo* can act as sub-contractors.	20 D.I (*Jfa*)
Wagenführ to Jco 30 May 1918. Insists that 20 fighters be built by Jfa and that the completed machine be sent to Adlershof for type testing.	
***Jco* to Seitz, *Jco*, Berlin 26 July 1918.** Urges that 10 D.I fighters be sent to Front as soon as possible for evaluation.	10 D.I (*Jco*). *Was order split 10 to* Jco *and 10 to* Jfa*?*
***Jco* to Seitz, *Jco*, Berlin. 1 August 1918.** Report on status D.I at Jco. 1). 3 long fuselage D.I ready. 2). 3 D.I today in assembly. 3). 5 D.I ready beginning Sept.	12 D.I (*Jco*) plus one static test machine (D.5180/18)
Wagenführ to Jco 21 August 1918. Expects fusion of *Jco* and *Jfa*, thus awards an open contract for 100 metal aircraft, from which 10 are to be D.I monoplanes.	10 D.I (*Jfo*/*Jfa*)

J 9 (Military D.I) Production Contracts

Idflieg Contract*	Type	By	No.	Serials
Nr.181/3.18	J 7	*Jfa*	1	D.2266/18
Nr.556/2.18	D.I	*Jfa*	10	D.3110/18 – D.3119/18
Nr.683/5.18	D.I	*Jfa*	10	D.5170/18 – D.5179/18
Nr.683/5.18	D.I	*Jco*	10	D5180/18 – D.5189/18
Nr.168/8.18	D.I	*Jco*	10	D.9160/18 – D.9169/18
Nr.168/8.18	D.I	*Jco*	20	D.10307/18 – D.10326/18

Note: * *Idflieg* changed the numbering of their letters in 1918, each month they started from "1" again. This means that Nr.xxx/2.18 gives the order as of February 1918 and so on. Earlier they numbered them in sequence through all years. Note by R Zankl.

The Only Surviving Junkers D.I on Display in the Musee de l'Air in Paris. (Photo Pyperpote)

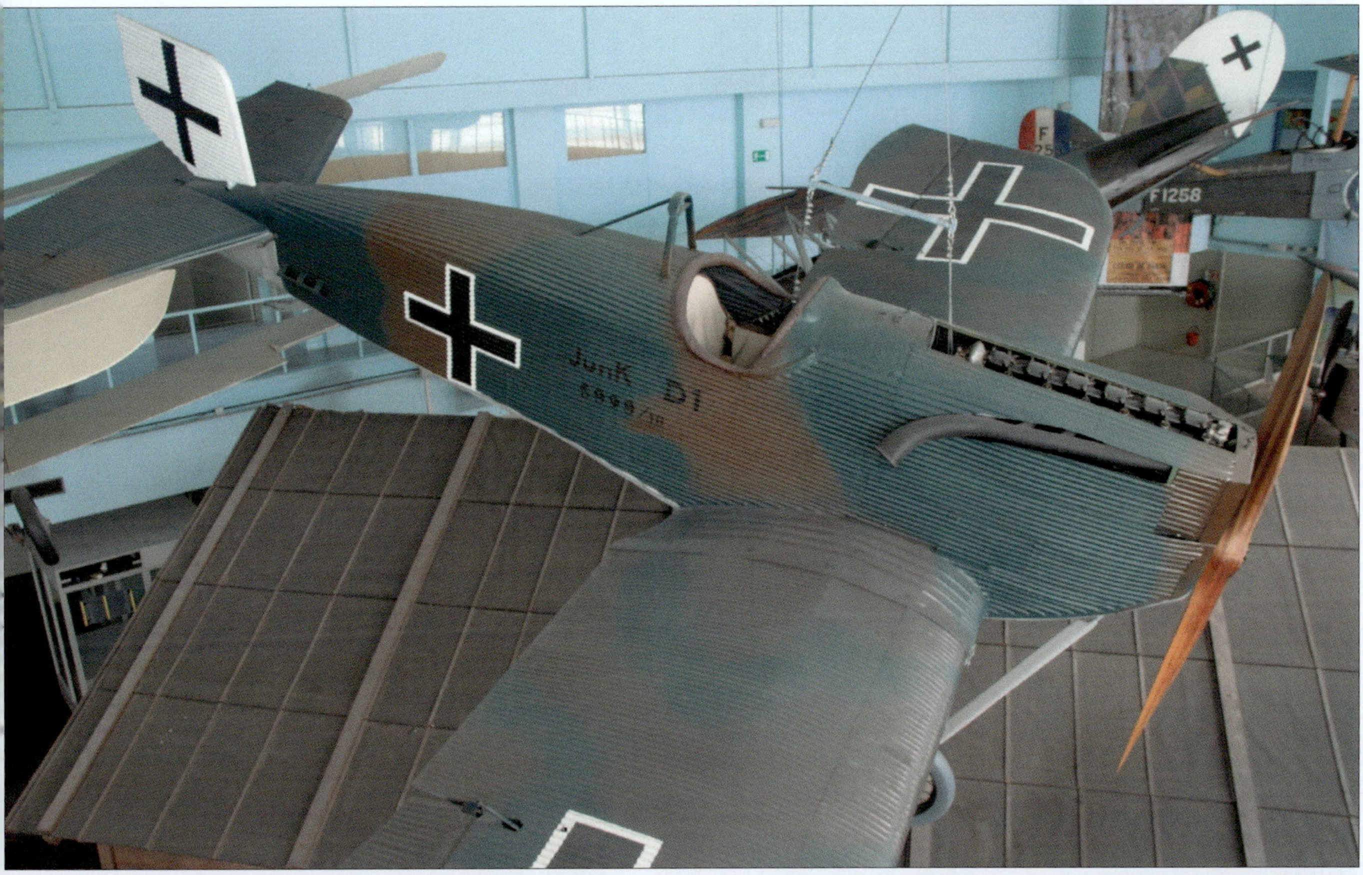
Junk D I
F1258

F1258

JUNKERS J.9 (D1)
1917

Junk D1

D1

End Notes Chapter 8

1. Polysius AG still exists. It was founded in 1859 by Andreas Ernst Gottfried Polysius, master machinist, opened his own workshop in Dessau. From 1890 the company specialised in machines for crushing, grinding and processing raw materials, and in 1907 constructed a complete cement factory in Egypt. In 1946, after the Second World War, Polysius made a fresh start in Dessau.
2. Junkers actions to ensure that Jco was not left out of production orders was successful. The *Flugzeugmeisterei* sent a letter to Junkers at Dessau on 30 May 1918, wherein they acknowledged that 20 *Probeflugzeuge* (test aircraft) Type Junkers D would be allocated to *Jco* from *Jfa*, and in particular, the already finished aircraft, that was *Typenprüfung* (Type tested) at Adlershof, as a sample aircraft. Copy via Bruno Schmäling.
3. Wagner states that the first fight of the J 9 was in April 1918. Wagner, W. P.111. Op Cit.
4. The Benz engine was based on the Hispano-Suiza that was in widespread service in Allied aircraft. The German aircraft engine industry did not produce a good reliable V-eight engine during the war.
5. 26.07.1918. Notes from Junkers internal notes and correspondence via L Andersson.
6. Wagner calls this machine a J 7 and confirms that it has a good climb rate and speed but was considered still not manoeuvrable as a front line fighter. Grosz and, Gray and Thetford designate this Junkers fighter a D.I.
7. Copies of the original typed report and the printed version are located in P.M. Grosz Collection Box 491.
8. This Report was republished in *Flight* from 1 April 1920. All quotations in this section are from this Report unless otherwise noted. Despite the publication of the Reports on the J.I and the D.I, the Junkers system appears to have had no impact on British aeronautical design.
9. AEF, USAS, Paris, Technical Section. Report on: Junkers All-metal Monoplane, Type R.E.-5. 28.01.1919. Report prepared by Major J.C. Riley, Chief of Division of Technical History and Research. Copy P.M. Grosz Collection Box 491.
10. Wagenführ to Junkers-Fokker-Werke AG, "Delivery of Aeroplanes Type Junk D.I. 28.05.1918. Copy via Bruno Schmäling. Also notes from Junkers and *Idflieg* letters in P.M. Grosz Collection Box 482.

11. Wagenführ had given the company orders for years, so the claim that none of them had the authority to grant orders was false. Report of telephone call with *Idflieg*. 17.04.1918. Copy via Bruno Schmäling.
12. Letter to Idflieg from Junkers and Co, signed by Sp (Spaleck), 08.05.1918. Copy via Bruno Schmäling.
13. It is obvious that *Jco* had 11 aircraft under construction on 1 August 1918, and at least six were initially completed. Notes in P.M. Grosz Collection Box 482.
14. Sachsenberg was credited with 31 victories. He trained as a pilot in 1916 and started his career flying Fokker E.III monoplanes with *Marine FA2*. Commanding *MFJ* 1 from 1 February 1917, in September 1918 he was made commander of *Marine Jagdgruppe* 1 (Naval Fighter Wing) in Flanders. He died on 23 August 1961.

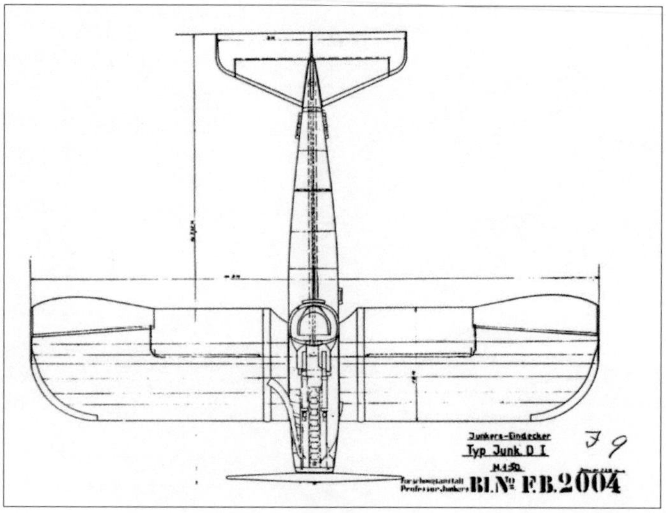

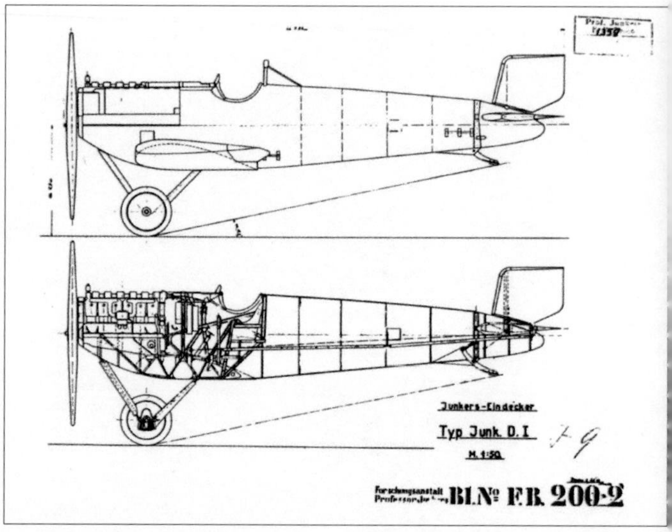

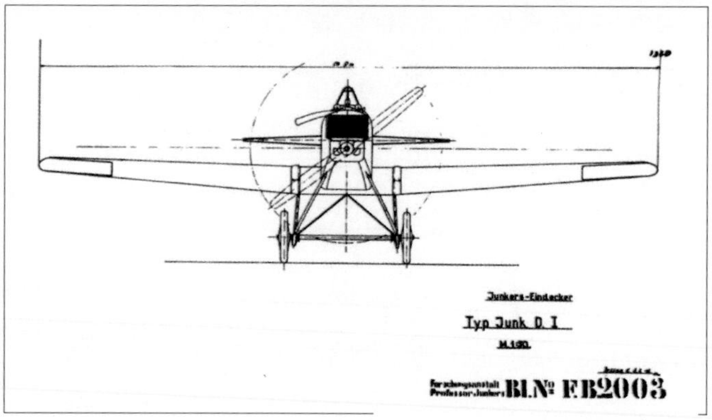

Above, Left, & Above Left: Junkers drawings of the D.I dated August 1918.

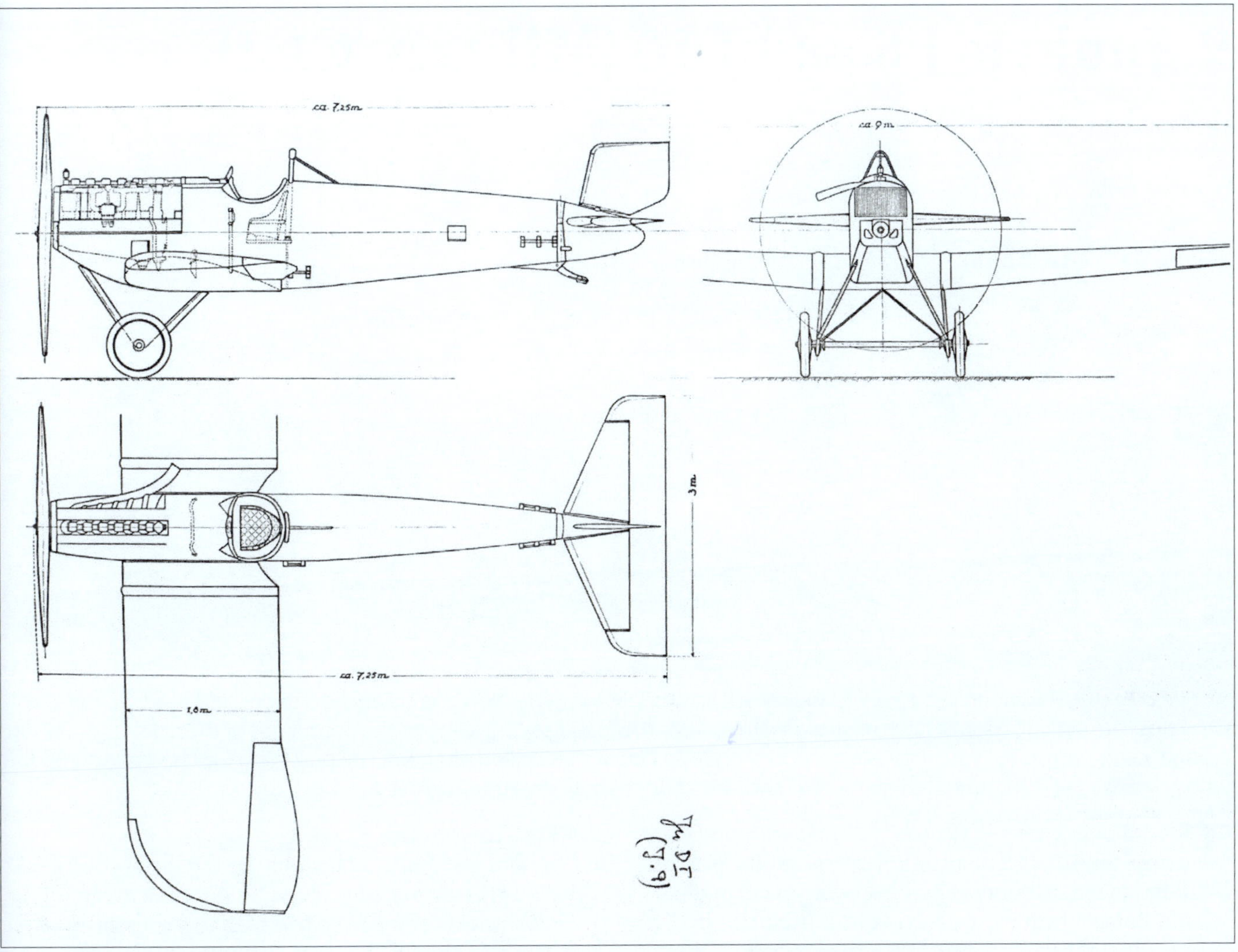

Above: Three-view drawing of the D.I. This drawing appeared in many aviation journals post-war.

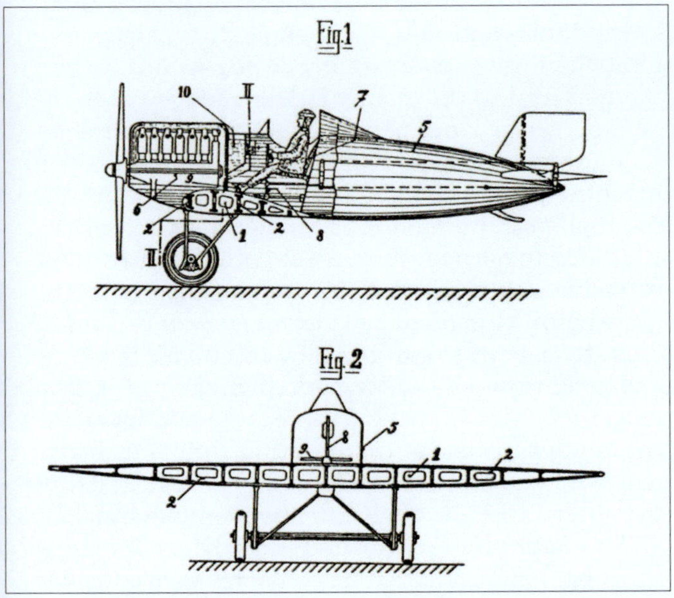

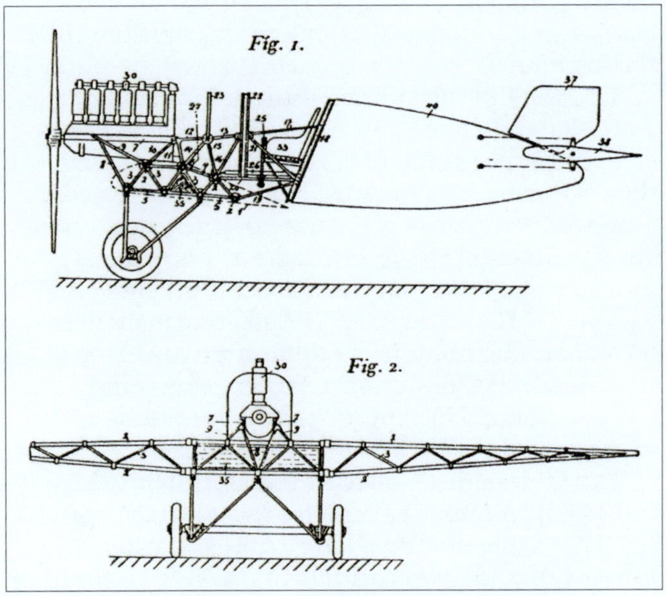

Above & Above Right: Drawings from the patent on the D.I.

9. Junkers J 8 and J 10 (Military CL.I)

Above & Facing Page: Junkers J 8 on 2 January 1918, the CL.I prototype. Note the balanced ailerons and the shape of the wing tips. The landing gear has two inverted V-struts from the fuselage centreline to the outer ends of the axle supports, and a single central strut. The wheel covers have "Junkers & Co Dessau" stencilled on them. The port wing root is strengthened with a walkway as the corrugated metal could not stand up to rough treatment. (AHT AL0459-220 and SDAM)

The J 8 was a two-seat monoplane developed from the J 7. It had a Junkers nose radiator and large balanced ailerons. The observer was armed with a Parabellum on a gun ring and the pilot had a synchronised machine gun. Power was supplied by a Mercedes D.III engine. It was designed for close infantry support to replace the Halberstadt and Hannover CL aircraft used in these operations. It was not armoured.

The story of the J 8 is confusing. Most references state that only one J 8 was constructed, it serving as a prototype for the J 10. According to Wagner[1], the J 8 was built to Junkers' requirements in secret around December 1917. Grosz however, notes that an experimental single-seat fighter was ordered in December 1916, but the three prototypes were C-types (C.701/17 to C.703/17). The secrecy may have been due to Junkers building a two-seater machine when the authorities were expecting a single-seater. Until more documentation is discovered this can only be speculation.

The J 8 was first flown on 10 December 1917, from Halle airfield, a year after the contract was let. That same month Fokker wrote to Professor Junkers that the two partners in *Jfa* were committed to develop a C-class machine (that is a two-seat machine with armament for the pilot and observer). Fokker stressed the advantages of the J 8 with its field of fire for the observer and its high speed, concluding that it would have many uses at the Front.

Fokker flew the J 8 on the 14th, a few days after he damaged the J 7. He was impressed with its performance. Fokker's test pilot, Schmidt, then flew tests for climb rates and speeds on 8 January 1918. During this flight fog rolled up obscuring the landing field. Schmidt then experienced engine failure when the fuel feed to the engine failed, and he had to make an emergency landing. Fortunately, discovering a hole in the fog, he put the J 8 down in a field but the machine turned over. Schmidt was unhurt and the monoplane suffered minor damage.

Idflieg must have been aware of the machine as it recorded in the February 1918 monthly report that the machine had been developed by *Jfa* and the aircraft, that was powered by a 160-hp Mercedes, had gone through the type acceptance tests. A final judgement on the machine's flight characteristics could not be made at that point in time but the firm had been given a test order for 20 machines in order to gather experience with this type of machine.

The *Baubeschreibung* drawing of the CL.I shows the long, balanced ailerons of the J 8. It is considered that the J 8 was type tested and accepted for the production version, the J 10 (Military CL.I). This was

Above: The J 8 on the airfield, presumably for testing. Note the Morrell airspeed indicator on the starboard wing. The undercarriage has the central strut omitted but the two inverted V-struts are still in place.

J 8 Chronology

Dec 1916	Junkers experimental single-seat fighter ordered.
4 Dec 1917	J 8 completed. To be tested following week.
10 Dec 1917	J 8 on Halle airfield for tests.
16 Dec 1917	During altitude test flight Schmidt suffers forced landing at Landsberg bei Halle.
17–22 Dec 1917	New undercarriage and new engine installed.
6 Jan 1918	Halle airfield, with *FEA* 14, ready for altitude flight.
14 Jan 1918	Altitude flight made with C-type. AUW to 5,000 m with 450 kg payload. Excellent performance, 3,000 m in 19 mins. Total flight time 42 mins.
20-27 Jan 1918	Competition tests at Aldershof.
Source: P.M. Grosz Collection Box 494.	

Above & Below: First flown on 4 May 1918, CL.1802/18 was the production prototype for the CL.I. These photographs give a good idea of the size of the neat, two-seat fighter – an enlarged D.I. Note the revised non-balanced ailerons. The wing crosses are carried around the leading edge of the wings. There is one synchronized Spandau machine gun.

not uncommon, the Fokker V 13 being accepted for the series production of the Fokker D.VI. Further it would seem that the J 8 was included in the order for three prototypes as it is not recorded as accepted by the Army.

The J 8 accompanied the J 7 to the First *D Flugzeug Wetthewerb* along with the J 7 with a new set of wings and balanced ailerons. The two

Above: Junkers CL.I 1805/18. Two camouflage colours are visible on the upper and side surfaces. Note the two pilot's synchronized Spandau machine guns.

Above: Another view of Junkers CL.I 1802/18.

machines were not to take part in the performance evaluations but were presented as demonstrations of the future aircraft under consideration for production. They were flown by service pilots from the Front including the redoubtable Manfred von Richthofen.

Specifications J 8					
Source	**1**	**2**	**3**	**4**	**5**
Dimensions, m					
Span	12.25	12.04	12.25	40 ft 7 in	40 ft 21/8 in
Length	7.90	7.90	7.90	25 ft 10½ in	26 ft 0 in
Height		2.66	3.10		
Wing Area		23.40 m^2	23.40 m^2	253 ft^2	
Weights					
Empty		710 kg	708 kg	1,560 lbs	
Gross		1,050 kg	1,050 kg	2,310 lbs	
Fuel			39 kg		
Oil			4 kg		
Crew			160 kg		
Payload			139 kg		
Speed					
		161 km/h(max)		116 mph	
Max at G/Level			180 km/h		
Cruising at G/ Level			160 Km/h		
Ceiling			5,000 m		
Range			500 km		
Endurance			3 h		

Notes: * Competition with minimum fuel load (< 1 h)
Source:
1. Junkers GA drawings of J 8.
2. Green and Scarborough.
3. Wagner, W.
4. Cowin, H.W. *The Junkers Monoplanes*, Profile Publications, UK, 1967.
5. J. Morrow shows different dimensions for the span of the J 8 and J 10 in his plans that accompanied Bowers, P.M. "Professor YOOnkers' Tin Donkeys." *Air Progress*, Spring 1961, P.64.

The J 8 story now becomes intertwined with that of the J 10.

The J 10 (Military CL.I)

Whether the other two prototypes were the same or similar to the J 8 with the extended balanced ailerons is unknown.[2] The *Idflieg* report for March 1918, mentioned the two-seat machine and states that it had a good flight characteristics and performance. However, the Junkers machine proved difficult to manufacture due to a lack of organisation at *Jfa*. In May *Idflieg* reported problems with the wings in flight. Considering the time frame this must have happened to the production machines, now designated CL.I, as the J 8 had been flying since the end of 1917 without any such problem being evident. The J 10 had only made a few flights by May 1918 when the complaints about the wing were made. Changes were made that overcome the problem in four weeks.

The 180-hp Mercedes D.IIIaü and 185-hp BMW IIIa were used in the J 10. The higher powered BMW engine proved to offer little improvement over the Mercedes at the low altitudes that the J 10 operated at. It was only at higher altitudes that he advantages of the BMW engine came into effect.

The production version of the J 8, the J 10, arrived too late to see front line service before the end of the war.[3] It appears to have been identical to the J 8 except that the plain ailerons within the wing contours were now fitted. The first few had the same undercarriage as the J 8 but this was redesigned for

Specifications J 10 (Military CL.I)								
Source	**1***	**2***	**3***	**4**	**5**	**5**	**6**	**7**
Dimensions								
Span	12.2 m	12.040 m	12.25 m	12.2 m	12.15	12.00	36 ft 1¼ in	36 ft 1¼ in
Length	7.9 m	7.900 m	7.90 m	7.9 m	7.90	7.90	25 ft 10½ in	26 ft 0 in
Height	3.1 m	2.657 m		3.1 m	3.10	3.20		
Chord		2.230 m						
Track		1.980 m	2.00 m					
Wing Area		23.40 m^2	23.40 m^2	253 ft^2	23.70 m^2	23.00 m^2	233 ft^2	
Weights								
Empty	735 kg			735 kg	735 kg	735 kg	1,620 lbs	
Fuel					110 kg	110 kg		
Oil					15 kg	15 kg		
Crew					160 kg	160 kg		
Payload					135 kg	115 kg		
Loaded	1,155 kg			1,155 kg	1,155 kg	1,135 kg	2,345 lbs	
Speed	120 km/h			190 km/h	190/175*	190/175*	118 mph	
Range					525 km	525 km		
Endurance					3 h	3 h		
Engine					Mercedes D.IIIaü	BMW Bz IIIa		

Notes: * These sources all show the balanced, extended ailerons.
Source:
1. *Jane's All the World's Aircraft 1920.* (*Jane's* has the designation recorded as the CLS as does *Jllustrierte Flug-Welt.*)
2. *Baubeschreibung* three-view.
3. Junkers three-view drawing 1779.
4. *Jllustrierte Flug-Welt*, Vol.1, 1919, P.376.
5. Wagner, W.
6. Cowin, H.W. *The Junkers Monoplanes*, Profile Publications, UK, 1967.
7. J Morrow data. From Morrow's plans that accompanied Bowyer's article: "Professor YOOnkers' Tin Donkeys." *Air Progress*, Spring 1961, P.64.

the majority. The first flight of the J 10 was on 4 May 1918. An order for 10 had been placed on 27 March 1918, followed by another on 25 September, then 20 more on 15 October and a further 20 on 9 November.[4] Given the military designation CL.I the machine had the new 185-hp BMW IIIa engine, redesigned landing gear, unbalanced ailerons and was overall lighter than the J 8. None saw service on the Western Front, they were too few, too late. Only 43 were constructed in total. It was utilised along with the J 9 on Germany's border wars immediately after the Armistice. They are known to have operated from Wainoden, Brieg in Poland, and Peterfeld in Lithuania.

A photograph of 11 men standing on each wing of a CL.I, in a Fokker like demonstration of the strength of the wings, was published in the *Aeronautical Engineering* supplement to *The Aeroplane* in its issue of 8 January 1918. In typical C.G. Gray[5] fashion the photograph was captioned: "A Fallacious Test: A German attempt to persuade the public of the strength of the Junker all metal freak machines."[6] Like so many involved in British aviation he failed to see that metal construction was the wave of the future.

The "Summary of Technical Air Intelligence for Friday, 8th November, 1918", listed the Junkers

This Page: Further views of the prototype CL.1802/18. Note the stencil *"Hier anfassen"* bordered by two arrows painted on the wingtip in the photo above. This aircraft has one synchronized machine gun mounted for pilot. A Morrell airspeed indicator is mounted on top of the left wing.

CL.I Monoplane under "New Types of Aircraft." It described the monoplane as follows:

The fuselage is rather long and tapers to the tail. The main wing has a wide chord, it is not swept back and is square at the wing tips, but the trailing edge is cut away on either side of the fuselage. The ailerons are balanced and have extensions beyond the wings. The tailplane forms a wide-angle triangle. The elevator is one piece and rectilinear; it is not balanced.

Approximate dimensions were given as:

Span (including ailerons)	40 ft 0 in
Overall length	27 ft 0 in

Above: Dated 19 June 1918, this photograph of CL.1802/18 appears to be in the same series as those on thee preceding pages.

Above: The photograph number, 1266, and the date, 19 June 1918, ties these photographs of CL.1802/18 together. Note the radio transmitter antenna visible under the fuselage beneath the cockpits. (AHT AL0459-219)

Above & Below: CL.1803/18 without any markings other than its serial. It had one sychronized machine gun for the pilot. Only six CL.I fighters were completed before the Armistice. The Junkers all metal aircraft were favourites of the pulp magazines of the 1930s, usually with misleading captions. This photograph appeared in Flying Aces magazine with the caption: "Here's the last game effort of the Germans to build an armoured trench fighter to stop the final rush of the Allies in 1918. This is the Junkers all-metal monoplane, which boasted of an armoured cockpit for trench strafing." The CL type was designed for trench strafing as one of its duties but the Junkers machine was not armoured.

Above: Completing CL.1806/18 in the Junkers factory. One D.I, three CL.I, and one J 4 fuselage can be seen in the background. The crowded conditions did not allow for ease of manufacture.

Above: This CL.I appears to have hit the port wing and then turned over. This attitude after landing seems to have been common for Junkers types and is a comment on the rough landing strips they were compelled to use. Note how the wing crosses are painted continuously over the leading edge of the wings. There is a notable contrast between the white cross outlines and the underside blue color paint. (From the August Quoos album.)

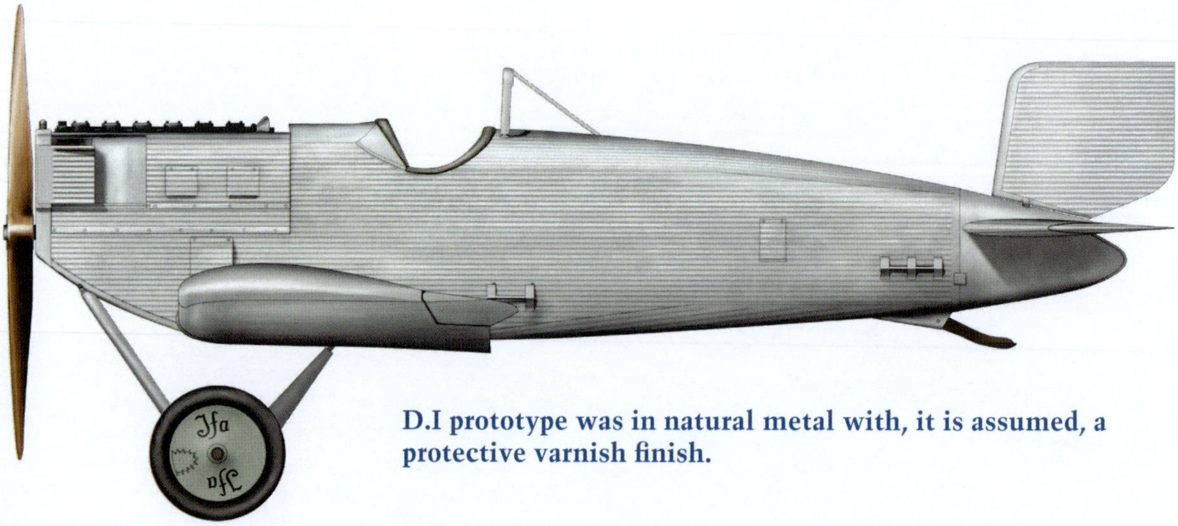

D.I prototype was in natural metal with, it is assumed, a protective varnish finish.

D.I 9166/18 with standard upper surface camouflage and assumed to have light blue under surfaces. The logo and serial were applied in black.

The subject of the British report, this D.I was noted as having a chocolate brown fuselage with white undersides and tailplane. The upper surface of the wings were finished in standard green and mauve camouflage.

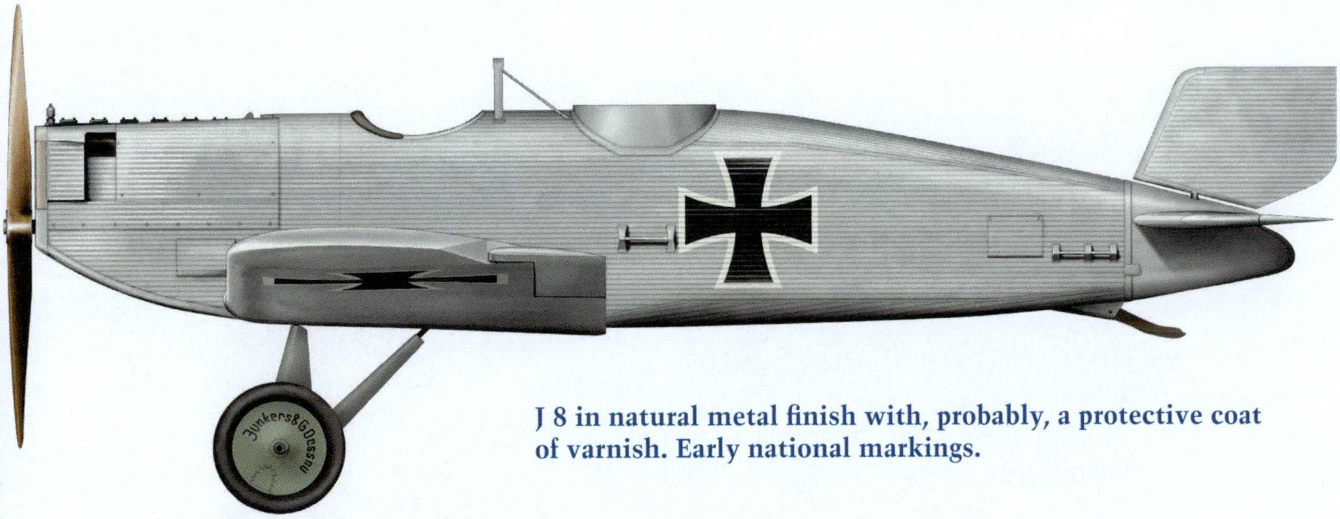

J 8 in natural metal finish with, probably, a protective coat of varnish. Early national markings.

CL.I 12613/18 is probably unique in carrying a personal insignia. Dark shield with white "J"/ Assumed to be in usual camouflage scheme.

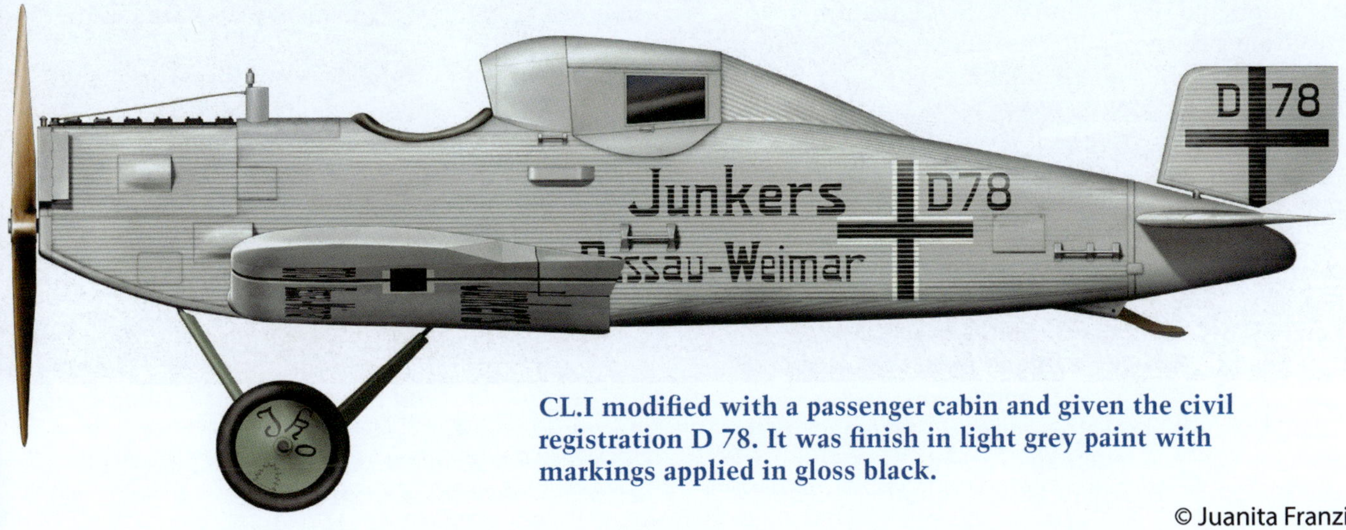

CL.I modified with a passenger cabin and given the civil registration D 78. It was finish in light grey paint with markings applied in gloss black.

Above: August Quoos in the cockpit of CL.12608/18 that was delivered on 18 February 1919. *FA* 431 was based at Wainoden in Kurland to protect Germany's eastern borders and the German population in the Baltic states. The unit was in action against the Red Army. (From the August Quoos album.)

A note to the report shows that the Allies were aware of the development of the CL.I before the date of this particular report.[7]

The *Kampfgeschwader Sachsenberg* was made up of volunteers from *Ltn* Gotthard Sachsenberg's old unit. As one of the *Freikorps* units it was attached to 1 Garde Reserve Division. Formed at Jueterbog it consisted of one fighter squadron, one assault squadron and one reconnaissance squadron, one machine gun company, one quartermaster unit, one cavalry platoon and one artillery platoon. It became one of the best known of the units supporting the *Freikorps*. Composed of *FA* 413, *FA* 416 and *FA* 417 it was based at Wainoden in Kurland. For their operations against the Soviets they were provided with the latest aircraft from Germany including Junkers CL.I and D.I monoplanes. The unit was to protect Germany's eastern boarders and the German populations in the Baltic states.

The Red Army was able to push the German 8th Army back as far as Riga and Mitau. In February 1919, the unit went into action. An advance party selected the Wainoden airfield with its two airship sheds next to the Libau-Schaulen railway. The rest of the unit arrived by the end of the month. The unit had the latest Fokker D.VII, Halberstadt CL.IV and Hannover CL.III biplanes in addition to the Junkers monoplanes. Bombing and strafing attacks are carried out on railway stations, troop concentrations and depots. By mid-March 1919 the unit has won back Riga. The Allies ban on operations in the Baltic saw part of the unit returned to West Prussia but the main part remained fighting the Russians during the summer.

Sachsenberg was always a promoter of Junkers aircraft and on 8 September 1919, he wrote to Professor Junkers as *Kommandeur des Kamfgeschwader Sachsenberg*, of his experiences with the Junkers all-metal aircraft in the East after the Armistice. He was concerned with the establishment of the main squadrons in the East and already was a supporter of Junkers aircraft.

As a result of my experience gained during test and comparison flights in Junkers D and C aircraft and keeping in mind the great weather durability of Junkers aircraft I asked on establishing my squadron for the East that a proportion of the airplanes be ordered from Junkers. As the Inspection

Above: CL.I of *FEA* 9 at Thorn, 1918. The camouflage separation between the upper and lower surfaces is not a straight line on the wing leading edge. This view displays the plain undercarriage, without the aerodynamic fairings, to advantage. (AHT AL0093-23)

had at that time already received a large number of C and D airplanes from Junkers my wishes were granted. I took about 30 Junkers Type aircraft with me made up equally of C and D types. The Junkers type has exceeded all expectations at the front. The "weatherability" of the aircraft is so good that it was possible to leave them in the open for weeks on end during March, in the thaw, in the ice, snow and rain. A cover over the engine and propeller was sufficient to provide adequate protection. As there were no tents or hangars available at the time it would have been impossible to operate in Russia with any other aircraft than the Junkers-metal-aircraft type. The flight characteristics particularly of the C aircraft made it possible to use the Junkers aircraft for all military purposes. The aircraft was employed by the squadron for reconnaissance and photography, bombing in the enemy's rear areas and most frequently at very low level for ground attack. The high speed of the aircraft in all these flights was much appreciated by the squadron, particularly in the ground attack mode. The opposition defence, especially with machine-guns, which was very heavy now and then, resulted in slower aircraft returning home totally shot up and riddled while the Junkers C returned from ground attack sorties invariably untouched. The few hits the aircraft sustained, even when major engine bearers were hit, never resulted in any form of unserviceability. After initial reservations were overcome all squadron pilots liked to fly the Junkers types over the front, particularly the C type. Relatively little (damage) occurred in crashes and emergency landings. Overall the type far exceeded all expectations I had for it. With further improvements, the Junkers metal aircraft will undoubtedly be the premier combat airplane as soon as it is introduced in large numbers. The advantage of its durability, extraordinary speed and resistance to damage negate all other minor faults and ensure that the Junkers type will be the first in combat aircraft ranks of the future.[8]

Above: Remains of a crashed Junkers CL.I. CL.I of *FA* 417 on 22 May 1919, after it was apparently hit by ground fire. Even the rugged Junkers construction could not stand up to the impact that his CL.I made. The corrugated covering has torn loose off both wings. (SDTB)

Many J 10 monoplanes were destroyed under orders of the Inter Allied Aircraft Control Commission (IAACC). This body was set up in June 1919 to ensure that the German Government kept the terms of the Peace Treaty. Junkers had converted four J 10 monoplanes to a passenger craft with a hinged hood covering the rear cockpit that could accommodate one passenger or a small amount of freight. He started a limited short-lived passenger service from Dessau to Weimar. They had *Junkers Dessau – Weimar* painted on the fuselage sides but retained their military markings.

Known civil J 10 monoplanes are D-77 (w/n 375 ex 1802/18) and D-78 (w/n 379 1806/18). The latter was operated by Lloyd-Luftverkehr Sablatnig. Two cabin Junkers went to France as reparations, and one was brought to the UK and was at Martlesham Heath in 1923 where it was photographed without its tyres.

Latvia obtained a CL.I in 1919 that the Germans had abandoned at Spilve. It was considered airworthy, with the fuselage and wings requiring some repairs, except for the lack of an engine.[9] Brought into Latvian service it received the serial No. 10.[10] On 17 June 1921 it was recorded as returned to service after an overhaul and repairs. Taking off the same day under the control of Vitn Jakubovs the aircraft had reached an altitude of about 50 m when the engine failed and landing downwind the machine ran into a ditch. It was repaired as it was in service on 22 March when it crashed on ice. *Vltn* Kraulis was flying, with *Ltn* Deprejs as observer, to the aid of German ships frozen in the ice near Riga. Engine trouble caused a forced alighting on the ice. The crew and aircraft were rescued by the German transport *Hanover* that returned them to Ventspils. This time it was not considered repairable and the wings were removed and the fuselage used for an airman's funeral carriage.

Above: An aircraft of *Kapmpfgeschwader Sachsenberg. FA* 417 on a reconnaissance mission over Kurland in March 1919.

Below: This aircraft was wrecked during a forced landing at Peterfelde in June, most probably due to fuel problems. (AHT AL0752-021)

Above & Below: Junkers CL.I in flight over Kurland (Latvia), possibly the aircraft at the top of the preceding page.

Above: A CL.I in flight. (SDTB)

Below: A CL.I taking off. (AHT AL0156-17)

Facing Page, Bottom: Another view of the prototype CL.1802/18.

Above: A pilot and observer with CL.12613/18. Note the serial application and the individual insignia. This machine has the windscreen. The weighted radio aerial fairlead may be seen under the fuselage. This machine appears to have been at Peterfelde in April 1919. (AHT AL0156-140)

Below: This CL.I in the Wainoden hangar appears to have the serial CL.12600/18. The pilot's guns are present but no windscreen. Note the LVG C.V behind. The Sachesenberg units remained at this location until March 1919, when they moved to the Vitini (Weitenfeld) airfield near Vecauce (Alt Auz), Latvia. (AHT AL072-008)

Above: 7 March 1919. *Vzfw* Herman Hackbush with CL.12600/18. The landing gear proved weak in service, and although not known for sure, this may have been the reason that some CL.I monoplanes are seen with the additional inverted V-strut undercarriage. Note the colour of the rear fuselage under the tailplane. The Zeppelin shed in the background identifies the location as Wainoden on the Kurland Peninsula (now in Latvia). (AHT AL0752-015)

Below: Same location, CL.12600/18 in background. Original caption stated this was first flight of the CL.I fighters but the undercarriage was too weak causing the pictured result. *Fw* Fritz Tödheide was associated with this crash. (AHT AL0752-012)

Above: Children were always attracted to any aircraft that landed in their vicinity at Peterfelde, summer 1919. Note the way the radiator blocks extend beyond the margin of the fuselage nose. (AHT AL0156-118)

CL.I (1803/18) abandoned by the Sachsenberg regiment at Vainode was obtained by Russian forces. It bore a light (white) coloured band around the fuselage at the rear gunner's cockpit. This machine and a badly damaged 12604/18, together with a D.I, were found to be unserviceable and not placed in service but would have introduced the Soviets to the Junker's products. Junkers was to have a good relationship with Soviet Russia post-war.

The specifications of the J 10 as listed below are taken from reputable sources, however given that the *Baubeschreibung* drawing of the CL.I shows the wing arrangement of the J 8 with the extended balanced ailerons, what the true dimensions of the J 10 (Military CL.I) are, is open to debate until confirming Junkers data is found. The *Baubeschreibung* drawing represented the prototype and production aircraft could differ dimensionally.

End Notes Chapter 9

1. Wagner, W. P.109. Op Cit.
2. Wagner states that the second J 8 prototype was the one sent to Adlershof for strength testing.
3. The popular British magazine *Air Stories* published fiction and historical articles with a continuous series on "Aces." One series featured contemporary and historical aircraft that were illustrated by sketches (no photographs appeared in the magazine) and specifications. It described the Junkers CL.I as being designed for "ground straffing" and "it proved a formidable performer at this dangerous work. No official information is available regarding the type of engine used or the speed obtained." The article gives the impression that the CL.I was in service at the Front and is typical of the misinformation published between the two world wars. *Air Stories* Vol. 4 No.5 May 1937.

Above: Ground crew and airmen (*Ltn* Martin and *Hptm* Eberstein) pose with CL.12609/18 of *FA* 431 at Klein-Gandau (Breslau). This machine has the full serial application "Junk C.L.I. Jfa". Accepted on 20 February 1919, it appears to have an extra strut bracing the undercarriage.

Above: CL.12619 , accepted on 19 March 1919, has the pilot's windscreen fitted. The remains of snow still lie on the airfield.

Above: Junkers duo; CL.1802/18 with the J 7 single-seat fighter prototype with standard ailerons but radiator mounted in front of the pilot. The J 7 appears to have the fuselage overpainted but this may be due to the light reflecting off the corrugations. (SDTB)

Below: The serial of this CL.I cannot be read. It appears to be an early production CL.I. The port wing wing-walk is clearly displayed.

Above: Accepted on 19 March 1919, CL.15672/18 in as new condition. Note the serial on the wingtip. The pilot has a rear-view mirror but no windscreen. Note the wheel covers. (STDB)

Above: A line up of Fokker D.VII fighters with an Albatros , Halberstadt CL.II, Junkers Cl.I, and another Halberstadt. Details of the location and unit would be welcome.

4. P.M. Grosz Collection Box 493.
5. Charles G. Gray was the long-time editor of *The Aeroplane*, and from 1916, also edited *Jane's All the World's Aircraft*. A man of strong convictions, his editorials had an influence on the British aviation scene. He left The Aeroplane in 1939, his strong support of fascist movements playing a part in his dismissal. He died on 9 December 1953. His obituary was published in the journal *Flight*, 18 December 1953, P.803, and revealed he was a gentle and kind man unlike the impression gained from reading his perverse and acid comments over the years.
6. The January 1919 *Jlluftrirte Zeitung*, Berlin, showed a photograph of 11 men standing on the starboard wing of a Junkers CL.I.
7. NARA RG45 Entry 520 Box 142.
8. Sachsenberg to Professor Junkers, 08.09.1919.

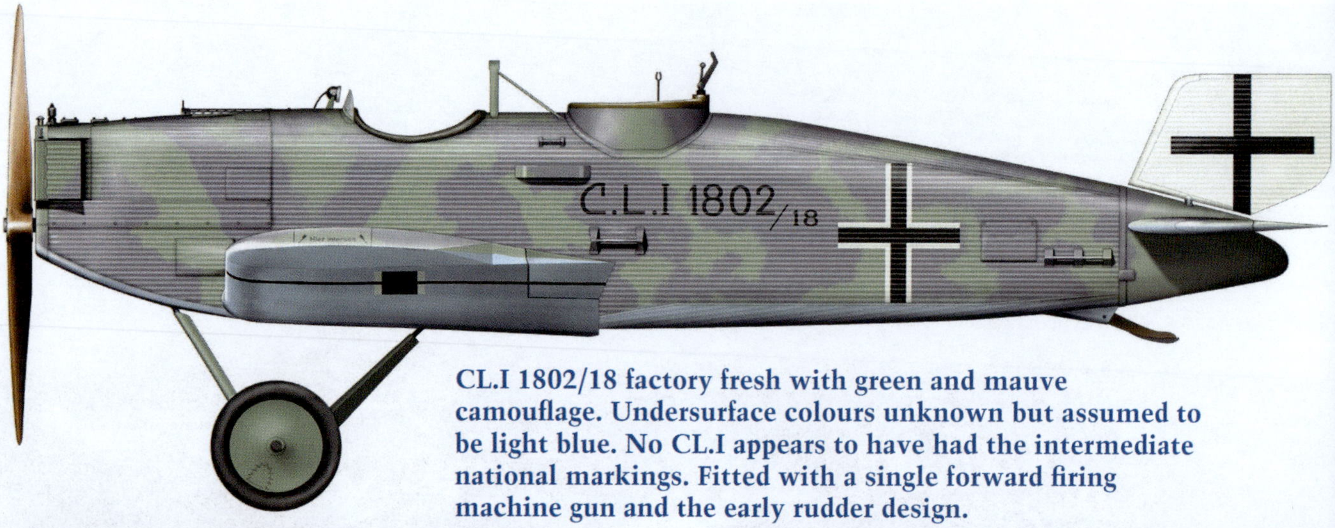

CL.I 1802/18 factory fresh with green and mauve camouflage. Undersurface colours unknown but assumed to be light blue. No CL.I appears to have had the intermediate national markings. Fitted with a single forward firing machine gun and the early rudder design.

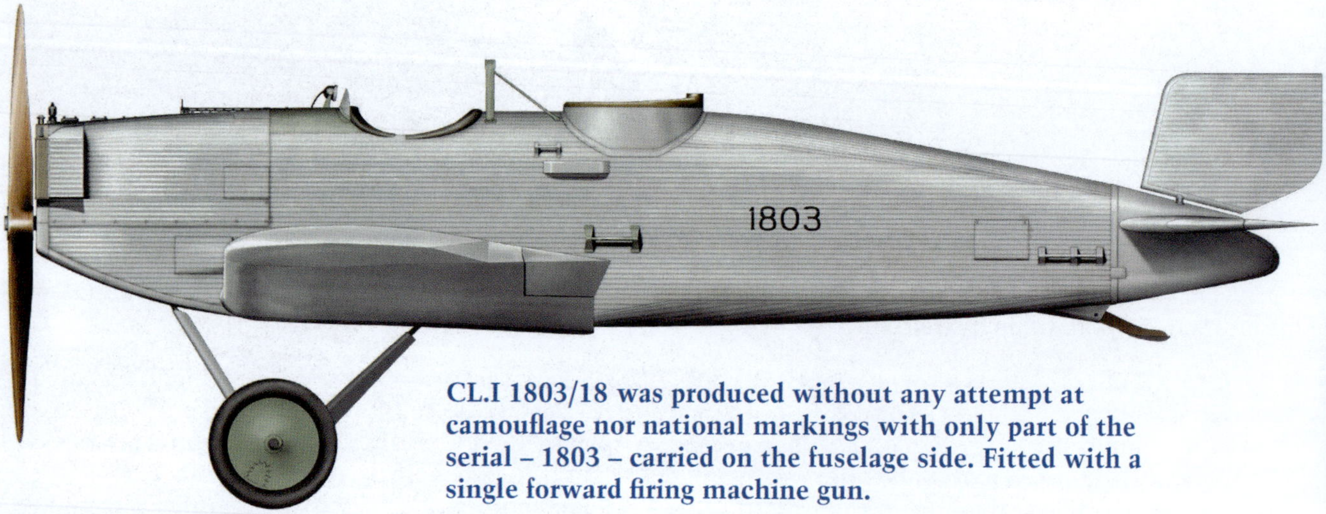

CL.I 1803/18 was produced without any attempt at camouflage nor national markings with only part of the serial – 1803 – carried on the fuselage side. Fitted with a single forward firing machine gun.

CL.I 12921/18 was in active service as denoted by the white fuselage band with dark (black) letter. Usual green and mauve camouflaged upper surfaces. Fitted with two forward firing machine guns.

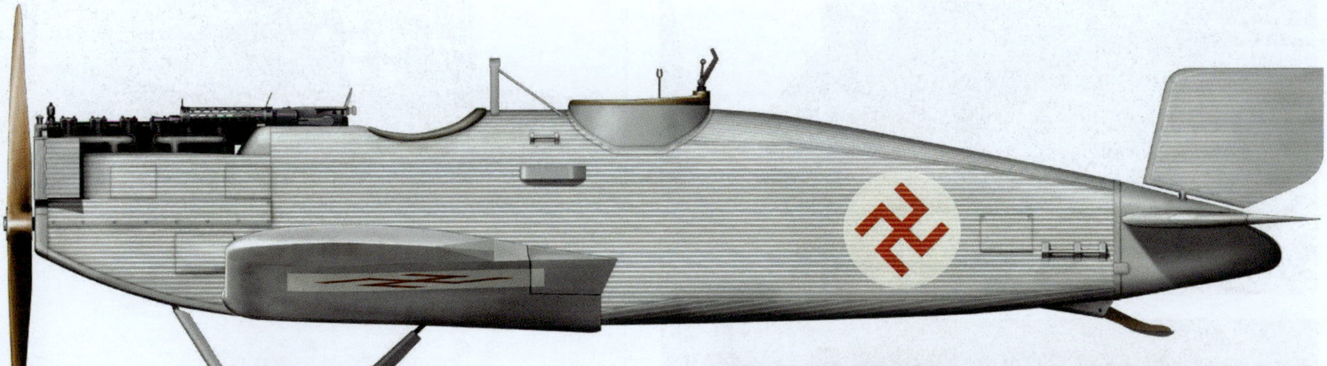

Latvian CL.I in natural metal finish with red on white national markings. Unusually the wing swastikas were not presented in a white circle but on a square.

This Page & Two Following Pages: As with many ex-military aircraft after the war, a hinged cabin was cobbled together for one passenger or a small amount of cargo in what was the observer's position. Here is the Junkers modification of the J 10, complete with military crosses before the reintroduction of civil registrations. The service operated briefly in March 1919 between Dessau and Weimar, the first airline service by an all-metal aeroplane. This set of photographs were obviously posed to show how the aircraft could transport passengers and cargo. Photograph dated 12 March 1919. (STDB)

12.3.18

Junkers
Dessau-Weimar
Junkers

Below: D-78 on the first German civil register was a conversion of CL.1806/18. On the original photograph the registration can be seen on the wing under-surface.

Above: Forward view of a J 10 civil modification. Note the way the fuselage panels have been built up behind the pilot's cockpit and the oversize radiator. Aerodynamically it would be very inefficient and at odds with Junkers' design philosophy. The Junkers J 10 is without a doubt the first all-metal aircraft to have operated an air service.

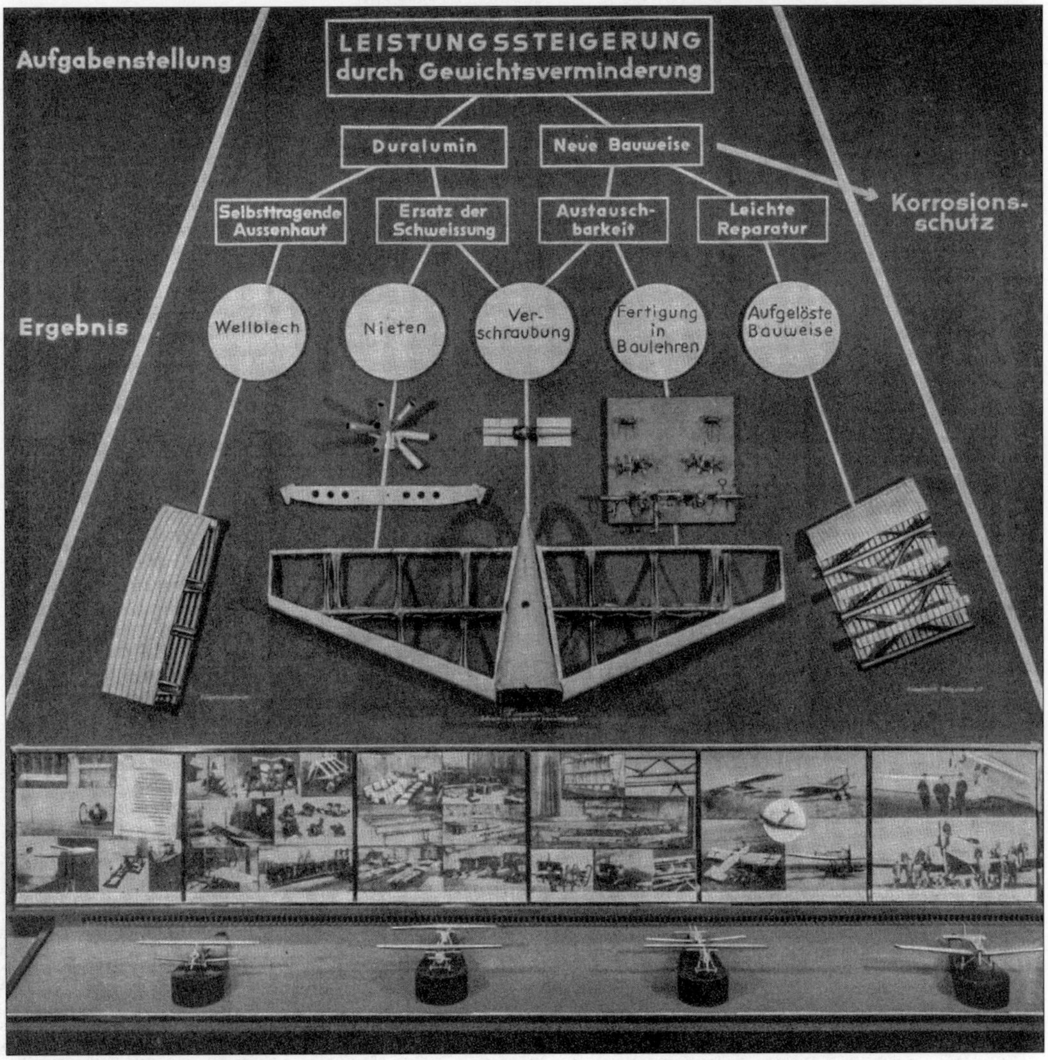

Right: The display in the Junkers technical museum between the world wars showing the evolution of the civilian post-war Junkers types from their military antecedents.

Schlachtstaffel des Geschwaders Sachsenberg,
die im Osten gegen die Bolschewisten hervorragende Dienste leistete.

Above: The remains of CL.I aircraft "M" of the Sachsenberg unit. The engine has fallen completely out of the fuselage, turned upside down and faces the remains of the machine.

Facing Page, Top: This CL.I is reportedly 12925/18. It has the white fuselage band of the Sachsenberg unit. The tailplane also appears to be white.

Right: The remains of a white fuselage band may just be discerned on this wrecked Junkers CL.I.

Facing Page, Bottom: Latvian CL.I in the workshops. Note that the wheels do not have tyres fitted.

Below: Latvian line-up for an official inspection with the CL.I at the start and Sopwith 1½ Strutters behind.

Junkers CL.I (Jfa) Shipping Dates from List Ending June 1919

Month	Prototypes 701–703/17		1800–1809/18		12920–12929/18		12600–12619/18		Total
Order			Nr.556/2.18		Nr.556/2.18		Nr.227/10.18		
1918									
Jan			1800	1					1
Feb									
Mar			1801	1					1
Apr									
May									
Jun									
Jul									
Aug									
Sep									
Oct			1805, 1807, 1808	3					3
Nov									
Dec									
1919									
Jan			1803, 1804, 1809	3	12920–12929	10	12600–12603	4	17
Feb							12604–12609	6	6
Mar							12610–12619	10	10
Apr							15671–15674	4	4
May									0
Jun									0
Repurchased			1802, 1806	2					2
Total		3		10		10		24	44

Source: R Zankl
Known serials for the CL.I include:
1802/18 Mercedes became D.77
1806/18 Benz became D.78.
1803/18 and 12604/18 captured by Soviet Russia.
12609/18 of *Kampfgeschwader Sachsenberg*

Copy via Bruno Schmäling. The C-type referred to by Sachsenberg was the Junkers CL.I. Apparently no J.I armoured types were used.

9. The serials 12921/18 and 1320 are given for this machine. Latvian Aviation web site. http://latviniaviation.com.Junkers.html. 16.07.2005.

10. "The Civil Aircraft Register – Germany" on the *Golden Years of Aviation* website lists D-77, a civil J 10, as having being obtained by the Latvia air force as No.10.

Above: Soviet Navy Junkers J20 built on the development of the J 10 and J 11. They were delivered in the Winter of 1923–1924 and remained in service for many years.

Weights of the J 8 or J 10

Item	Kg	Notes
Empty	301.7	
Pilot	85	
Observer	80	
MG & ammunition	65.5	1 MG & 500 rounds for pilot. 1 MG & 3 x 200 rounds for observer.
Instruments	1	
Fuel & Oil	108.5	133 litre main tank, 27 litre auxiliary tank, 11 litre oil tank. 138 kg total weight when full.
Motor	277.7	
Exhaust manifold	5.3	
Starter	2.0	
Radiator	16.8	Empty
Water	18.0	18 litres
Airscrew	19.0	With hub
Fuel tanks	25	
Oil tank	2.0	
Engine accessories	22.5	
Miscellaneous	20.0	
Gross weight	1,050	
Note: from the BB card for CL-I Type Test in February 1918.		

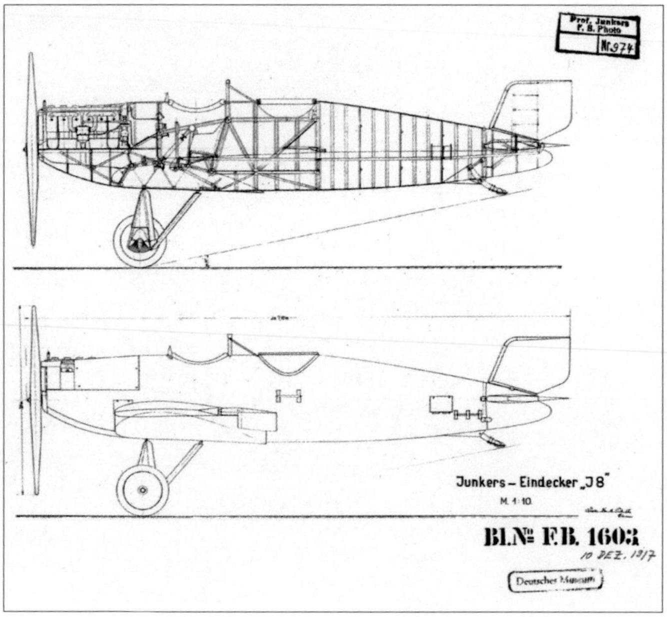

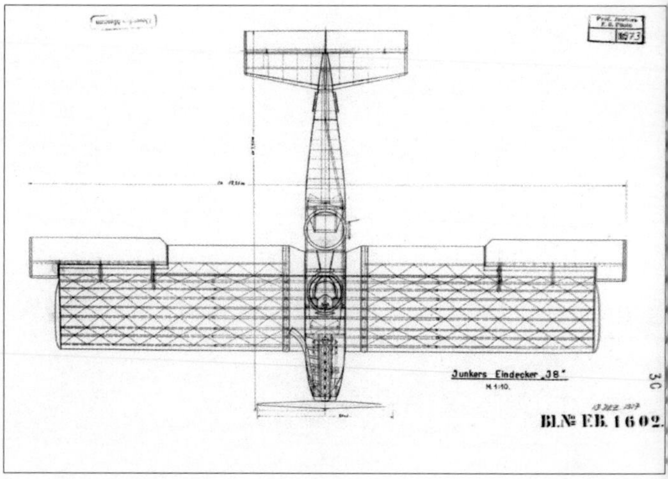

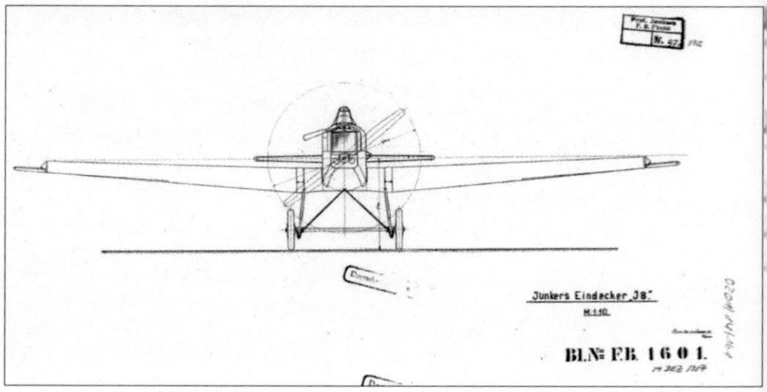

I. Nutzlast. JUNKERS CL I mit 160 PS MERCEDES-Motor	kg.
a. Insassen 1 Führer 85 kg 1 Beobachter 80 kg M.G. Schützen ... kg	165,0
b. Bewaffnung 1 starres M.G. ... kg 1 bewegl. M.G. ... kg 1 Gurt mit 500 Patronen ... 12 kg; 3 Trommeln zu je 200 Patronen ... 22,5 kg	65,5
c. Bomben ... Bomben zu ... kg ... Bomben zu ... kg	
d. Lichtbildeinrichtung	
e. F.T. Einrichtung	
f. Instrumente u. freibleibend	1,0
g. Betriebsstoffe: ausreichend für 3 Std. in 0 km Höhe; 1 Benzinhaupttank zu je 133 l, 1 " HILFSTANK " 27 l (160 l); 1 Oeltank mit 11 l Oel (ohne 3 l Luftraum). Bei vollen Tanks insgesamt 138 kg Betriebsstoffe. Bei Abnahme Tanks 4/5 gefüllt, Benzin gerechnet zu ... kg, Oel ... kg	108,5
I. Nutzlast = kg	340,0

II. Leergewicht.

1/ Triebwerk.	kg.	
a/ 1 Motor (einschließlich 6 l Oel im Gehäuse)	277,7	
b/ Übersetzungsgetriebe (falls nicht im Motor eingebaut mit Zwischenwellen, Lagern u.s.w.)		
c/ Auspuffsammler: mit Befestigungen	5,3	
d/ Anlaßvorrichtung	2,0	
e/ Kühleranlage: leer	16,8	
f/ Kühlwasser: 18 l	18,0	
g/ Luftschrauben; mit Naben	19,0	
h/ 1 Benzinhaupttank; mit Befestigungen i/ 1 " HILFS-tank; mit Befestigungen	25,0	
k/ 1 Oeltank	2,0	
l/ Motorzubehör (Drehzahl, Druck, Benzinstandmesser, Leitungen, Hähne, Schalter, Hebel, Kabel, Pumpen u.s.w.)	22,5	388,3
2/ Flugwerk:		
a/ Hauptrumpf, oder Schwanzträger mit Verkleidung, Deckblechen u.s.w.	73,0	
b/ Nebenrümpfe; mit Verkleidung		
c/ Rumpfzubehör; Sitze, Spanntürme u.s.w. STEUEREINRICHTUNG	41,7	
d/ Fahrgestell; vollständig mit Streben, Rädern, Befestigungen u.s.w.	45,0	
e/ Schwanzsporn; mit Abfederung		
f/ Steuereinrichtung; mit Befestigungsteilen		
g/ Sämtliche Flügel; vollständig mit Klappen, Gelenken, Stielen, Kabeln und Steuerzügen	123,0	
h/ Höhen u. Seitenleitwerk; mit Befestigung und Steuerzügen	19,0	301,7
3/ Rumpfeinbauten; soweit nicht zur Festigkeit erforderlich und nicht unter Nutzlast gerechnet z.B. Befestigungsteile für M.G., F.T. Bombenaufhängevorrichtung u.s.w.	20,0	20,0
II. Leergewicht		710,0
III. Gesamtgewicht G =		1050,0

BEIM TYPENFLUGZEUG: 2 BENZINTANKS IN DEN FLÜGELANSÄTZEN JEDER MIT 67 l FASSUNG

Heft-rand

A3. 816a JUNK. CL.I.

Left & Facing Page: *Baubeschreibung* drawing and performance details for the CL.I. Note the machine selected for this was one of the prototypes with the balanced ailerons. The second page of the report is at left.

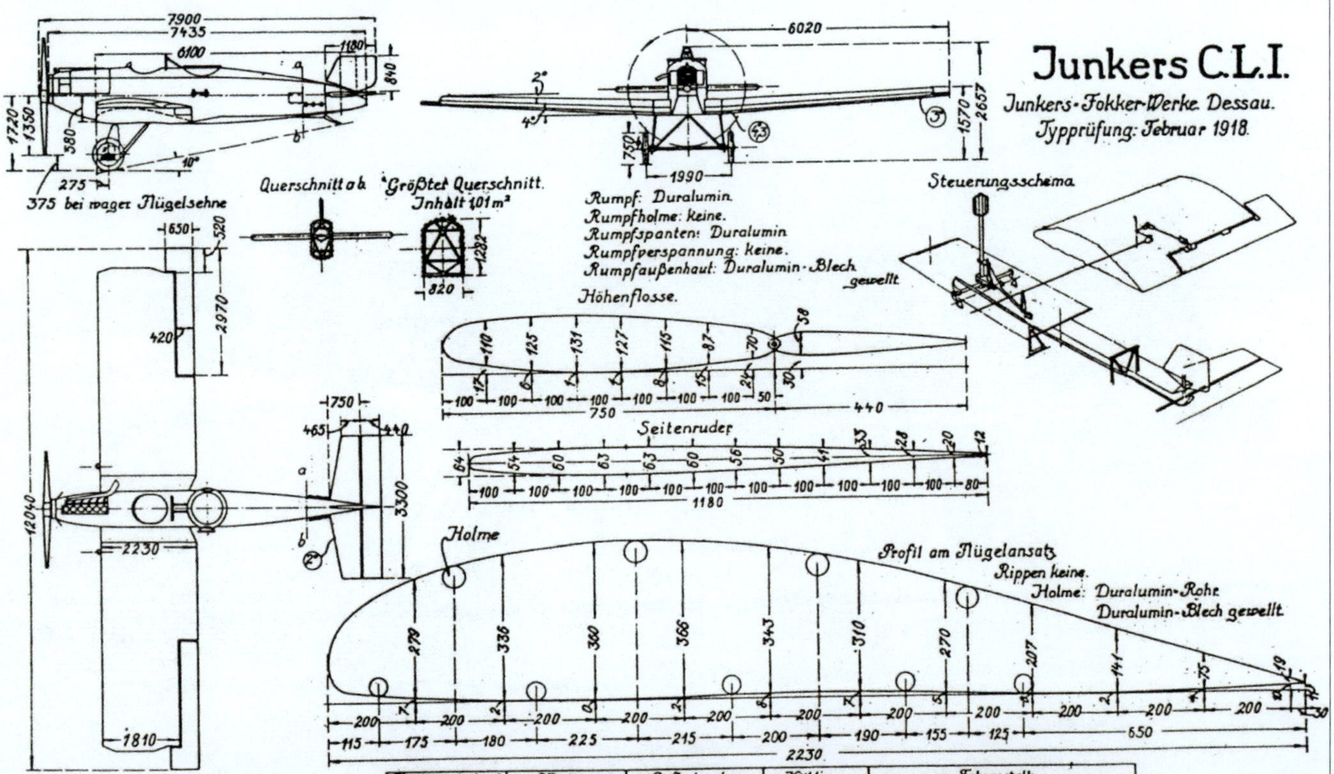

Flächeninhalt m²	Motor.	Luftschraube.	Kühler.	Fahrgestell:	
Beide Flügel mit Querruder 23,40	160 PS Mercedes Bremsleistung N ~ 170 PS. n ~ 1400 Umdr/min.	Axial, Holz, 2 flügl. Durchmesser 270 cm. Blattbreite: 23 cm. Steigung: 210 cm. n ~ 1400 Umdr/min.	Stirnkühler. Jbt. Junkers u. Co. Inhalt - 57,5 l. Gesamtes Kühlwasser 18 l.	Streben Stahlrohr 35/33 Fütterung keine	Federung: Drahtspirale. Federungsweg: 120 mm. Nabe: Breite: 160 mm. Durchmesser: 56 mm.

Heft-rand

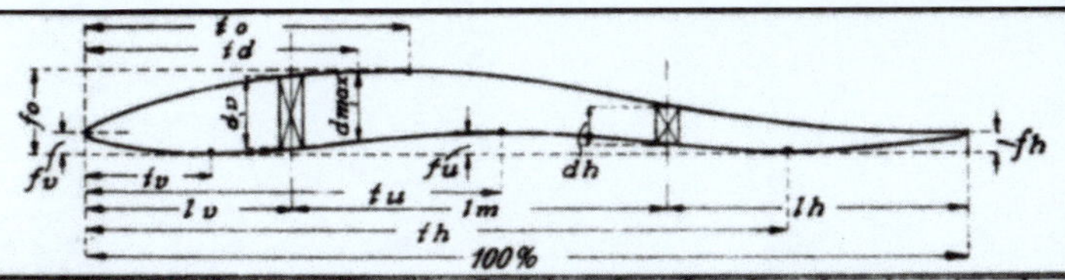

% d. Rippentiefe	f_v	f_h	f_u	f_o	d_{max}	d_v	d_h	t_v	t_h	t_u	t_o	t_d	l_v	l_m	l_h
Profil am Flügelansatz	4,04	0,67	0,90	16,60	16,60	—	—	21,75	79,60	55,40	30,70	29,60	—	—	—

Eigenschaften: Steigklasse: 50/45

Anlauf: gef. 80 m. erreicht m. Auslauf: gef. 80 m. erreicht: m.

Nutzlast 340 kg.

Steigzeiten auf Jahresmittel umgerechnet:
gefordert: 1 - 5, 2 - 6, 3 - 7,7, 4 - 10,3, 5 - 16 km, min
erreicht: 0, 3,9, 1 - 4,7, 2 - 6,4, 3 - 9,2, 4 - 19,3, -

Geschwindigkeit: gefordert: mindestens 165 km in 5 km Höhe
erreicht: in 2900 m 161 km, in 3350 m 158 km, in 4300 m 156 km/Std.

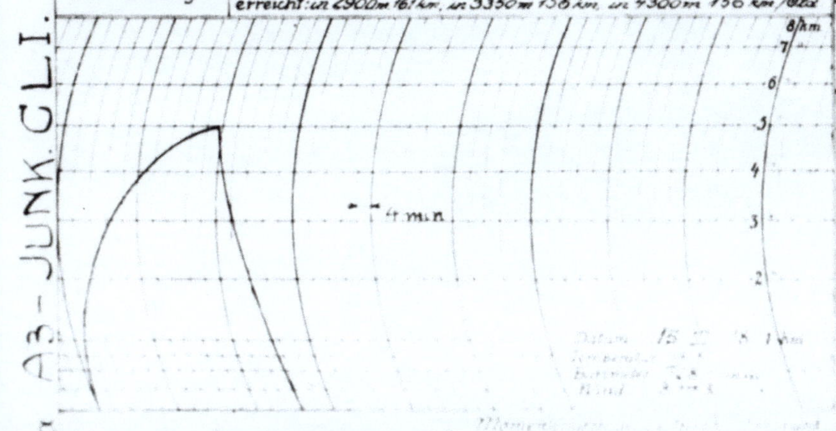

Flächenbelastung: (vergleiche Gewichtstabelle)
$\frac{G}{F} = \frac{1050}{23,4}$ kg/m² = 44,9 kg/m²

Leistungsbelastung:
$\frac{G}{N} = \frac{1050}{170}$ kg/PS = 6,18 kg/PS

Gewichtsanteil:
des Triebwerkes = $\frac{II^1 \text{ kg}}{III \text{ kg}} = \frac{388,3}{1050}$ = 0,370 kg.
des Flugwerkes = $\frac{II^2 \text{ kg}}{III \text{ kg}} = \frac{301,7}{1050}$ = 0,287 kg.
der nützlichen Last = $\frac{I + II^3 \text{ kg}}{III \text{ kg}} = \frac{360}{1050}$ = 0,343 kg.

Einheitsgewicht:
der Flügel = $\frac{II^2 g \text{ kg}}{F \text{ m}^2} = \frac{123}{23,4}$ = 5,25 kg/m²
des Triebwerkes = $\frac{II^1 \text{ kg}}{N \text{ PS}_e} = \frac{388,3}{170}$ = 2,285 kg/PS$_e$

Behälterzuschlag:
$\beta = \frac{II^{1 (h+i+k)} \text{ kg}}{I_g \text{ kg}}$ = 27

Fahrgestell soll so abgeändert werden, dass es von den Flügeln wechselbar wird.

This D.I was found with others at Hombeek, Belgium post-Armistice. All had a dark over-painted fuselage. This machine had a two colour band partially around the fuselage. The dark colour is unknown but assumed to be red. Wings show the usual green and mauve camouflage.

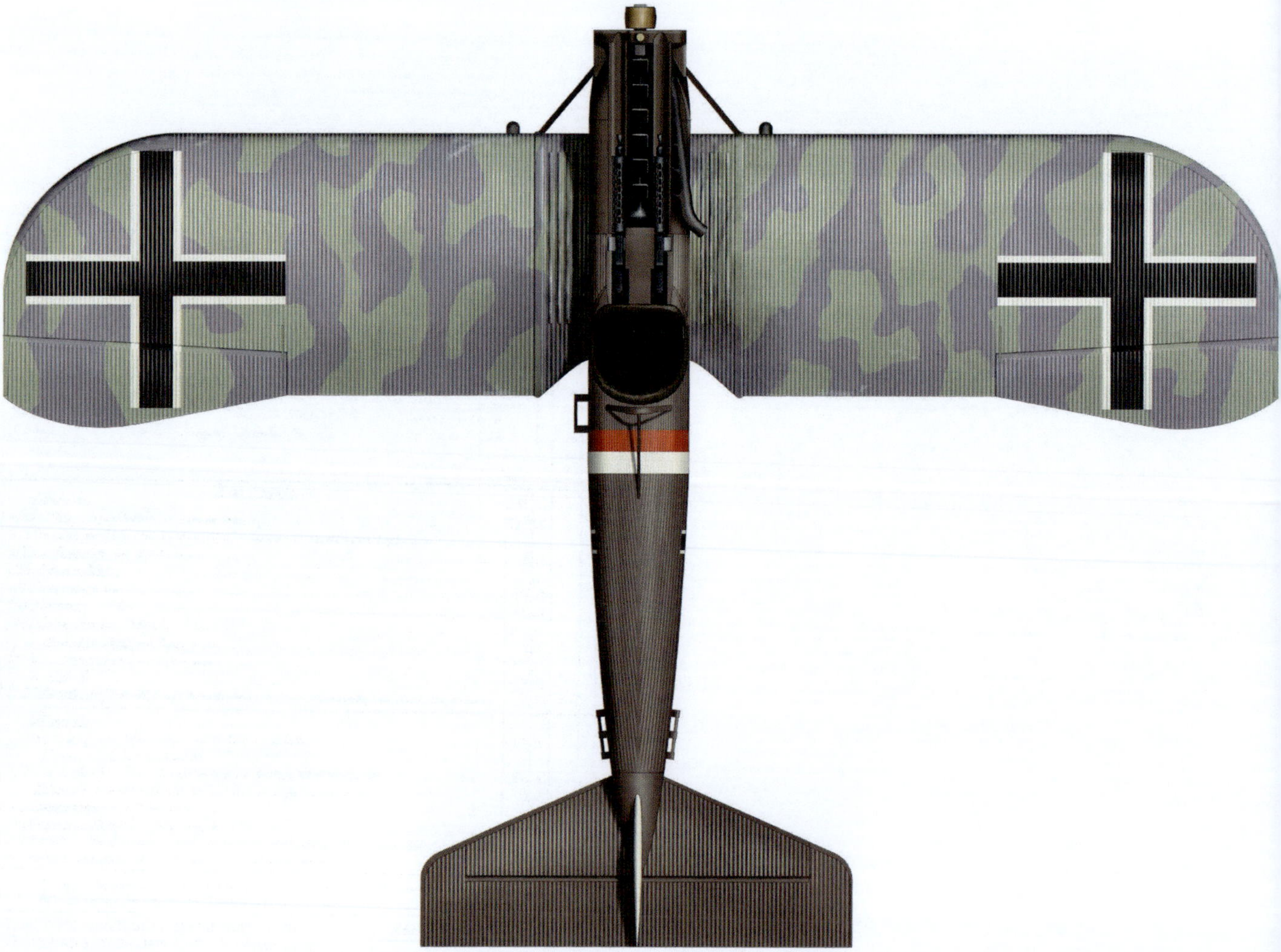

10. Junkers Marine Aircraft

Above: Marine Nummer 7501 has the number in the Army's style rather than the Navy's. This is the first of the three at the Seaplane Testing station at Warnemünde. Richard Thiedemann, the naval pilot who test flew the machine was impressed with its performance.

The next Junkers aeroplane in sequence was the J 11, however before entering into its story, it is necessary to go back to the beginnings of Junkers relationship with the German Navy's *Reichmarineamt (RMA* – State Marine Authority). Junkers had good contacts with the *RMA* due to his ship's engines. In June 1916, Junkers prepared the design of a single-seat fighter floatplane to be powered by a Mercedes D.III engine. The biplane, *Junkers-Marine-Flugzeuge* 2 (J.M.2) was designed by Jaekel who had joined Junkers from Sablatnig, which explains the lines of the proposed fast machine.[1]

The following year another single-seat fighter monoplane floatplane was proposed. This machine was to have a wingspan of 18.80 metres and an area of some 45 square metres. No sketches of this aeroplane, the J.M.2 I, appear to have survived.

The J.M.2 II project was ordered by the *RMA* in January 1917. Powered by a Mercedes D.III the project was marked out as a biplane or monoplane with project sketches and estimates of performance sent to the *RMA*. The machine was designed to give the pilot the best view upwards and downwards.

The J.M.2 600 proposal was apparently designed with an increased gap over that of the J.M.2 II, as it was thought that the latter might have dangerous spin characteristics.

The J.M.2 III monoplane fighter was put forward in March 1917. This was a low wing floatplane with a thick cantilevered wing. This machine featured the wing centre section being part of the fuselage to which the outer panels were attached.

There are drawings but no data on the J.M.6 Ia and Ib projects. A two seat floatplane that appears to have had wheels mounted within the floats. It is presumed to have been designed as a reconnaissance machine.

The J 11

Junkers did not have any success with marine aircraft until the J 11. Metal floats were being experimented with but the concept of an all-metal seaplane must have aroused the interest of the German Navy. Whether Junkers approached the Navy or the other way around is not known. In late

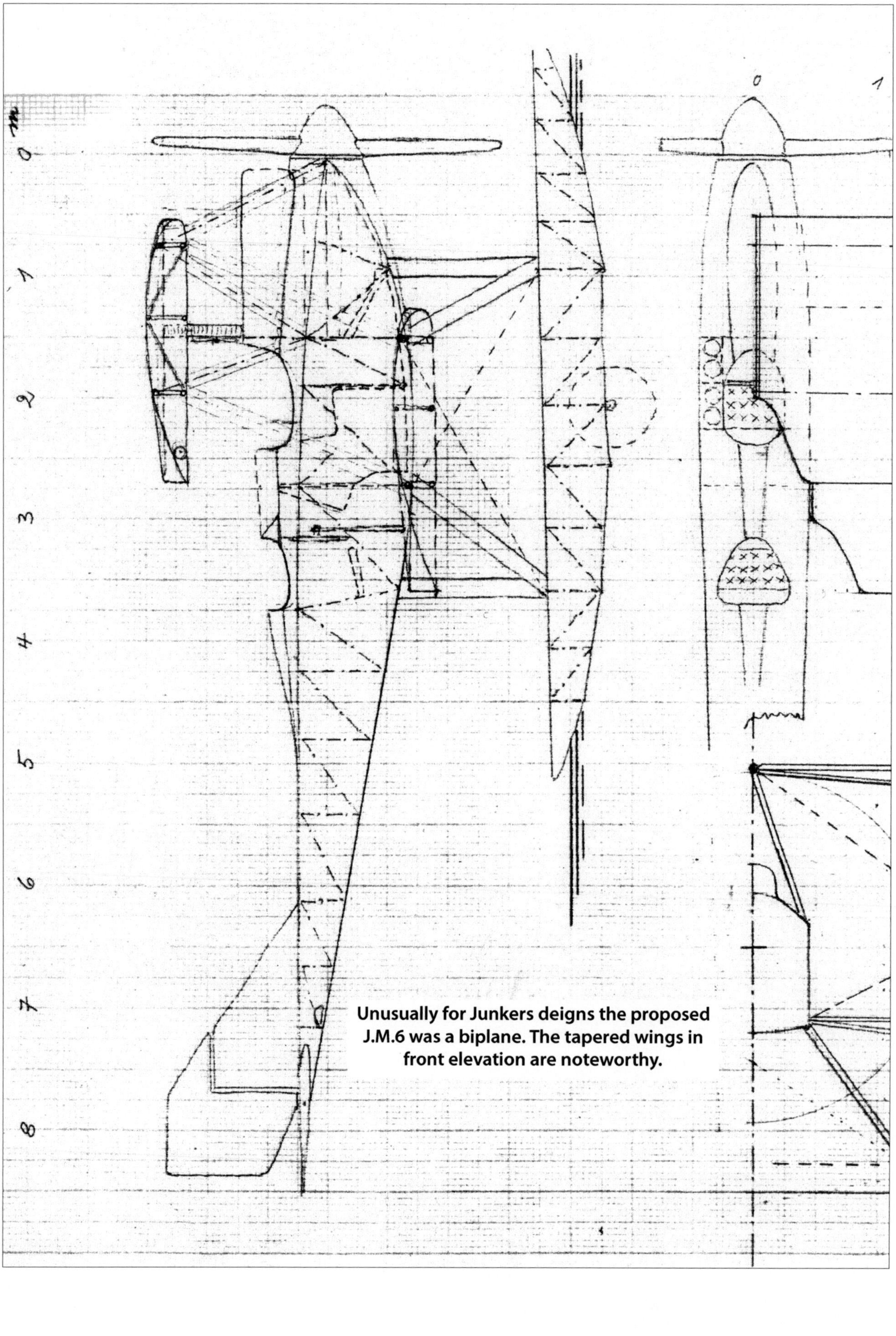

Unusually for Junkers deigns the proposed J.M.6 was a biplane. The tapered wings in front elevation are noteworthy.

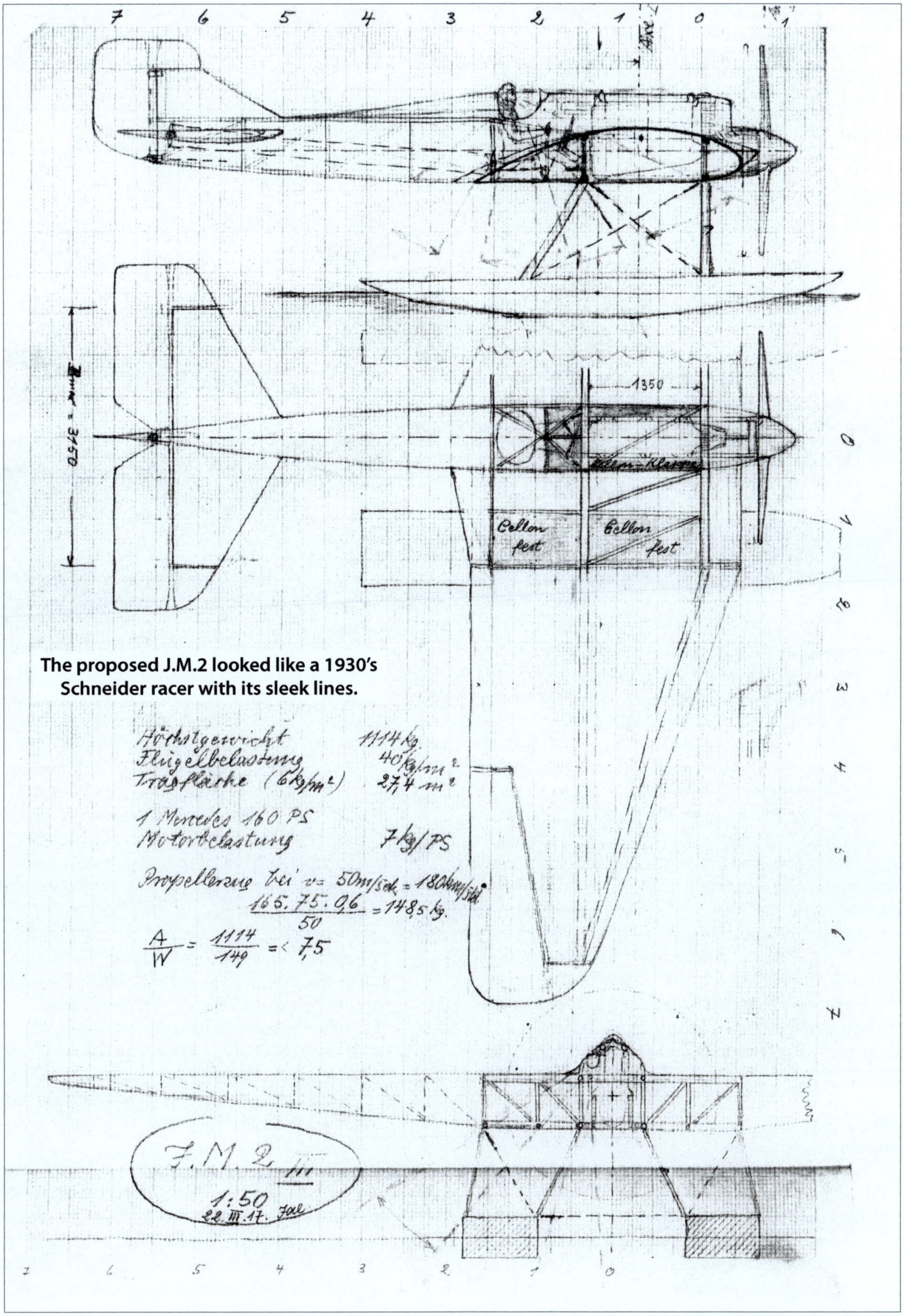

The proposed J.M.2 looked like a 1930's Schneider racer with its sleek lines.

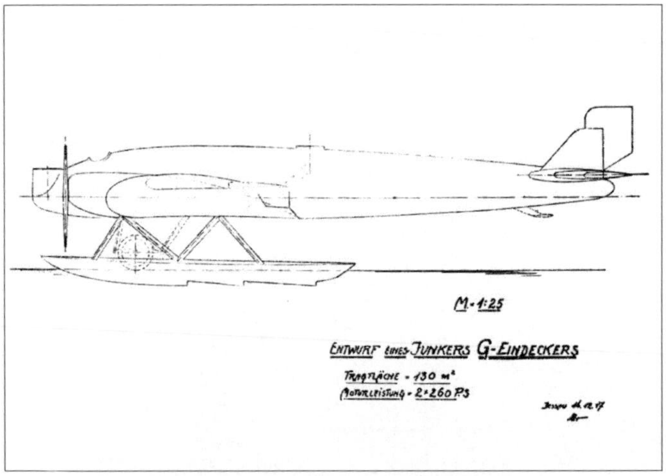

Above: Proposed twin engine G type with float/wheel undercarriage. This may be the design that was proposed to be built as a landplane in order to test it aerodynamically before placing the machine on floats.

1917, the *RMA* decided to order a two-seat all metal floatplane in the C3MG Class. At that time only the Junkers and Zeppelin-Werft-Lindau companies were capable of building in metal aircraft that would be fit for service use, and so they each firm was given an order for three aircraft.

In a letter to Professor Junkers in May 1918, Seitz recorded that he had received a visit by father and son Osterkamp together with *Ltn* Sachsenberg. Osterkamp had just inspected "the new factory and the D-machines with the 200 Benz engine. He advises accelerating the completion of the machines as soon as possible." Osterkamp was to return to the Front on the 25th but would return to the type acceptance testing, alternating with *Ltn zur See* Sachsenberg.

Ltn der Reserve Sachsenberg (our Sachsenberg) has been informed about the order from the undersecretary-of-state of the *Reichsmarineamt* dated 6.6.1918, for three G-type and three C-type aeroplanes. "He is of the opinion that the Marine, who want to see something from us, must not be disappointed and that we must start with this order."

Seitz was worried that this letter had not been answered and asked for instructions. He recommended that the *RMA* be informed that they were anxious to start, and that *Jfa* did not give the impression that the order had been "rejected by us. Sachsenberg advises to build one C-prototype first of all and send it to Warnemünde for tests."

The suggestion of *Idflieg* regarding the order for one R-plane must not collide with the building of the Marine C-plane. "It should not be difficult to achieve an agreement and a practical allotment of supplies, perhaps ideally that we voluntarily give up this marine order with floats when a substantial direct Marine order for D-type aeroplanes is secured." An experimental C-type aeroplane with floats could be built on the side.

Ltn Osterkamp reported that the marine Chief of Operations had spoken to *Kogenluft* (the Commanding General of the Air Force) about why the *RMA* would prefer to assign orders to *Jco* and *Kogenluft* said he was favourably disposed to the suggestion. "I will at once exploit this well-disposed attitude."[2]

From this document, it can be seen that the J 11, already on order, was considered more as an afterthought, possibly being given an impetus when the order for D.I fighters from the Navy did not eventuate. Another document gives the date of the order for the "delivery of three C-type marine aeroplanes with cantilever wings and 195 hp Benz V-form engine" as 1 December 1917. It appears from surviving documents and comments by Peter M Grosz that this was common practice, the final order for the construction of the approved design being given after the three prototypes had proven themselves.

The document asked for the aircraft to be *entirely built from Duralumin, is intended to be a light C-type with 3 fixed and one movable machine gun.* (A handwritten note in the appendix records the fixed guns as 2 in number). *The aeroplane should have good fighting characteristics, i.e. good manoeuvrability, good visibility, ability to climb in a turn, have a good field of fire for the moveable machine gun, a maximum speed of at least 170 km/h, and a landing speed of not more than 90 km/h. The aircraft is intended to be a twin-float machine. You can obtain detailed information on the form and type of floats from Bauaufsicht* (this is thought to be an organisation responsible for the specifications of aircraft parts). *The floats shall also be constructed from Duralumin. The distance between floats shall be 25% (biplanes) or 20% (monoplanes) of the wing span. The aeroplane may be built as a biplane or a monoplane. The general arrangement drawings shall be sent to the RMA and the static calculations to the SVK (Seeflugzeug-Versuchskommando* - Seaplane Test Command*) for examination. … You are to submit a quotation of the price and delivery time.*

The detailed appended list noted that the machine was to be a tractor powered by the Benz Bz.IIIb engine. The propeller had to have at least 400 mm clearance over the water. The two fixed machine guns were to have 500 rounds each. Fuel was to be carried for 2½ hours with a ½ hour gravity tank

Above: A Marine Cs.I under construction, 15 October 1918. (SDASM)

Above: A Marine Cs.I in the Junkers factory, 5 October 1918. Note the style of the national insignia. (SDASM)

Specifications J 11						
Type	**Original Tailplane**				**Final Tailplane**	**Final Tailplane**
Source	**1**	**2**	**3**	**4***	**5**	**6****
Dimensions in m						
Span	12.75		12.75	12.75	12.75	12.75
Length	8.800		8.95	8.8	8.950	8.8
Height			2.95	3.22		3.22
Wing Area, m²		27				
Weights, kg						
Empty		914	914	914		914
Loaded			1,420	1,420		1,420
Speed, km/h			180	180		180

Notes: * Designation given as C.I. ** While the three view is the same as 5 above, the data appears to be that for the unmodified machine.

Source:

1. Junkers factory elevations. September 1918. (Note that the *Typeuprüfung* drawing of November 1918, shows a span of 12.550 m)
2. March 1919 data via L Andersson.
3. Thetford & Gray.
4. *Jllustrierte Flug-Welt*, Vol.1, 1919, P.376.
5. Junkers three view of final tail configuration. Archives of Technology AP00069.
6. *Jane's All the World's Aircraft*.

capacity.

With a load of 435 kg the take-off run was to be 25 seconds; climb to 3,000 m in 25 minutes, and the climb to 5,000 m was to be reported. The horizontal speed at 300 m was to be 170 km/h. With this load the machine was to be seaworthy in high seas corresponding to a wind speed of 8 to 10 m/sec.

The biplane was to have a cantilevered upper wing. The factor of safety was to be 5. Double ailerons were recommended and one of the aircraft was to have stick control.[3]

The floatplane that eventually was built, the J 11, was a seaplane version of the J 10 monoplane, possibly desired to replace the Hansa-Brandenburg monoplanes of that service. The machine has been designated CLS-I in many publications, (including Thetford and Grey), however in official documents this designation has not been found to date. It is referred to as the "Marine C" or "Cs.I" or similar. The J 11 met the Navy's C3MG category - C Class (two-seat) with three machine guns. The pilot had two fixed synchronised machine guns while the observe/gunner had a single Parabellum on a ring mount. The additional side area of the floats led to a triangular fin installed ahead of the rudder. This proved insufficient and an entirely new tail assembly was designed and trialled in early 1919.

Three prototypes were ordered in December 1917 (*Marine Nummern* 7501-7503).[4] The J 11 had a larger wingspan than the J 10 to compensate for the weight of the twin floats.[5] The engine was only a 185-hp Benz IIIa and, although the engine was set up to develop its full power at ground level, the seaplane was underpowered.[6] Its performance is depicted as not being any improvement over conventional floatplanes already in service, that is the Hansa-Brandenburg monoplanes, and this was the reason that no more were ordered. However, examination of the original documents shows that this is not entirely true.

On 23 October 1918, Navy pilot *Oberflugmeister* Richard Thiedemann[7] performed the first flight at the *SVK* at Warnemünde. Problems with the machine were soon apparent, especially with the rudder. The fragility of the corrugated sheet covering was a problem and would deform, particularly in the engine area. The metal covering had to be wiped down with oil soaked cloths after each flight to prevent salt corrosion. The floats, provided by Firma Luftfahrzeuggesellschaft Bitterfeld, were poorly constructed and the noses of the floats broke away on the first flight.[8]

Brandenburg provided a detailed account of the trials and tribulations of the J 11 prototype during its testing at Warnemünde in a series of telegrams and letters. It was not only the aircraft and the military that caused him problems, Junkers own organisation could not arrange the wages for their own crew.

Junkers (*Jco*) Navy Aircraft Orders

Date of Order	No.	Marine Nummer	RMA No.	Notes
30 Apr 1917	3	1481–1483	Bx 5899	Submarine flying boat, cancelled.
	3	1574–1576		Three-engine aircraft, cancelled
1 Jun 1917	3		Bx 7721	Single-engine floatplane, cancelled
24 Nov 1917	3	7801–7803	Bx 16953	Two-engine floatplane, cancelled 26 Nov 1918.
1 Dec 1917	3	7501–7503	Bx 17128	J 11 floatplane.

Note: There are different dates listed in the Junkers records. The Navy orders are taken from Naval and Junkers records.
Source: P.M. Grosz Collection Box 483.

On 28th Brandenburg wrote:

On the 28.10 (Monday) Thiedemann and the undersigned (Brandenburg) *made the first test flight to check the alterations that had been made. During this flight, I observed that in the air the rudder only moves slightly and flutters considerably.*

In series construction we most likely will need to use 3/10 instead of 2/10 sheet metal.

After this flight Th. had the trailing edge of the rudder bent back a little towards the middle and flew again with a sailor.

After this a small adjustment to the right aileron was made as it did not lie symmetrically. Followed by a short flight as above. Following this there was a correction to the rudder again. Followed by another flight as above. After this flight Th. deemed the aircraft ready to be flown (by others).

First to fly was Oberltn. Bücker. (four flights). After that, also in the morning, Oberltn. z.S. Heisseck (Frontstation Norderney).

In the afternoon of 28.10, Oblt. Bucker flew once again (four flights) followed by Oblt. z.S Freude (three flights).

In the group discussion with Th. the following was mentioned:

During the flights of Fr. (Freude) *with the J11, Bü.* (Bücker) *flew a Hansa-Brandenburg mono plane with BMW engine. Both aircraft flew over the launch area beside each other at about 300 m.*

At this point J11 pulled away from the Hansa B. A competitive climb was not carried out due to a misunderstanding. Bü. (Bücker) *suggested that Th. conduct another climb and pull up much harder than in the first so as to improve the result (then v=180 km/h average climb speed)*

Th. immediately did so. The aircraft was ballasted according to the requirement (514kg) and Th. took off with me.

Lift off was at 120 km/h.

Speed in the climb 150–160 km/h. Landing speed 120-130 km/h.

We could only get to just above 1000m due clouds.

The Barograph showed 7 minutes/1000m so no improvement.

After this flight another was conducted by Ltn. (?) Schürer.

The verdict as current can be summarised as follows:

Climb, about the same as the Hansa-Brandenburg, with comparable barograph readings.

Speed, *Superior to the H.-Br.* (Hansa-Brandenburg*). The landing speed is of no concern to pilots with feel for the airplane, others however make real awful tail down landings, most likely caused because the relevant pilot does not dare to allow the aeroplane to wash of speed in a horizontal glide.*

Elevators *generally not faulted. One pilot noted that in a turn the elevator became limp (perhaps blanketed by the wing slipstream?).*

Rudder, *By far the most criticised, and seems rightly so. Bücker is continually asking for a lengthening of the fuselage. In a roll the effect of the rudder is just sufficient. In flight the control effect of the floats is great. Apparently the keel fin extension also has a negative effect on the rudder. It is difficult to come up with clear proposals when the observed faults cannot be clearly defined. For one the aircraft enters an uncommanded left turn, another says it is prone to sideways accelerations. Even Th. cannot make any positive conclusions. I have suggested to him that he fly without the keel fin to establish whether control is increased or diminished thereby. This will be done as soon as the propeller arrives*

Above & Below: Two more photos of Marine Nummer 7501 at the Seaplane Testing station at Warnemünde, the first of the three aircraft of the batch. The serial number in the Army's style rather than the Navy's was probably due to it being the first aircraft Junkers built for the Navy.

Above: The Junkers Marine Cs.I, Marine Nummer 7503, probably at Dessau, note the camp ovens in the background. This machine has the new fin and balanced rudder. The wings have been overpainted, possibly to reduce the effect of salt water on the airframe. The fuselage national marking has not been overpainted.

from Wolff (should arrive Thursday noon.).

On the 29.10, I spoke with Oberltn. Bücker. I wanted his advice as to when we could get the aircraft accepted. I advised him that our risk in flying as on the 28.10 was not small. His view was that it would be paid for if a Marine pilot crashed it. He could give no firm date for the delivery of 7501 as in his opinion it would be some time before the tests were completed. He must also invite a number of combat pilots to fly it. Their opinion would be needed before any orders would be forthcoming.

On the 29.10 the inspection by the department of Baumeister (Constructor) *Neesen and the M.G. installation was planned. The former is taking place at present. The firing took place but had to be stopped as the cowling in the vicinity of the muzzle was torn by the blast.*

Th. is making a reinforcement from mild steel. In the afternoon of 29.10. at 2 pm the weekly meeting led by Kapitan z.See Hering to which company representatives are also invited took place. After discussions about the R-aircraft as well as the companies Albatros, Friedrichshafen, Sablatnig and shipyard Danzig, 7501 was discussed.

The status of this airplane was noted as extremely important by Kap. Hering.

Oberltn. Bü. (Bücker) *duly emphasised the good qualities of speed (superior to the H.-Br)* (Hansa-Brandenburg) *and climb and described the effect of the rudder as poor. Very widely discussed was the observation by Schurer on the 28.10. that a standing observer greatly reduced the effect of the rudder.*

The question as to whether a similar effect was noted in the land plane I could deny.

As to the question of a solution I proposed changes to the keel fin and rudder and perhaps eventually a fuselage extension.

Kap. Herring said that as soon as possible a meeting should take place at which Bauminster Neesen can report the results of his inspection so that he could make a decision about series production.

I assume that this meeting will take place on 30.10. Should the opportunity present itself I will work towards a handover of 7501.

Depending on the outcome of this meeting and the result of a flight without the keel fin I will come to Dessau to discuss necessary modifications to the fuselage. I would point out that Hering is of like mind. The rudder now has this shape.

The danger that the rudder could be blanketed by observer is hereby avoided. The result of the discussion with Neesen will follow by telegram.

Letter of 28.10. with enclosure for Th. Received. Neesen has not yet studied drawings. Enclosed wages tally and copy of my telegram of 28.10.18.

Signed
Brandenburg.[9]

By telegram on the 29th Brandenburg informed Junkers that

The top two engine cowlings were removed in order to attach the steel reinforcements necessary to protect them from the gun blast. At the time we discovered that as a result of the numerous flights on the 28th the cowls were cracking in every edge and corner. We will repair this cowling as good as possible here but will immediately have new smooth cowls made from Duralumin or aluminium as per the unhatched part of the drawing. Please also do this for the next two aircraft and strengthen this smooth cowl in the vicinity of the MG muzzle with steel sheet until a gap of at least 80 - 100 mm exists between the bullet path and the cowling. We hope to have finished this new cowling in the next two days. The old one should last until then even if there is a lot of flying. Apart from this, other modifications have been made that need to be incorporated into the next aircraft and series production machines.

The keel fin was removed on the 29th but the reduction in weight (2 kg) was not compensated for. *Kapt* Hering was consulted the following day and was "most obliging and urged completion." When he was told that a flight without the fin was planned he told Brandenburg to consult Dr Munk (aero dynamist) for any doubts I had. As to the risk, "he said the same as Bucker, namely that the Navy would pay if one of their pilots crashed the aircraft – except Thiedemann, who is our pilot and flying for our company's interest, also told me it could not be handed over yet."

Brandenburg then talked to constructor Neesen who suggested that, in comparison with other aircraft, about 300 mm be added to the fuselage length. A 2 pm meeting with Dr Muck, Dr Stier and *Oblt* Bucker "was also unable to offer any suggestions to improvements as the results of measurements had not been provided as yet."

Bucker was of the opinion that while the machine flew well in good weather he was afraid that in turbulent weather the controls would be inadequate as the aircraft did not track straight. Dr Muck was satisfied from his data that the size of the rudder should be adequate. "The moment of the rudder could not be directly compared as it depended on the wing loading." While acknowledging that lengthening the fuselage may help, Brandenburg pointed out that the potential loss of time resulting from this, especially if it required relocating the engine. Following this, other possibilities were discussed.

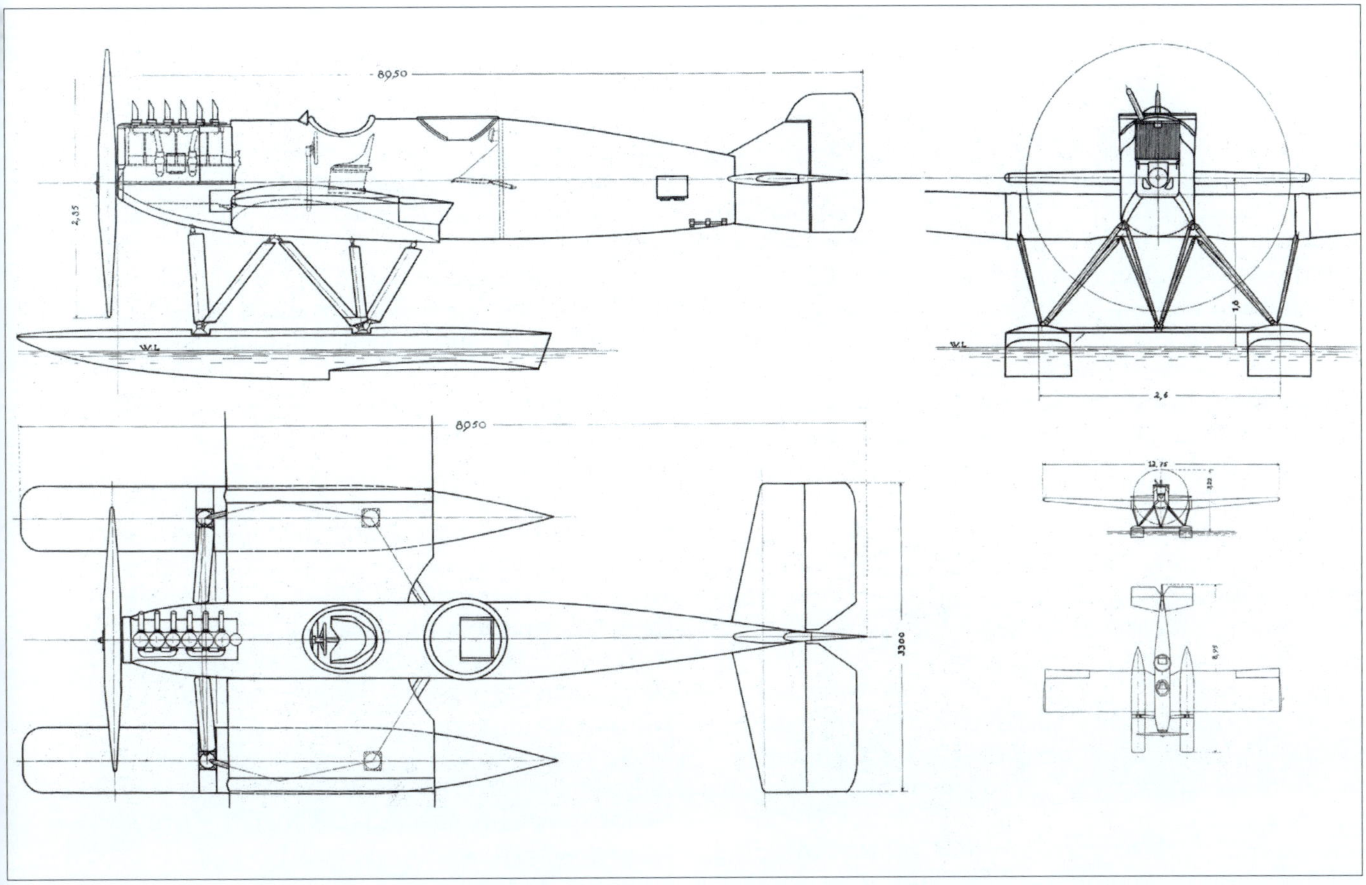

As to the removal of the keel, Brandenburg could only point to the land machine (CL.I) that did not need one, however he acknowledged that the danger of instability created by the floats could not be refuted. Neesen and Munk proposed a variable fin above the fuselage; a second fin below the fuselage was not recommended. It was agreed that Thiedemann fly the aircraft without the fin immediately, followed by Bucker to establish the result of removing the keel, even if it was a negative. Bucker also faulted the "dead action" in the rudder. Brandenburg assured them that this would not occur in a precisely manufactured series aircraft. Then Bucker again mentioned the effect of a standing observer.

The machine was ready for flight without the fin at 4.15 pm. Thiedemann took off with the sailor Schulz at 4.32 pm. "On the water the control seemed to have improved. Thiedemann showed me, by overflying, that in the air the rudder inputs did not cause the aircraft to deviate from its path. After this flight Thiedemann said that in the air there was no improvement and perhaps even a slight deterioration was evident. He did not pass on his findings to Bucker who then made two flights. Bucker's comments were that the aircraft was much better and, even with a standing observer, he could not find fault. He insisted that he would still have to fly the aircraft in turbulent conditions."

Thiedemann said that Bucker "really needed to learn to fly the machine. This was probably the reason for his contradicting reports." The only real problem with the floatplane was the ineffectiveness of the rudder probably caused by the fuselage blanketing the airflow. Thiedemann reported that

Without banking the aircraft's rudder input will cause the aircraft to turn; on centring the rudder the machine should fly straight ahead but does not. It has to be corrected with opposite rudder.

Brandenburg then went on to "hope that Bucker sticks to his verdict of this evening, thus removing the main point of contention." This would leave only the sea trials and four-hour flight to end the test phase. The following day Munk wanted to carry out another accurate speed test.

On 30 October Brandenburg noted that the third exhaust pipe broke and requested a replacement by express post. Drawings arrived and the SVK cleared them. These are assumed to be for modifications revealed by the testing of the machine. "For Thamm no wages have been received since he started here. I have requested more money."

With respect to the rudder he considered that it might be possible to increase its effectiveness by extending it below the fuselage where the fuselage would not blanket it.

"This should extend as far as possible in the flight direction but only so deep that it is not submerged too much during landing. Compare with the Hansa-Brandenburg monoplane rudder."

On 1 November, Brandenburg asked *Oblt* Bucker what was the opinion of the other two pilots who had flown 7501 after him on 31 October. Originally he indicated that both were satisfied but later said that *Oblt* Freude was not. Bucker indicated that the Navy was happy to have a competitor to Hansa-Brandenburg and asked about possible delivery. Brandenburg told him "4 aircraft 4 weeks after the first order and 10 more in the second month after that. He asked me to confirm that."

The enlarged rudder was ready at midday. Thiedemann flew first for some time. His verdict is the enlarged rudder provides no advantage (over the original). *The machine pitches into the turn and is difficult to fly. Afterwards Kapt Ltn Mans flew the machine, his first flight, and it was raining. He found that the machine turns off to the left but the rudder had insufficient control effect and there was mechanical interference in the controls.*

The following flight was by Ltn Schurer. He pushed the machine quite strongly, almost standing it on its wing. He found manoeuvrability excellent but criticised the small elevator. This had not been noted before but appears to be due to Schurer being the first to really push the aircraft into a steep turn. Thiedemann advised an enlargement.

Bucker advised I seek advice from Neesen on the modifications to the rudder. I did and came to the following arrangement: See diagram. The hatched tip area will be halved and the rudder will be extended upwards at an angle.

For the next series of trials the machine would be altered as shown on a diagram that accompanied the letter.

According to Theo the opinions on the aircraft in its old form without the keel fin were quite satisfactory. All this testing has been caused by the fact that the test pilots should have first got used to the aircraft. Theo said that it would only take one "Big Name" to say the machine is good and everybody would immediately shout "I told you so!" Unfortunately, the actual man responsible for the machine is on holidays and Bucker is apparently frightened by the responsibility. This is why he is constantly talking of inviting front line pilots (to fly the aircraft). *This morning he spoke of the sea trials. I hope this last alteration will satisfy everybody so that next Tuesday a decision will be made. Further delays and changes are, in my view, to be strongly resisted....Despite our people being here for two weeks no wages have arrived. The RM 300 sent to me had to be immediately paid out for overdue wages. As a result I immediately require a much larger sum so that I can give Master Gorner and the two sailors here fulltime their money (RM 800).*

As an addendum to the letter Brandenburg enclosed a carbon copy of a telegram indicating Hansa-Brandenburg were using Hirshfeld exhausts for their monoplane. This would have been in response to the breaking of exhausts on the J 11 as noted above.

On 9 November, after a thorough inspection of the machine's condition

we could only find a radiator leak. The loss of water appears so little that it is difficult to attribute the state of the engine after the landing on the 9th to it. Thiedemann insists that the engine ran without fault during the climb and only faded in the transition to horizontal flight. According to the Barograph (2000m in 13 min. 3000 m in 25 min. more accurate calculated figures to follow) this would appear to be correct.

According to Brandenburg's observations the radiator must have been at the uppermost of its performance limits so that at higher altitudes it started to form steam, especially when like the day before, it was unusually warm.

I have also made another observation to which I still seek an explanation. Despite the radiator system being topped up continuously I observed for the first time that the radiator lost water thru expansion during warmup. It did not do this yesterday. Also the temperature control thermometers seem not to work. The currently installed instrument does not go past 50C at run-up. It would also seem that the water in the long pipe between the radiator and thermometer is noticeably cooled. I will install a normal mercury instrument tomorrow.

The rudder in the form sent from Dessau, as already reported, was unsatisfactory. We are now returning the aircraft to its original form as delivered except that the trailing edge of the rudder will be reinforced and bent a little to the left to make it track a little to the right. The later supplied rudder will be modified by cutting off the top and adding to the bottom to achieve the form that Oblt Bucker wants to try. Should we have appropriate sea states before this work is completed we can start trials with the original rudder providing the engine was not damaged. That we will find out on the 11th.

The new rudder should be finished that day also. Should this, as one must unfortunately expect also prove unsatisfactory, then I would suggest that further trials with this fuselage are useless. It would then only be useful with this machine to prove its sea-worthiness. This possibility, with the current weather, could be some time off.

Should it become evident tomorrow that the engine is seriously damaged I will telegraph you for instructions as to proceed.

With the situation in Berlin and our results thus far it would appear useless to try to persuade Herring for an order. After the transfer of Government into new hands it is unlikely that there will be further talk of War material orders. Should, as is most likely, the Armistice provisions be accepted tomorrow, then a total embargo on war production is to be expected. If the situation is clearer in Dessau please advise us by telegraph, whether there is any further point in remaining here.

With the remaining funds we could remain till the end of the week. Should a longer presence here, be required then a further sum should be transferred via telegraph. In the event that any communication is impossible I will try to get to Dessau towards the end of the week.

The problems with the rudder vibrating, the radiator, and stability were overcome. As a result of these modifications an exceptional floatplane was developed.

Post Armistice, *Marine Nummer* 7503 was a completed with a new tail empennage. It is not known if 7501 was finally modified to the same standard. At least one J 11 served on mine spotting duties post-war.

The Allied Armistice Commission report lists Warnemünde twice; once as an Experimental station, and secondly, as a Service station, but then uses "Warnemünde Testing Station" when listing the 153 aircraft undergoing testing at the time of its 14 December 1918, inspection. Only Junkers J 11, *Marine Nummer* 7501, is listed although the last two of the order were delivered in November and December.[10]

The British prepared a report on German naval aviation and noted that the "Junkers Two-seater Monoplane Seaplane"

which is manufactured by the Junkers-Fokker Werke, was seen at Warnemunde (sic), *and embodied an "all-metal" construction. Many of its characteristic features were similar to that of the Junkers Infantry aeroplane. It was stated that the machine inspected was the third sent for trial, and that the results obtained had been quite satisfactory – the overall weight being not more than that of seaplanes embodying a more conventional design.*

The engine was noted as a Benz IIIa, "that is a *supercompressed* 150 H.P. Benz." The engine was sunk well down in the fuselage with the top being practically level with the top of the fuselage.

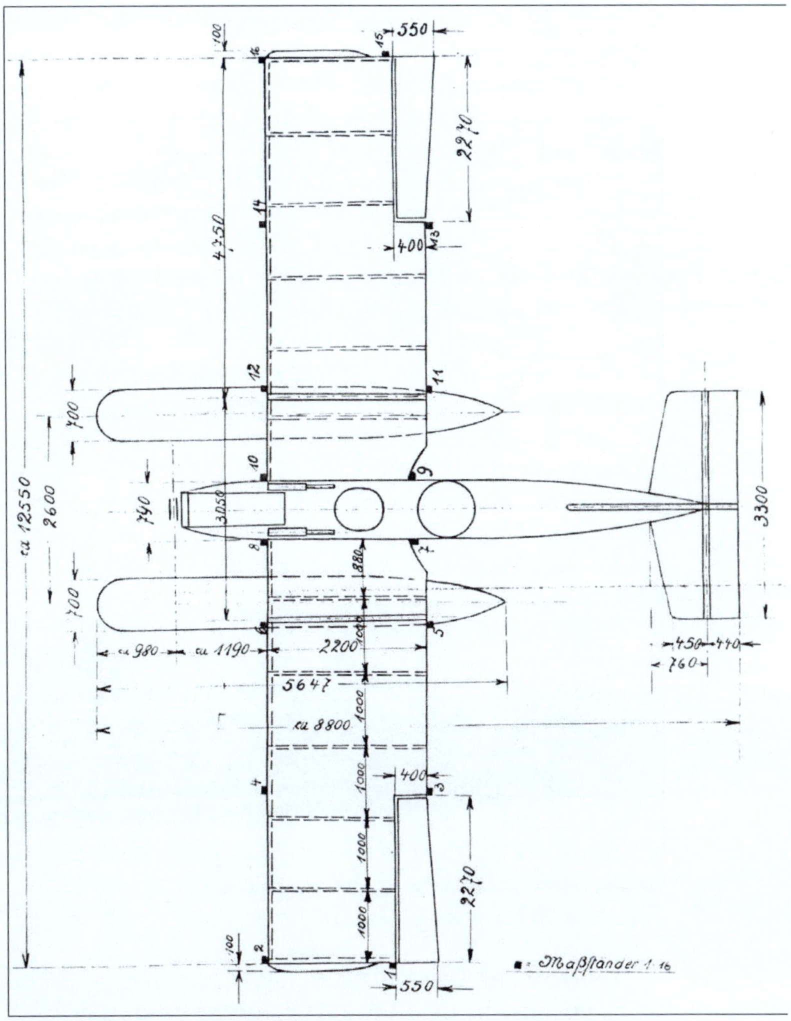

The wings were covered with corrugated sheet aluminium, the direction of the corrugations being in the line of flight and with a pitch of about 50 mm. There were short wing extensions from the sides of the fuselage to which the wings were attached. Like the other Junkers monoplanes, the wing structure carried through the fuselage. The wing was rather flat on its lower surface.

The fuselage used the usual Junkers tubular steel construction covered with corrugated sheet. The pilot sat well forward close to the rear of the engine, with the observer in line with the trailing edge of the wings. The observer had a ring mounted Parabellum machine gun. The pilot had two fixed synchronised Maxim machine guns fixed to the extreme sides of the fuselage at about the level of the top longerons. No gun sights were fitted.

The main float struts had an M configuration when viewed from the front. They were connected at the point of the middle V to the centre of the two horizontal cross bracing ties. The struts formed a reversed N when viewed from the side. The floats were made of sheet metal but none were attached when examined by the British.

The frontal radiator was fitted such that the boundaries of the radiator were faired off by the sides of the fuselage.[11]

Thiedmann wrote the following appraisal of the J 11. Acknowledging his relationship to the Junkers' organisation, it is still a good indication of what the machine could have achieved if time had allowed.

The performance of the aircraft with a disposal load of 510 kg can to be outstanding. No other seaplane with a 185-hp engine and with such a disposable load has reached a speed of 180 km/h. To date the rate of climb has not been surpassed. The aircraft floats well on the eater, the design of the floats making it possible to take off and land smoothly. The float supports are strong enough such that a landing with a wind speed of eight metres per second is possible.

As there is no bracing, assembly is extremely easy and carried out in a very short time. Because of the special construction of the wings distortion is impossible and therefore the flying qualities remain constant.

A modification of the type was later built in the Soviet Union with a 300-hp Hispano-Suiza engine where it was known as the Junkers A.20. Junkers established a factory in the Soviet Union in 1922 at Fili, near Moscow.

Other Naval Orders:

The second volume of the *Atlas Deutscher und ausländischer Seeflugzeuge* contains an intriguing entry under Fokker-Junkers entry. Marine Nummern 7801–7803 are assigned to a Fokker-Junkers T type (*Torpedo-Flugzeug*) Torpedo carrying marine machine with two 260-hp Mercedes motors. The three Type T machines were ordered in November 1917 before the J 11 None are shown as delivered, the same as for the J 11 monoplane. According to Wagner the aircraft that received the *Marine Nummern* 7801–7803 were three G-Type twin-float machines with FT equipment and were ordered on 24 November 1917. Junkers advised that they wanted to build three C-Type machines first, and that before trying the marine G-Types they should be built as a landplane to gain experience with the type's construction.[12] This is mentioned in the discussion of the J 11/Cs.I above. Apart from this nothing further is known about this proposal, but it appears that construction of these G-Types was never begun.

End Notes Chapter 10

1. Jaekel, first name unknown, was a ship designer until 1915 when he joined Sablatnig. He learned aircraft designer here and left to Join Junkers where his first design was the J.M.1.
2. Seitz to Professor Junkers, 17.06.1918.
3. *RMA* to Junkers 01.12.1917. P.M. Grosz Collection. Box 494.
4. The *Atlas Deutscher und ausländischer Seeflugzeuge* shows that three machines were ordered but does not show any as delivered.
5. The J 11 was not a J 10 on floats as stated by Wagner, though its relationship to the J 10 is easily seen. The serials applied to the three machines were *Marine Nummern*, not *werke nummen*. Wagner, W. P.118. *Op Cit.*
6. The *Atlas Deutscher und ausländischer Seeflugzeuge* shows the motor as a "195B" – a 195-hp Benz. In correspondence the engine is referred to as a Daimler-Mercedes 160-hp D.IIIa.
7. Thiedemann was sent to Warnemünde during WWI for experimental flights in the J 11. In November 1919, he joined the *Junkers Flugzeuwerke* as a test pilot and became an operational director. In 1924 he became a technical director at *JFA*. By 1937 he was the manager at *Junkers Flugzeug-und Motorenwerke AG*. He remained in this position until the end of WWII. Post-war he was on the board of directors of *Henschel Flugzwerke AG* in Kessel.
8. "Junkers, of course, could not, as a matter of prestige, use the well-proven Duralumin-floats from KWL (*Zepellin-Werft-Lindau*) which from 1917 were delivered to a number of other firms, like Flugzeug Friedrichshafen." E-mail from M.Schmeelke.
9. "*Flugversuche in Warnemünde ab 19.10.18.*" Brandenburg, 28.10.1918.
10. *Report of the Aircraft Section of the Allied Naval Armistice Commission*, HMS *Hercules*, December 1918. This report is reproduced in Andersson, L & Sanger, R. *Retribution and Recovery, German aircraft and Aviation 1919 to 1922,* Air Britain, UK, 2014.
11. *Report on the German Naval Air Service – Seaplanes and Airships*, Air Ministry, No date, but post-Armistice. Copy in NARA File A-1-q.
12. Wagner, W. *Op Cit.* P.134-135.

11. Junkers *Riesenflugzeug* Projects

Above: Wind tunnel model of Junkers R.I.

In January 1917 Junkers received a contract for a study of an R-plane. The Staaken and Siemens-Schuckert R-planes had proved themselves in combat however the improvements in the Allies fighter aircraft led to the decision to develop a new generation of R-planes that were capable of daylight operations. Junkers all-metal construction was one concept that was felt could be utilised for this second-generation of R-planes. *Idflieg* probably gave Junkers a contract in 1917 for the R.I.

The Junkers design department proposed a 35-metre span monoplane in March 1917, that is referred to as the R.I. The R-1 was a four-engine concept with the engines buried within the thick cantilevered wing. Each pair of engines drove a single airscrew through a complex right-angled gearing mechanism. This arrangement was necessary as the engines were arranged transversely along the wing axis. The wing was typically Junkers thick cantilever construction, the centre section behind incorporated with the fuselage with two detachable outer wing panels. The wing was thick enough to enable a mechanic to service the engine in flight.[1]

Wing tunnel model testing was so promising that the contract was modified to include two prototypes (R.57/17 and R.58/17). Unfortunately the engine gearing proved extremely difficult to solve and the machine was not complete when the Inter Allied Armament Control Commission arrived at the Junkers & Co factory in late spring 1919.

Drawings of a second Junkers R type (called the R.II, but this is not confirmed) survive. This machine had a 38.5 m wing span and twin rudders. The drawing shows that the engines were aligned with the line of flight, two coupled engines serving each airscrew, eliminating the right-angle gear box of the R.I. This machine differed greatly from the first as comparison of the three-view drawings will show. The fuselage height was increased to 3.6 m. The rear fuselage was now oval with the problems of manufacture that would have represented. Junkers had obtained Patent No.313692 of 23 March 1918, covering a R type.[2]

A four engine giant aircraft was started at the Junkers factory in 1920. It would have been an extension of the previous work carried out on the design of the R-plane for the government. Designated JG1 this would be "4 motor Junkers plane" reported on by the US attaché in April 1921. He noted that it was of the same tubular construction as the small

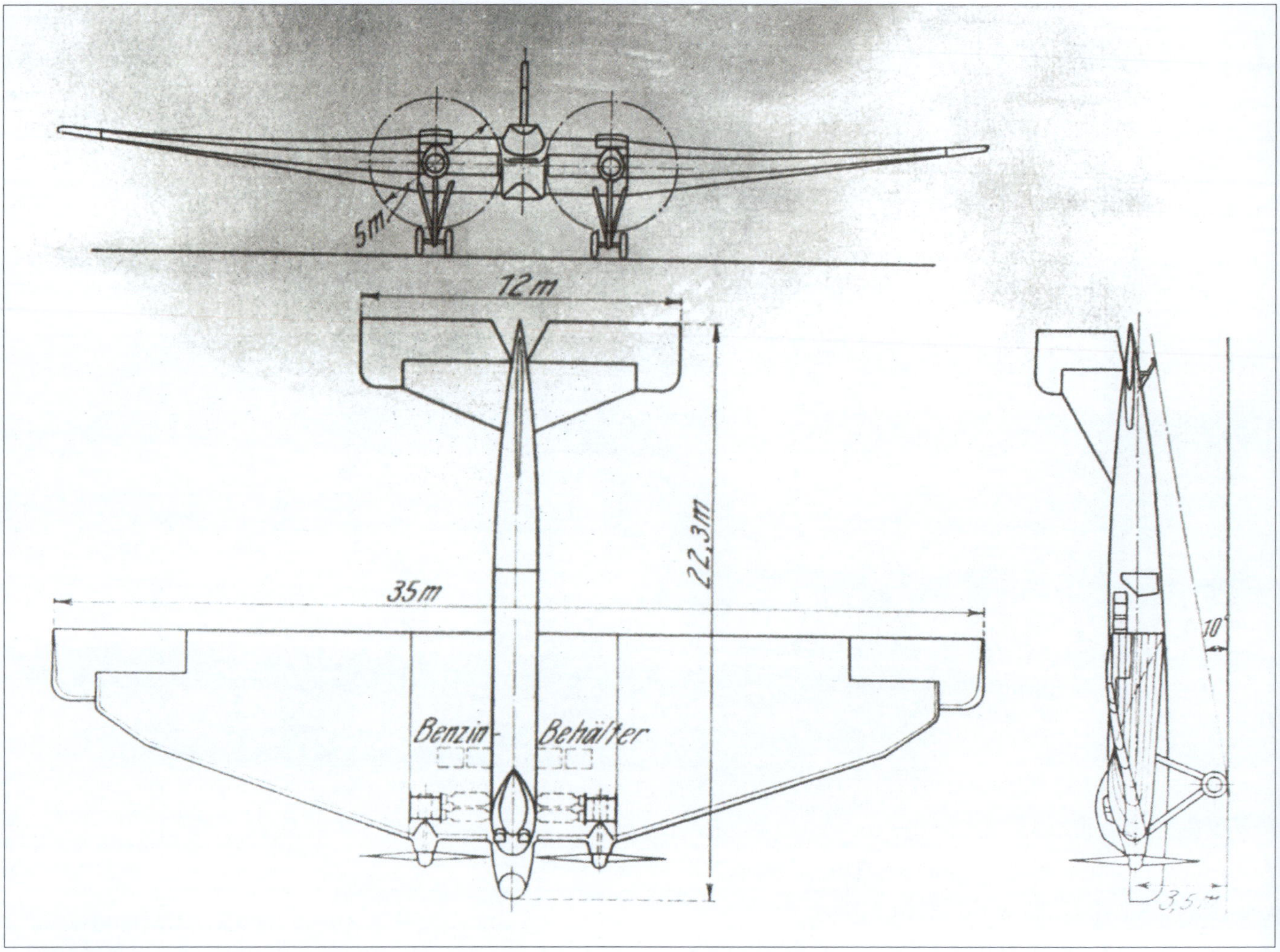

Above: Three view of the R.I with 35 m wingspan.

types.[3]

The "new Super-Junker" was described by 1st Lt E.E. Aldrin, USAS.

It was to be driven by four B.M.W. engines. A monoplane of 52 metres span, and an average wing chord of six feet, the greatest thickness of the wing near the body was four feet. Its internal construction was essentially like the "JL-6" with the same kind of pipe couplings, having duralumin tubes about six inches in diameter for spars, and there were welded steel webs to which the couplings were attached. The fuselage had a unique shape, in section a spherical triangle with the vertex at the top, and approximately a six foot altitude.

The large wing had a barrier at the tips to decrease end loss. "This surface may have been added for fin effect also. The ailerons were of the balanced type used on the Fokker. The duralumin corrugations in the Junkers machine are stamped. They make two waves at a time."[4]

The rear fuselage and wings were completed when the IAACC ordered Junkers to cease work in December 1920. The wings were to be sent to France but no rail car could carry them and it is assumed they were destroyed along with all surviving parts.

Junkers also proposed an enormous R-Type flying boat in June 1918. This machine would have a wingspan of 80 m and was a biplane. This machine remained a paper project only. It was to be 1928 before the giant G.38 transport was constructed with a wing span of 44 m.[5]

End Notes Chapter 11

1. Servicing the engines in flight was one of the requirements for a machine to be defined as an R plane.
2. On 30 March 1918, Wagenführ had noted that he intended to let Linke-Hofmann build C and D-type Junkers aircraft under licence. Drawings of the J 9 and J 10 were ready and it was considered that construction could start. The order for R-aircraft was to be cancelled as no work had been done. Notes from Junkers internal notes and

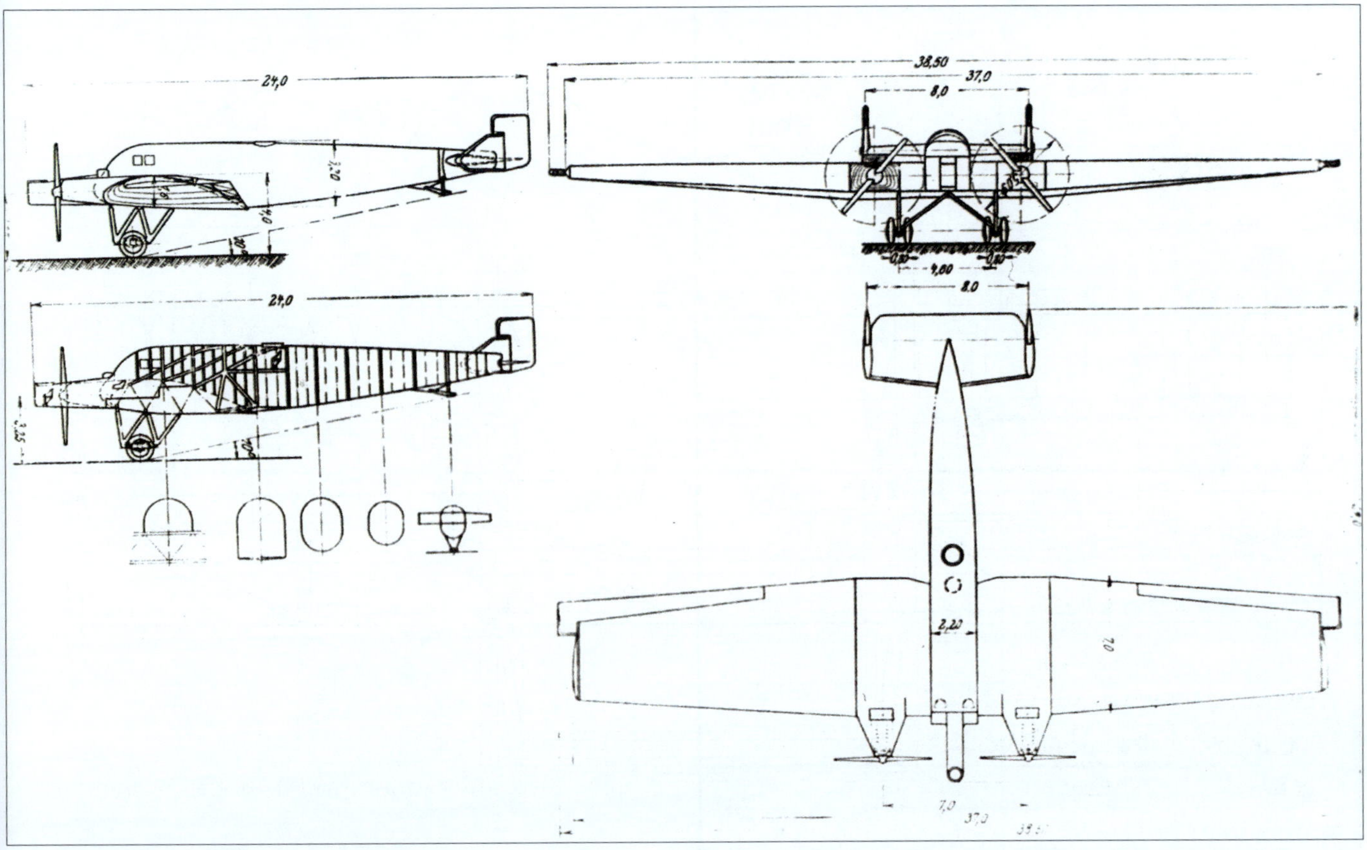

Above: Three-view of the Junkers R project with a 38.5 m wingspan.

correspondence via L Andersson.

3. US Attaché's Report No.58, 26 April 1921. Copy in P.M. Grosz Collection Box 483. In passing the Attaché noted that Junkers had a patent taken out some time previous to the war that gave him the sole right to install motors and gas tanks in the wings. "In connection with this, the constructor of the Staaken metal plane stated that to avoid complications, the motor of the Staaken E4/20 monoplane was so placed as to protrude forward and slightly above the wings."
4. Memorandum for Maj Bane. Subject: *Preliminary Report on Visit to Junkers Plant at Dessau, Germany*. 1st E.E. Aldrin, USAS. Lt 01/10/22. Copy in P.M. Grosz Collection Box 482.
5. For a detailed coverage of the Junkers projected aircraft including multi-engine G-Type machines for the *Reichsmarineamt*, see Wagner, W. Op Cit.

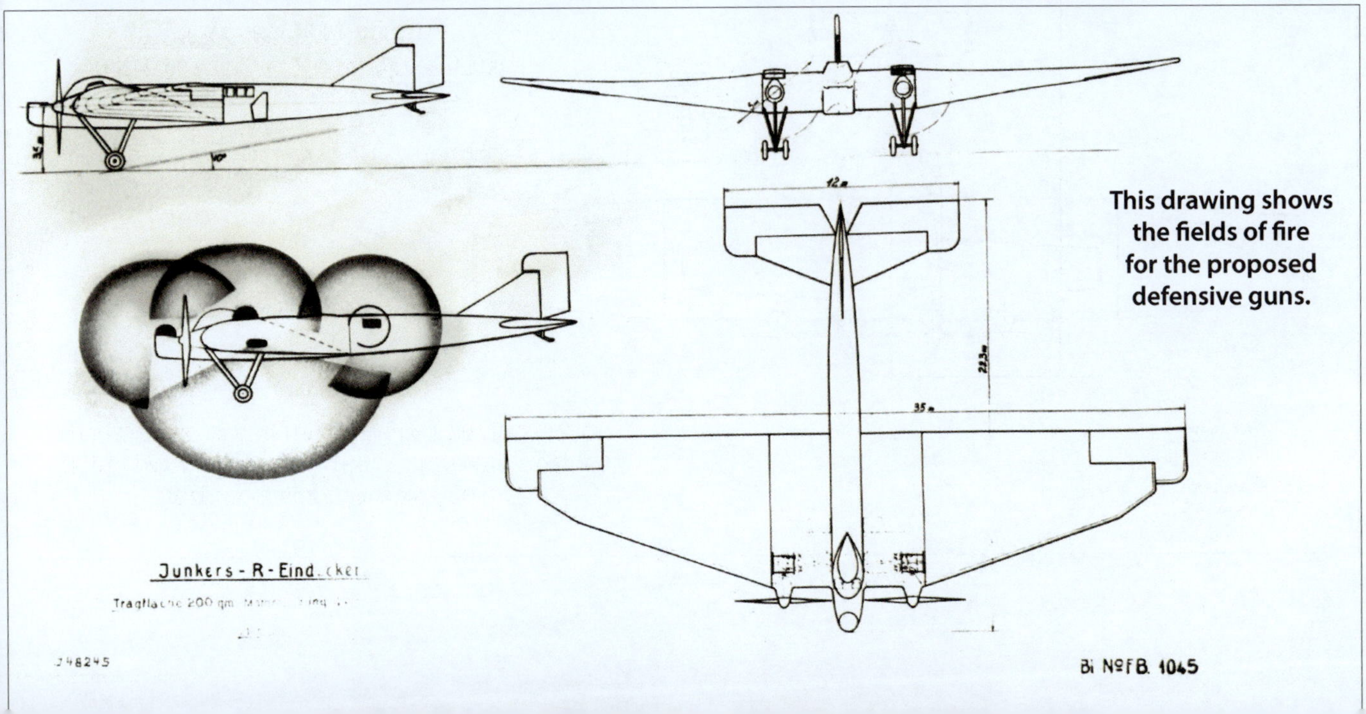

This drawing shows the fields of fire for the proposed defensive guns.

Specifications Proposed R-Types			
Type	**R.I**	**R.II (?)**	**Flying Boat**
Dimensions in m			
Span	35	38.5	80
Length	22.3	24	38
Height	9	6.5	9
Weights, kg			
Empty	6,000		
Military load	4,000		
Total	10,000		48,000
Speed, km/h			180
Climb to:			
1,000 m	4.6 min		
2,000 m	10.8 min		
3,000 m	19 min		
4,000 m	33 min		
5,000 m	76 min		
Ceiling in m	5,200		
Engines	4 x 260-hp Mercedes D.IVa		
Source: Haddow, G & Grosz, P. *The German Giants*, Putnam, UK, 1969.			

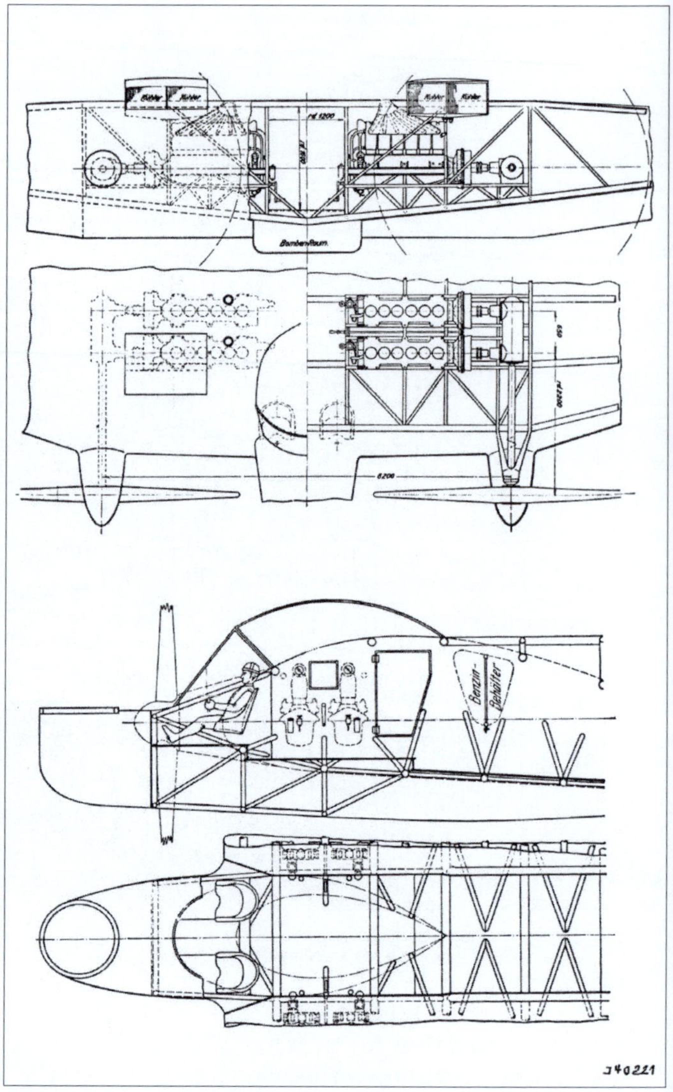

Above: Drawing showing the arrangement of the two coupled engines in each wing of a Junkers R-plane.

Left: *FA* 413 pilots in front of a Junkers at Peterfelde, 1919.

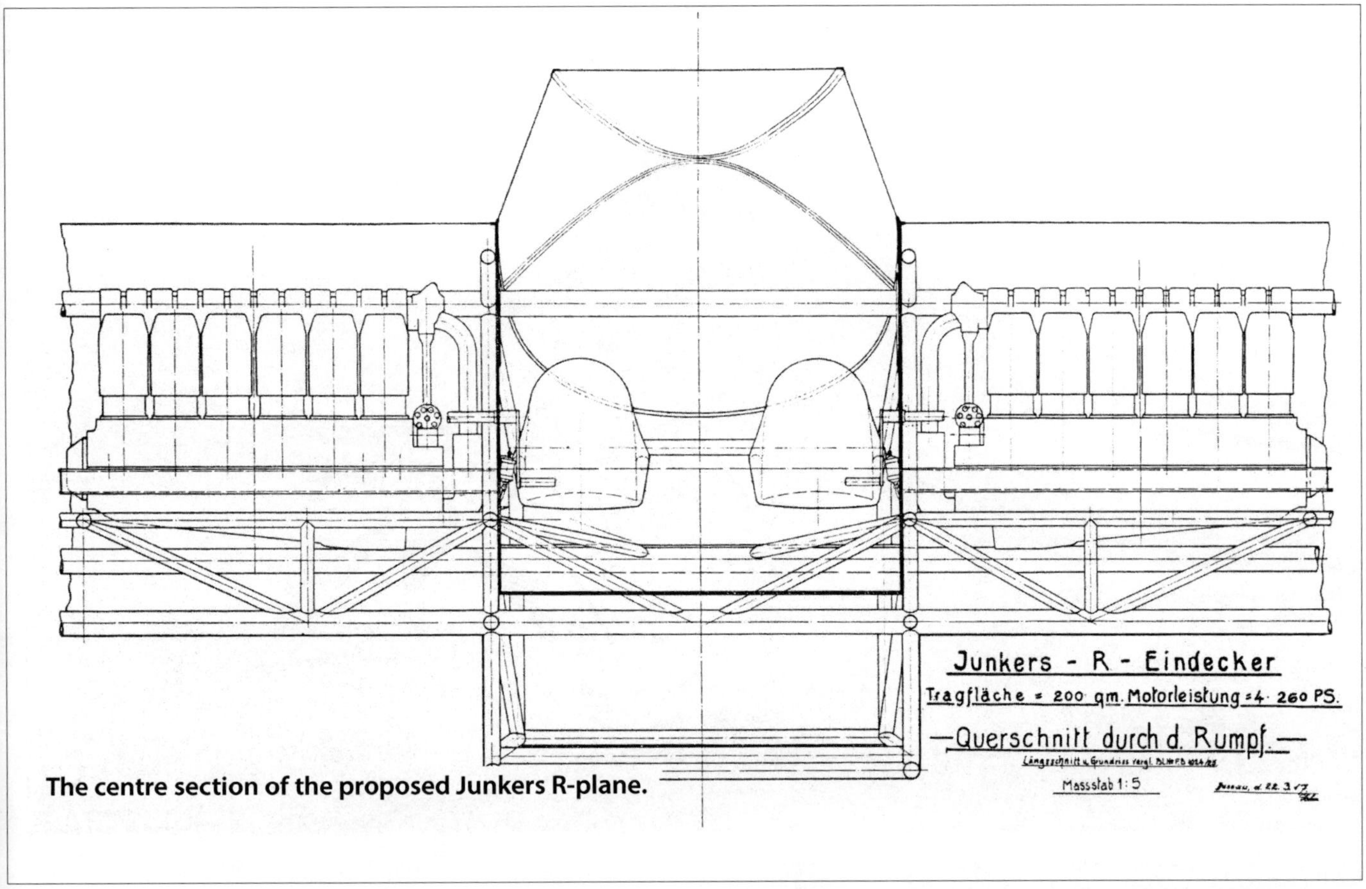

The centre section of the proposed Junkers R-plane.

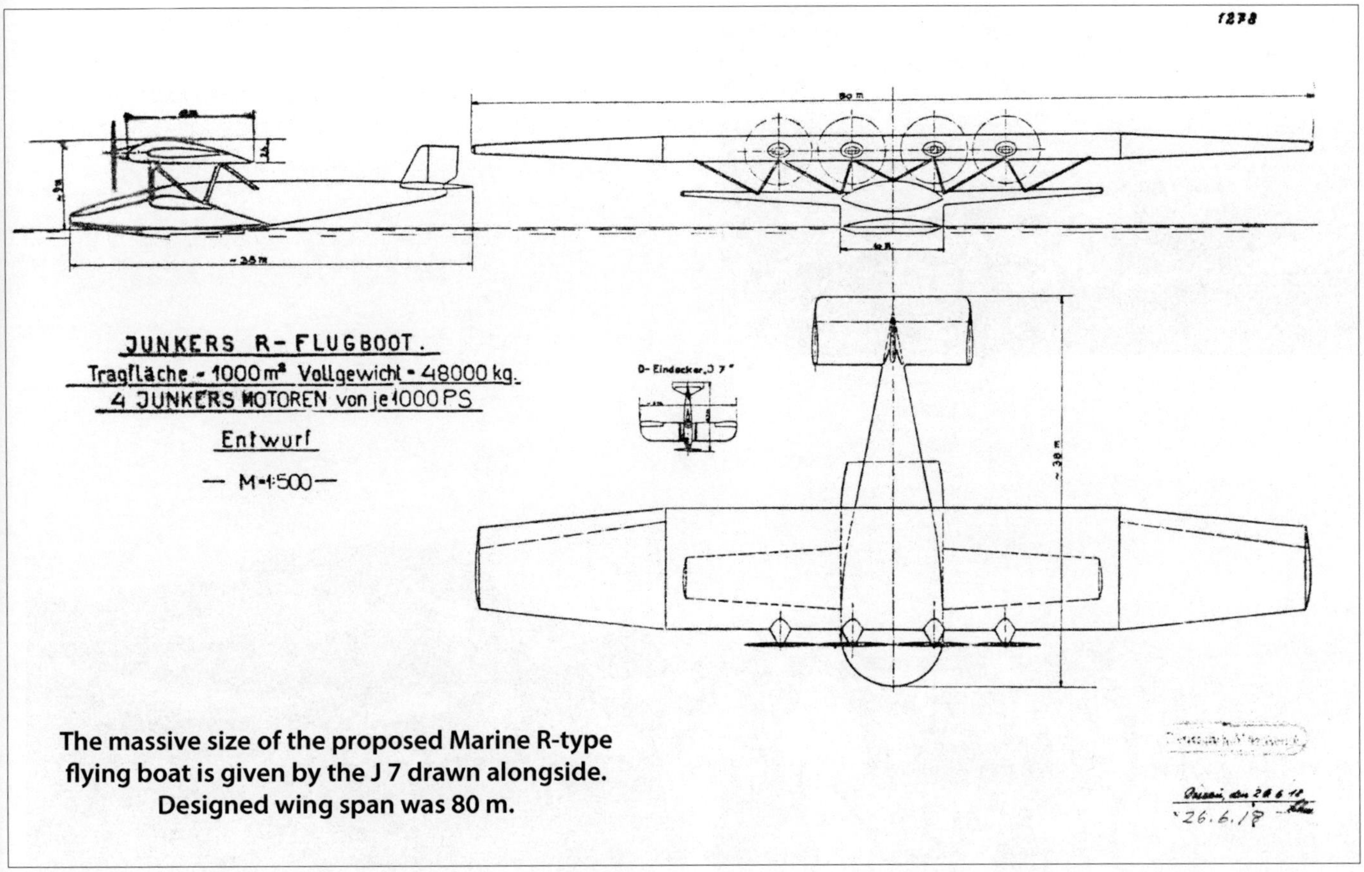

The massive size of the proposed Marine R-type flying boat is given by the J 7 drawn alongside. Designed wing span was 80 m.

A typical example of Junkers Construction. Partly covered wing of a large Passenger Carrier which was not allowed to be completed by the Commission of Control.

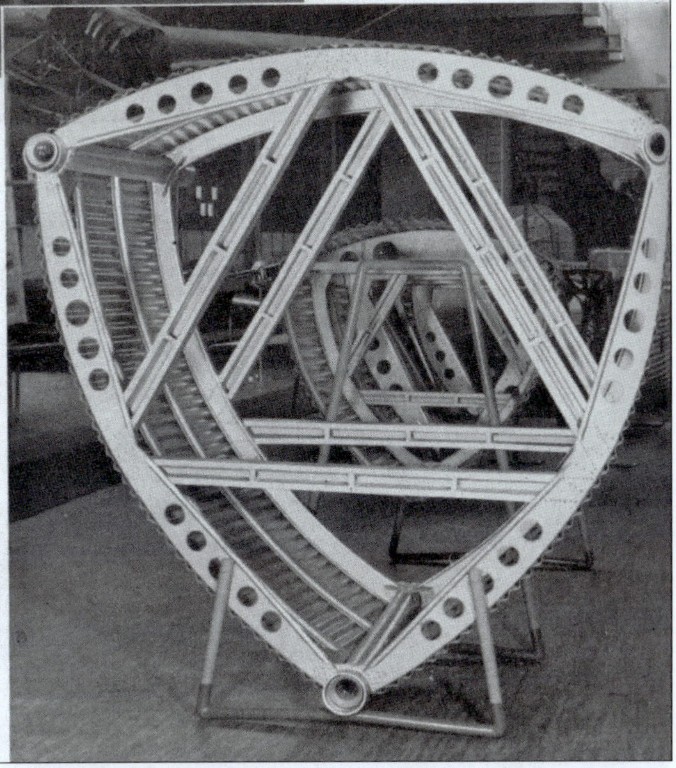

Parts of the JG.1 were saved and were on display in the Junkers Technical Museum before World War II.

36

Die letzten Stücke der JG 1, viermotoriges Verkehrsflugzeug, ca. 9 t Fluggewicht, 36 m Spannbreite, die auf Grund der Begriffsbestimmungen 1921 vernichtet werden mußten.

Facing Page, Bottom: Wing from a CL.I after the Soviets had opened it for inspection.

Below: The remains of CL.12604/18 in a Soviet junkyard. (via M Khairulin)

12. The Junkers Company Post-Armistice

Above: Junkers D.I in USAS hands at Romorantin. This monoplane may have been returned to the USA but requires confirmation. Note the light tailplane colour.

Orders from the *Demobilisierungsamt* dated 27 December 1918, stated that all work on Army orders must stop on 31 January 1919, however this did not apply where earlier arrangements had been made between factories and the acquisition authority.[1] The German Government cancelled all orders with all aircraft manufacturers from 11 January 1919. These covered the following Junkers aircraft (see table at right).

This represented a value of 16,5000,000 Marks, including 1,000,000 in spare parts. The Junkers Company held the view that on 11 January there were only 56 J-type aeroplanes to be cancelled instead of the 65; 35 C-type instead of 39 and of the D-type, 102 remained to be cancelled. This was a difference of only three machines and the company was pressing for the funds to be paid for these.

However, the same month new orders were placed for 20 CL.I and 10 D.I monoplanes and 30 J.I biplanes.

Junkers Aircraft Production Cancelled 11 Janurary 1919

Type	No.	Military Serial
J.I	65	J.740 to 804
D.I	100	D.10307 to 10326; D.5170 to 5179; & 70 without numbers.
C.I	35	Cl.701 to 703; C1.2608 to 12619; & Cl.15671 to 15690

Source: "New points of view to take into consideration for the suborders of 20 J-types, 20 C-type and 10 D-type machines." 17.02.1919. Copy via L Andersson.

On 13 January *Jco* had some 20-25 aircraft in the factory that had to be removed to make room for civil production. Junkers was considering buying back the J 11 floatplanes from the Navy. One was reported as destroyed, one was at

Above & Below: A large number of J.I biplanes were obtained by the USAS at Romorantin. Note all the wings stacked behind these two fuselages.

Above: Junkers wings stacked at Romorantin. Nobody read the Junkers manual as they are stacked on their leading edges.

In April 1920 the German Government Had the Following Junkers Aircraft in Its Inventory:

Type	*Fliegertruppen*	Air Police	Storage	Total
CL.I	1	2	11	14
D.I	3		1	4
J.I	17	2	4	23

Source: Anderson & Sanger, P.135.

Warnemünde and would have to be removed, and the third was ready, presumably at a Junkers facility. They were to be purchased if they could be bought for 10% of their value.[2] By the end of March 1919, the following had left the factory – 30 CL.I and 25 D.I monoplanes together with 22 J.I biplanes.

The German Government sold two Junkers CL.I monoplanes and 72 J.I biplanes between the Armistice and the signing of the Peace Treaty. The purchasers are not stated although Junkers did buy back some J.I biplanes that were then broken up.[3]

In April 1920 the German Government had the following Junkers aircraft in its inventory (see table above)

USA

The USA was interested in obtaining the latest German aircraft after the Armistice and gathered a large number together for selection as to which would be returned to the US.

"The Junkers All-Metal Monoplane Scout, which in certain respects is the most interesting of all the airplanes surrendered to the Allies by the Germans." Thus wrote Major J.C. Riley, USAS, on 22 January 1919. He noted that four D.I fighters were on a field at Hombeek, halfway between Brussels and Antwerp, and were "believed to be the only ones in possession of the Allies." He thought that the US could get the only good one left by asking the Belgium Air Service for it as they do "not seem to be interested in the slightest degree, and have left the planes unguarded on an open field where they are being plundered and wilfully destroyed by civilians....We could offer the Belgiums two Roland Scout planes in exchange of one of these Junkers, if necessary, as we have more Rolands than we want."[4]

Villers-la-Chevres airfield was situated on the

J 4 fuselage in the Museum of Science and Technology, Milano

Junkers Aircraft Entered On The First German Civil Register

Registration	Type	Registered to
D.32	D.I	Junkers
D.33	D.I	Junkers
D.77	CL.I 1802	Junkers
D.78	CL.I cabin	Junkers
D211	D.I	Junkers
D.212	D.I	Junkers

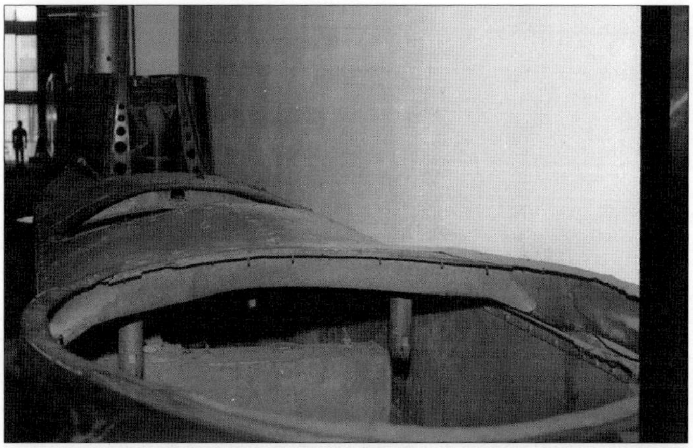

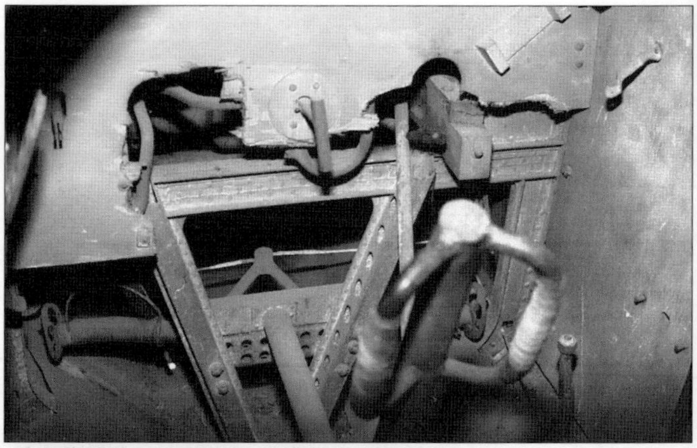

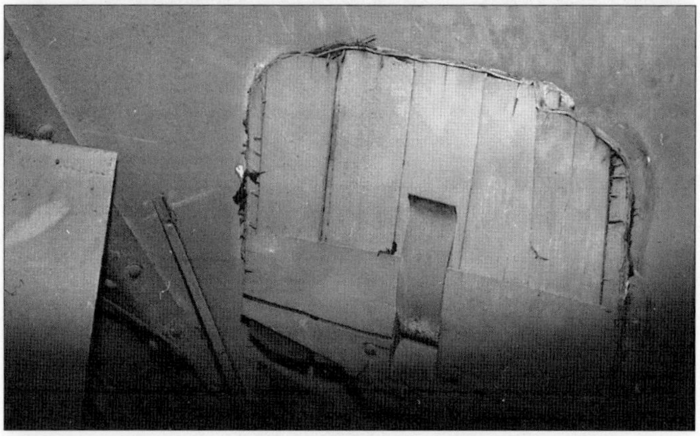

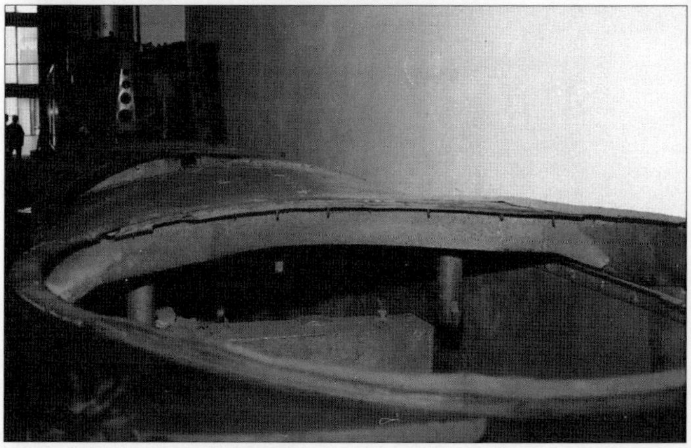

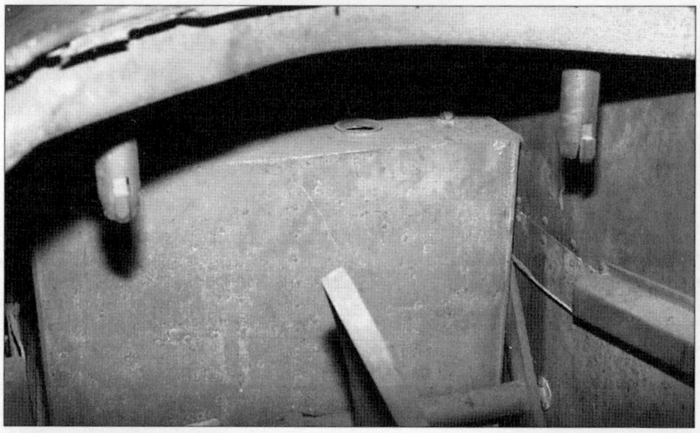

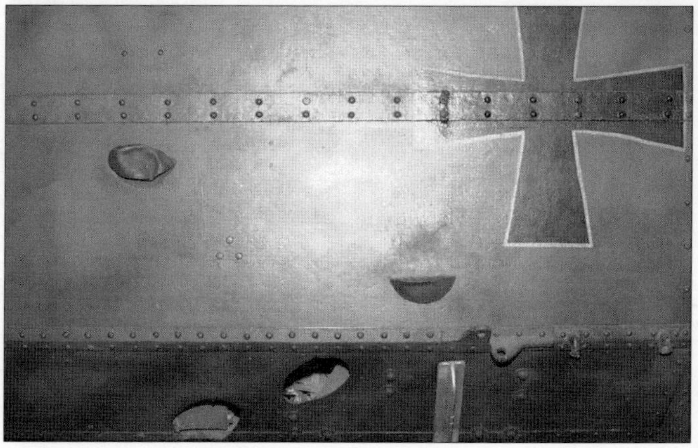

main road from Longuy to Laeguyon and the Germans abandoned a large number of aircraft here. They were rendered unserviceable by removing the magnetos and breaker points. Many had their new tyres slashed with a knife. Before the machines could be put under guard souvenir hunters had cut insignias from wings, fuselages, and tails, and had removed or broken instruments. The aircraft were initially left out in the open and inadequately guarded but were eventually placed into the hangars and many were crated up for shipment to the USA.

The Junkers J.I came in for special mention as a *type of airplane* (that) *is heavily armoured from the nose to the end of the observer's cockpit. The rest of the fuselage is covered with fabric. The frame of both fuselage and wings is metal tubing. The wings and tail surfaces are a thin corrugated metal instead of fabric. There are no wires and no struts between the planes at the ends.*

The following Junkers were recorded during an inspection 10 & 11 January 1919 (see table below).

It would seem that the lower wings were damaged near the fuselage by people standing on them to view the cockpits. The corrugations were fragile and this was often pointed out in German documents. In addition, there were two AEG G.IV and four G.V bombers and a Rumpler Rubild as well as a Fokker D.III that was classified as "scrap."[5]

Amongst the Roland D.VIb, Fokker D.VII, Halberstadt C.V, Hannover CL-V, Pfalz D.III, Albatros D.III, D.V and D.Va biplanes taken on to the US Army Air Service with US serial numbers was a Junkers type as A.S.94045. Unfortunately no designation is given for the type.

A list of August 1919 gives the following Junkers as being present in the USA.[6]

Type	Total
JFC C1	6
RE – V	1
Spares	10

A later list of 31 October 1919, gives the following with the spares being omitted[7]:

Type	Total
JFA C1	2
JFC C1	6
RE – V	1

Junkers Aircraft Recorded During an Inspection 10 & 11 January 1919		
Type	**Condition**	**Remarks**
J.I Jfa 595/18	Unserviceable	Lower wing battered in where walked on near fuselage. Tyres bad. Fabric torn from fuselage. (*Frontversand* 23–28.09.18) Junkers
J.I Jfa 584/18 (Benz good condition)	Unserviceable	Fabric torn from fuselage. Both tyres missing. Lower wings battered near fuselage. Cover of fuel tank gone. (*Frontversand* 16–21.09.18)
J.I Jfa 594/18	Unserviceable	Insignia cut from fuselage. Left wing crumpled near fuselage. Rudder bent. One tyre bad. Spark plugs gone. (*Frontversand* 23–28.09.18)
J.I 816/17	Unserviceable	Insignia cut from fuselage. Wings battered near fuselage. Starting magneto missing. General condition fair. (Armed with 2 angled machine guns. Crashed 20.07.18. (*Frontversand* 23–28.09.18)
J.I 876/18	Unserviceable	Fuselage fabric torn off. Wings crumpled near fuselage. Starting way gone. One tyre bad. One magneto gone. One unserviceable. (*Frontversand* 23–28.09.18)
J.I 596/18	Unserviceable	Fuselage fabric torn off. Wings crumpled near fuselage. Oil pressure gauge & starting magneto gone. One unserviceable. Solid tyres on wheels. (*Frontversand* 23–28.09.18)
J.I 586/18	Unserviceable	Fuselage fabric torn off. Metal torn off portion of lower wing. Lower wing crumpled near fuselage. One magneto and six spark plugs gone. Condition bad. (*Frontversand* 23–28.09.18)
J.I 593/18	Unserviceable	Fabric torn off fuselage. No tyres. Magneto breaker box broken. Handle gone from starting magneto. Lower wing crumpled near fuselage. Condition fair. (*Frontversand* 16–21.09.18)

The inability of those recording the inventory to correctly identify the Junkers aircraft makes it impossible to be certain of which aircraft are being discussed.

In June 1921 the following Junkers were listed[8]:

At McCook Field:

Type	Total
FAC	1
JL-6	3
At Fairfield Air Intermediate Depot:	
RE-5	1

From Major J.C. Riley's Report to the Chief Technical Section referred to above, it appears that the Junkers R.E. - V/RE-5 was a D.I. A Junkers "RE5" single-seat monoplane was turned over to the AEF in April 1919.[9] From photographs it is known that at least one D.I was acquired by the US in France.

The JL-6 was the Junkers F.13 as sold in the US by John M Larsen. Larsen immigrated to the USA in 1892 from his native Denmark. In 1919 he was in Europe intending to sell US aircraft but on seeing the F.13 arranged the founding of the Junkers Larsen Corporation in 1920. He managed to sell some of the modified F.13 monoplanes to the US Army and Post Office as the JL-6 (JL for Junkers-Larsen the US designation of the F.13.) After a series of crashed the JL-6 was grounded and the joint venture collapsed. A JL-6 was at McCook Field with the number P-145 in June 1921. Its fate is recorded as "Salvaged 11-5-23."[10] The other Junkers designations have not proved possible to be determined as to the correct type of aircraft. No other Junkers is listed as receiving a P-number. The allocation of a P-number meant that the machine was flyable. As McCook Field was the place where foreign and experimental aircraft were taken for examination and Junkers A.S.94045 did not receive a P-number, it is assumed that the machine would not have been in a flyable condition and the serial was allocated for clerical purposes.

The US Army Air Service Engineering Division tested the Junkers all-metal wing post-war.[11]

The German Junker (sic) *is the only sample of duralumin tubular and sheet construction of German manufacture that has been received for analysis in this country. As a matter of record and to assist designers in preparation of new designs in all-metal construction, a thorough study was made of this structure, special attention being given to the properties of the duralumin tubing, the duralumin sheets, and to the method of making joints and couplings.*

Above: CL.15674/18 was in a sorry state when it was one of the Junkers aircraft given to Japan post-war as war reparations. (SDTB)

Below: The colours of CL.15674/18 as depicted on this Japanese postcard are, unfortunately, incorrect.

ユンクル (YUNK. CL. I型) 單葉戰鬪機ダイムラー百六十馬力

The purpose of the investigation was stated to be:
(a). The physical properties of the materials used,
(b). The chemical composition of duralumin used.
(c). The design and construction of the wings, including couplings, splices, joints, welding, riveting, etc.
(d). The method and quality of workmanship.

The Junker wings are good examples of practical all-metal construction. With the exception of the strut values of the U section internal truss members, both the design and construction of the Junkers wings are very efficient and dependable, although it is possible that some of the joinery could be simplified to some extent so as to make a more practical production proposition.

The wings were covered both sides with corrugated sheet duralumin which was fastened to all of the spar tubes by lines of duralumin rivets spaced about two inches apart along the entire length of the tubes. The workmanship was good and the design and construction found to be efficient and dependable. Steel rivets were used for holding members to steel fittings and parts, but only duralumin rivets were employed for holding duralumin to duralumin. Although the Germans held to welding for uniting steel parts, no welding or soldering of duralumin parts was attempted in these wings.

Shortcomings were that the necks of some of the steel coupling parts were machined a little thin and the throats of some of the couplings were loose. The ductility of the tubing was erratic. Under tension test specimens necked very little and broke suddenly. The sheet duralumin showed a wide range of tensile strength. This was thought to have been due some specimens being oxidised more than others. Many specimens showed crystallization or granular appearance in the break. The wings had been given a coat of lacquer and had been painted green on the outside, but most of this had disappeared leaving the sheet duralumin to exposure to the elements. Inside the wing all parts were coated in lacquer, except the steel fittings that were given a coat of varnish.

Sometimes couplings, splices and riveted joints failed, and in other instances the attached tubing failed outside the joints, and that was recorded as indicating a well-balanced design.

The chemical composition of the duralumin averaged as follows:

Silicon	0.51
Copper	3.34
Iron	0.81
Magnesium	0.59
Aluminium	94.60

Australia

Such was the fascination with the Junkers all-metal aeroplane that a Junkers wing was received in Australia together with the German and Allied aircraft the Australian War Records Section brought back to Australia after the war for the proposed war museum. The type of Junkers it came from has not been determined, nor its fate. It was originally displayed in the exhibition held in Melbourne, but then disappeared and was presumably destroyed along with other priceless exhibits when the storage at the Exhibition Building, Melbourne, caught fire on 25 January 1927. A Fokker D.VII and D.VIII together with an LVG C.V that was shot down by Australian airmen in Palestine, together with the Bristol Fighter that shot the LVG down, and an R.E.8 fuselage, disappear from records about this time and all are presumed to have been destroyed in the fire. The material was being prepared to be transported to Sydney for another exhibition.

Belgium

Seven Junkers aeroplanes were given to Belgium as war reparations. They included CL.I, D.I monoplanes and J.I biplanes. Their eventual fate is unknown.

France

The French Navy operated a CL.I "cabin" monoplane from its Fr jus-Saint Rafael testing centre. It was one of two that had been converted into a passenger transport in 1919.[12]

United Kingdom

Britain received captured aircraft during the war including Junkers J.I 181/17 (G/3Bde/31) that was salved near La Vacquerie, there being no record of a J.I being brought down in British lines due to combat. It was destroyed in a hangar fire in 1921. G/5Bde/30 was recorded incorrectly as Junkers J.II 1566/18.

Post-Armistice it was thought advisable that a Junkers J.I be obtained "in view of the interest being taken in this type of construction."[13] The British received J.I biplanes 819/17, 820/17 (Benz 34230), 860/17 (Benz 35766) and 864/17 (Benz 33332) at Farnborough from France in September 1919. 586/18 was sent to Canada. Britain also received a CL.I that was tested at Martlesham Heath in June 1923.

Italy

Italy received seven Junkers aircraft, mostly in June-July 1920, as shown in the chart below. When the J.I fuselage that had been exhibited at the Museum of Science and Technology in Milano until 2006 was taken to the *Deutsches Technikmuseum*, Berlin,

Above & Below: Latvia operated a single CL.I with the serial number 10. The Latvian national insignia was a red swastika (*Ugnskrusts*) in a white circle. Here the wing insignia is applied as a white square. It appears that his machine has just missed landing in the water but did not have enough height to miss the bank on Kipsala Island in the Daugava. Note the two machine guns and the damage to the port wing. No.10 made a forced landing on ice on 22 March 1922, when the Latvians launched an effort to resupply German ships trapped by ice in the Gulf of Riga.

Above: The fuselage of the CL.I in Latvian markings. The CL.I wasobtained from stocks of abandoned German aircraft that included Albatros C.III, D.F.W. C.V, Hannover CL.III and Halberstadt C.V two-seaters and Fokker D.VII fighters.

Above: Strange bedfellows! A Latvian CL-I with a Sopwith 2F.1 Camel in British markings. When the British forces left in December 1919 they left seven Camels with the Latvian Aviation Park.

Above: After it was put out of service due to an accident, the fuselage of the CL.I was used by the Latvians as a funeral cortege for fallen aviators.

where it underwent restoration, the number 805 was found leading to the conclusion that this was J.805/17.

Since the J.I in the museum has an acceptance date of June 1918, it is conclusive proof that it is in the 800/17 to 899/17 batch as the other machines listed were not delivered until 1919.

Italy also received a D.I fighter in June 1921. This latter machine had been found hidden at the Junkers facility and had been confiscated by the Allies.

Japan

Japan received two J.I biplanes, 724/18 and 762/18. These were given to the Navy. 724/18 and a Junkers CL.I were displayed at Tokorozawa airfield. Of the two CL.I monoplanes that were received, 15672/18 and 15674/18, one went to the Army's Aeronautical School.

Latvia

Latvia received a single CL.I. The serial quoted as 1912/18 is incorrect and it is thought that it was CL.12921/18.

Russia

White Russian forces included the Awaloff-Bermondt's Western Volunteer Army that received at least one Junkers CL.I from German units that were being disbanded in the autumn of 1919.

The Red Air Fleet obtained two Junkers CL.I

Above: CL.1803/18, abandoned by the German Sachsenberg regiment it was obtained by the Soviets in Latvia at the end of 1919. The fuselage still shows the remains of the original camouflage. This photograph was taken in Moscow, note the Imperial Russian emblem above the hangar door. (via G Petrov)

Above: Hitler Youth examine an AEG J.I in the Luftfahrt Sammmlung, in Berlin, Museum prior to WWII. The Junkers J.I was the next machine in line.

monoplanes (Cl.1803/18 and Cl.12604/18) and one D.I (serial unknown). None were serviceable.

The Survivors

A Junkers J.I and D.I (identity unknown) were exhibited in the *Deutsche Luftfahrt Sammlung* in Berlin before World War II alongside an AEG J.I together with a marvellous collection that included an actual Fokker Dr.I that Manfred von Richthofen had flown. They were destroyed by Allied bombing in World War II. The surviving aircraft were railed to Krakow in Poland but no Junkers machine was amongst them. [19]

Canada received J.I J.586/18 as a war trophy

Right: The J 4 that was displayed in the Luftfahrt Sammmlung had the corrugated skin removed from the wings showing the internal structure. Of interest if the use of the "J" in the spelling of "*Infanterie Flugzeug*". This led to the armoured aircraft being called J-types.

Above: J.I 586/18 at Villers la Chevres. This is the aircraft sent to Canada and preserved in the museum.

Above: This post-war exhibition in Canada is probably the Canadian National Exhibition at Toronto in August 1919. A Fokker D.VII, AEG G.IV and Junkers J.I are on show with the fuselage of Sopwith Snipe E8102 on the right-hand side, the machine in which Canadian William Barker won the V.C. on 28 October 1918, when he singlehanded fought a large formation of Fokker D.VII fighters. Barker was credited with three Fokkers down in flames from the fight. Wounded in one arm and both legs, Barker crashed in Allied lines. Exhibitions such as this are known to have also taken place in the USA and Australia in the years immediately after the Armistice.

in 1919. As noted above it is presently with the Canadian Aviation and Space Museum.

A D.I survives in the Musee de l'air et de l'espace, collection in France. A D.I reproduction was built by Manfred Pfumm and is on display at the *Luftwaffenmuseum*, Berlin Gatow.

Endnotes Chapter 12

1. 10.01.1919. Notes from Junkers internal notes and correspondence via L Andersson.
2. 13.01.1919. Notes from Junkers internal notes and correspondence via L Andersson.
3. The serial numbers quoted by Anderson and Sanger go over those generally accepted as the

Above: J.586/18 on display in Canada's National Air Museum at the Ottawa/Rockcliffe airport. The airframe has suffered over the years in storage. It was not treated with the care that it requires being thought to be on a par with modern metal airframes.
Below: J.586/18 in storage but intact. The corrugated fin and rudder stand out well in this photograph.

Junkers Aircraft sent to the UK

In January a special mission was sent to Fienvillers to inspect the German aeroplanes stored there. It was thought advisable to have certain examples sent back to the UK for testing. In addition to a two-seat Gotha twin-engine "fighter", it was also considered "advisable to get over one of the Junker (*sic*) J.1 Allmetal (*sic*) machines in view of the interest being taken in this type of construction."[1]

The British Superintendent of Research requested in March 1919 whether it would be possible to be supplied with a sample of German aircraft armour plate as it was "desired to carry out photomicrographic tests and analysis to complete the information already obtained in regard to other German bullet resisting armour." As it was understood that some German armoured machines were to go to Martlesham Heath for testing purposes and requested some armour plate for testing purposes.[2] The request was granted and when the machines arrived at Martlesham Heath they would be notified so that they could take their sample.

The British had requested that three machines of each type be sent back to Martlesham Heath. In April an additional request was made for

one each of the following if three are not available:-
D.F.W.
Hannoveraner.
Roland.
Junkers Biplane.
Junkers Monoplane.[3]

On 12 September 1919, 18 rail trucks with German aircraft were sent to the RAE Farnborough.[4] The following were the Junkers content identified:-

Truck No.39517
2 R.H. Junker Top Planes.
1 L.H. " " "
3 Junker C/Sections
3 Left Hand Bottom Planes
4 Right " " "

Truck No. 39521
Junkers J.ii (*sic*). No. Number.
Benz Engine 34210 (Mags Plugs Compass & Instruments missing)
3 Junker C/Section. 2 L.H. Planes top Junk.

Truck No. 39596
Junker J.ii (*sic*). No. Number.
Benz engine 34230. (Mags Plugs Instruments & Compass missing).
Spandau Gun 4093

Junker J.ii (sic). No. Numbers.
Benz Engine 33766. (Mags Plugs & Instruments missing).
2 Spandau Guns 5908/5768.

1 Set Main Planes
Tailplanes Rudders & Elevators.

Truck No. 39610
1 Set Junkers Main Planes 1 Junker C/Section.
Junker Tail, Plane Junker Radiator, 1 case Junk Fins.

Truck No.
Junker J.i (*sic*). 819/17.
Benz Engine 33849. 2 Spandau Guns.
4 Instruments. Compass missing.

In April 1919, a Minute for the Asst Controller (Experiments) set put a list of German seaplanes that the British thought should be brought to Britain for testing at Felixstowe where the new testing base for seaplanes was to be established. These were:

Brandenburg Monoplane Seaplane (150 Benz or 185 Rapp)
BiplaneSeaplane (150 Benz)
Seaplane (260 Maybach)
Stakkener (sic) *Giant Seaplane (4 – 260 H.P. Maybach)*
Dornier Giant Monoplane Seaplane (4 – 260 H.P. Maybach)
Zeppelin 2 Seater Monoplane Seaplane (8 cyl. 190 H.P. Benz)
Junker (sic) *(all metal) 2 seat Monoplane Seaplane (150 H.P. Benz)*
Albatros Single Seater Fighter Seaplane (190 HP Benz)
Seaplane (260 HP Mercedes)
Brandenburg 2 Seater "Kannonen" Biplane Seaplane (260 Maybach)
Friedrichshafen 2 seater Reconnaissance Seaplane (230 HP Benz)

1. Minute. D.1 to D/D od D. No date. TNA Mun 8/34.
2. Minute to X2 from Lt Col Forbes, Head of Air. Arm.(G) 06.03.1919. TNA Mun 8/34.
3. To Capt Wilson, E.1.A from Ass Controller (Experimental), X4. 05.04.1919. TNA Mun8/34.
4. G Barfoot Baunt(?), HQ, RAF in France & Flanders, to General Brooke-Popham. 16.09.1919. TNA Mun8/34.

Gotha twin engined Seaplane (2 – 260 Mercedes)
Rumpler single Seater Seaplane (160 HP Mercedes)[5]

As far as is known the only German marine aircraft taken to the UK and tested was the Brandenburg W.29 *Marine Nummer* 2670. It would appear that no room could be found for the machines at Grain or Felixstowe and the opportunity for evaluating the latest in German technology was lost.

5. List with Minute, Asst Controller (Experiments) to E.1.A (Capt Wilson). Date received 11.04.1919. TNA Mun8/34.

batch numbers for the J.I due to their research into what happened after the Armistice when Junkers was still building aircraft.

4. Maj J.C. Riley to Chief Technical Section. Subject: *Attached Report on Junkers All-metal Monoplane R.E.-5.* 28.01.1919. P.M. Grosz Collection Box 491.
5. AEF US Air Service *Report on Inspection of German Airplanes at Villers-Le-Chevres, Cosnrs, East and West Fields, and Tellancourt.* 13.01.1919. A.E. Ferko Collection, UTD Dept of Special Collections. Also Notes on German service from P.M. Grosz Collection Box 427.
6. "List of Captured Enemy Material in the United States Inventories as of August 27, 1919." Via late R Cavanagh.
7. "Quantity Report of Overseas' Airplanes." Copy in RAFM JM Bruce Collection Box 72. The listing gives German, British and French aircraft.
8. "Monthly Listing of Aeroplanes, 4 June 1921. – Airplanes at McCook Files as of 31 May 1921." Copy in USAF Museum.
9. Note in P.M. Grosz Collection Box 482.
10. Typed list of McCook P-Numbers. Copy in USAF Museum.
11. *Investigation of Junker Biplane Wings,* Air Service Information Circular No.230, Engineering Division, Air Service.20.05.1921. I am grateful to Carl Bobrow for making this report available. Parts of the report had appeared in journals and magazines and the origin of these articles is now confirmed.
12. A photograph of a military style CL.I with an elaborate roll over bar at a French naval base appears in Ricco, P & Soumille, J-C. *Les Avions Allemands Aux Couleurs Francaises,* Tome 2, (Aicdoc, France) P.71. It also shows an F.13 that was apparently part of reparations payment to the French.
13. W/Commander RAF, D.1. Minute 18.09.19. TNA Mun 8/34.

Italian J.I

Delivery Date All 1920	*Werke Nr*	Serial	Junkers Shipping Date	Notes
25 June	N/A	J.752/18	26 Mar 1919	
		J.760/18		
		J.767/18		Listed as cancelled, possibly incorrect number.
28 June		J.750/18	March 1919	
29 July	209	J.803/17	July 1918	

Source: P.M. Grosz Collection Box 487. Gentilli, R. "WWI German Aeroplanes to Italy", *Windsock International*, Vol.13, No.1, P.18.

Above, Above Right, & Previous Page: Junkers D.I on display in the *Musee d l'Air et Space.*

Junkers D.1 Reproduction Luftwaffenmuseum Gatow

TNA Mun8/34.

14. For the story of the collection see Hundertmark, M & Steinle, H. *Phoenix aus der Asche, Die Deutsche Luftfahrt Sammmlung Berlin,* Siberstreif Verlag GmbH, Germany, 1985.

13. Camouflage and Markings of Junkers Aircraft

Above: On this machine the interplane struts appear to be a dark colour. The application of the cross on the bottom of both wings was not uncommon, being requested by crews as they were fired on by both sides.

As with so much of German World War I aviation, colours are an area that is not documented in as much detail as one would like. With the Junkers aeroplanes there is little information besides a few reports on captured aircraft. The best guess has been made with present knowledge; however, this is always open to change as more information comes to light.

J 1

The J 1 appears to have been given a light coloured coat of varnish/paint after static testing. At one time it may have been painted a light (blue) colour as shown in a 1918 Dessau photograph of the dismantled machine. Early iron crosses were applied without any white field.

1st Lt E.E. Aldrin, USAS, inspected the Junkers facility at Dessau in 1922, and reported that "the Junker (*sic*) machines were covered in a greenish finish. This my escort said, was ordinary good furniture varnish or lacquer with a slight green tinting put on to show they had been lacquered."[1] While this report was made post-war, the system of varnishing would have evolved from the varnishing of the earlier machines.

J 2

The first J 2 was painted overall a pale (blue) colour. Light blue was a common scheme for early German aircraft to mid-1916. Later aircraft appear to have had a dark colour (brown/green) applied to upper surfaces over the lighter colour as seen in the accompanying photographs. From close examination of photographs showing the demarcation line between the upper and lower colours, Richard Alexander has suggested that the dark colour was applied by sponges.

J 4 (Military J.I)

Early J 4 biplanes were painted in a two colour scheme with a solid colour on upper surfaces with light blue lower surfaces. The dark colour has been

Junkers J.I Factory Colors

© Piotr Mrozowski
Junkers J.I
(Ifa) batch 100/17 to 149/17
First part of this batch
April 2018

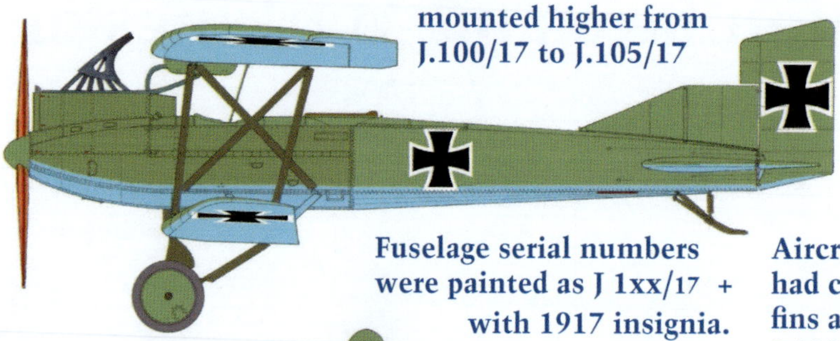

Flare container mounted higher from J.100/17 to J.105/17

Fuselage serial numbers were painted as J 1xx/17 + with 1917 insignia.

Aircraft in this batch had canvas-covered fins and rudders until J.140/17

"Ifa" or "Junkers & Co. Dessau" painted on the wheel covers

Some aircraft retained this camouflage to the end of the war; others had a grayish-violet color added to upper surfaces.

The armoured part of the front fuselage was covered with anti-corrsion paint, making it darker than the rest of the aircraft.

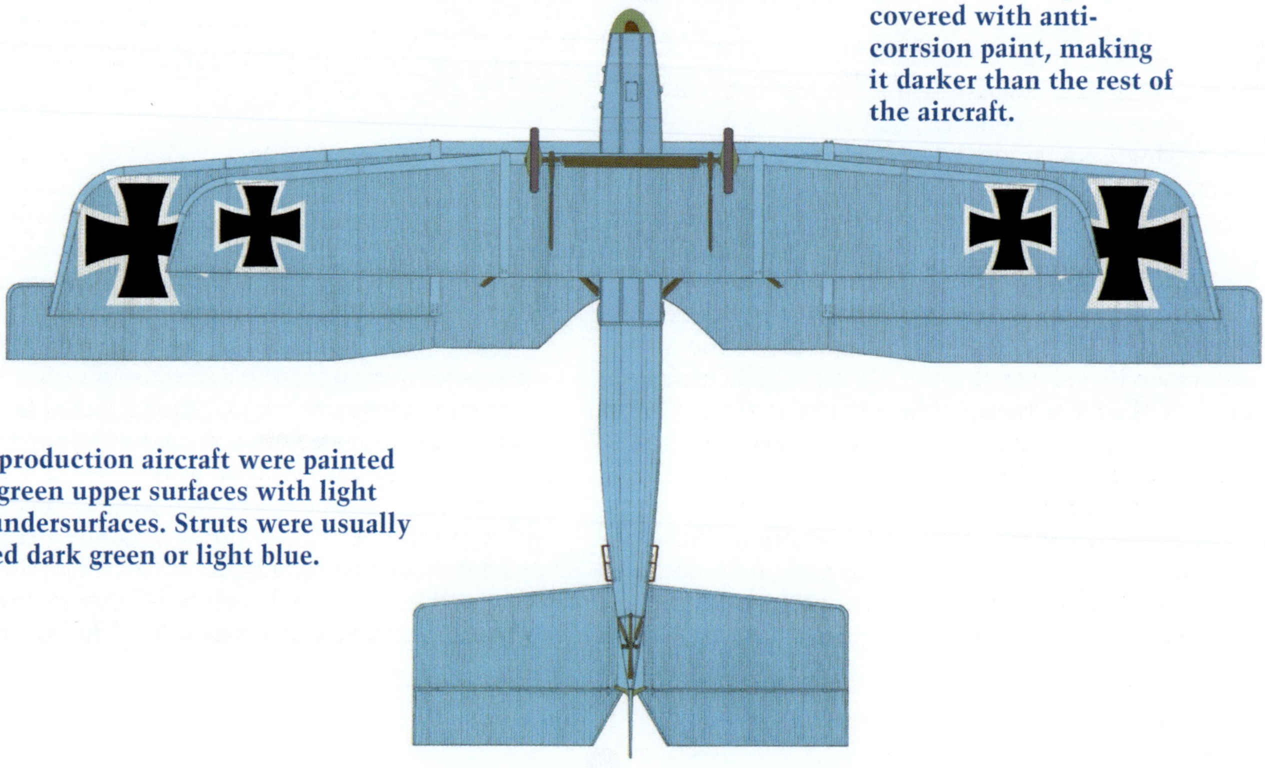

Early production aircraft were painted olive-green upper surfaces with light blue undersurfaces. Struts were usually painted dark green or light blue.

Junkers J.I
(Ifa) batch 100/17 to 149/17
From middle of this batch
April 2018

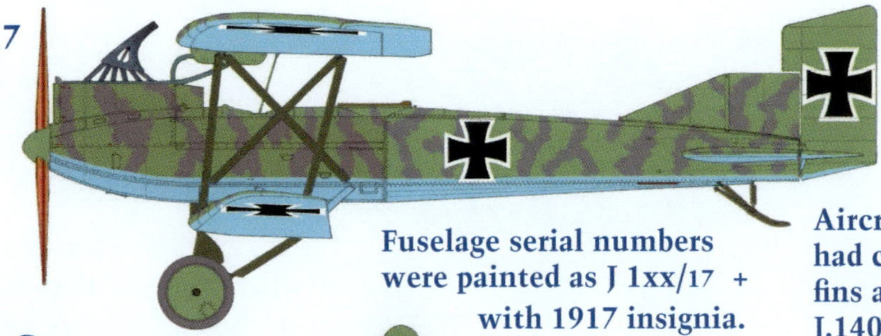

Fuselage serial numbers were painted as J 1xx/17 + with 1917 insignia.

Aircraft in this batch had canvas-covered fins and rudders until J.140/17

"Ifa" or "Junkers & Co. Dessau" painted on the wheel covers

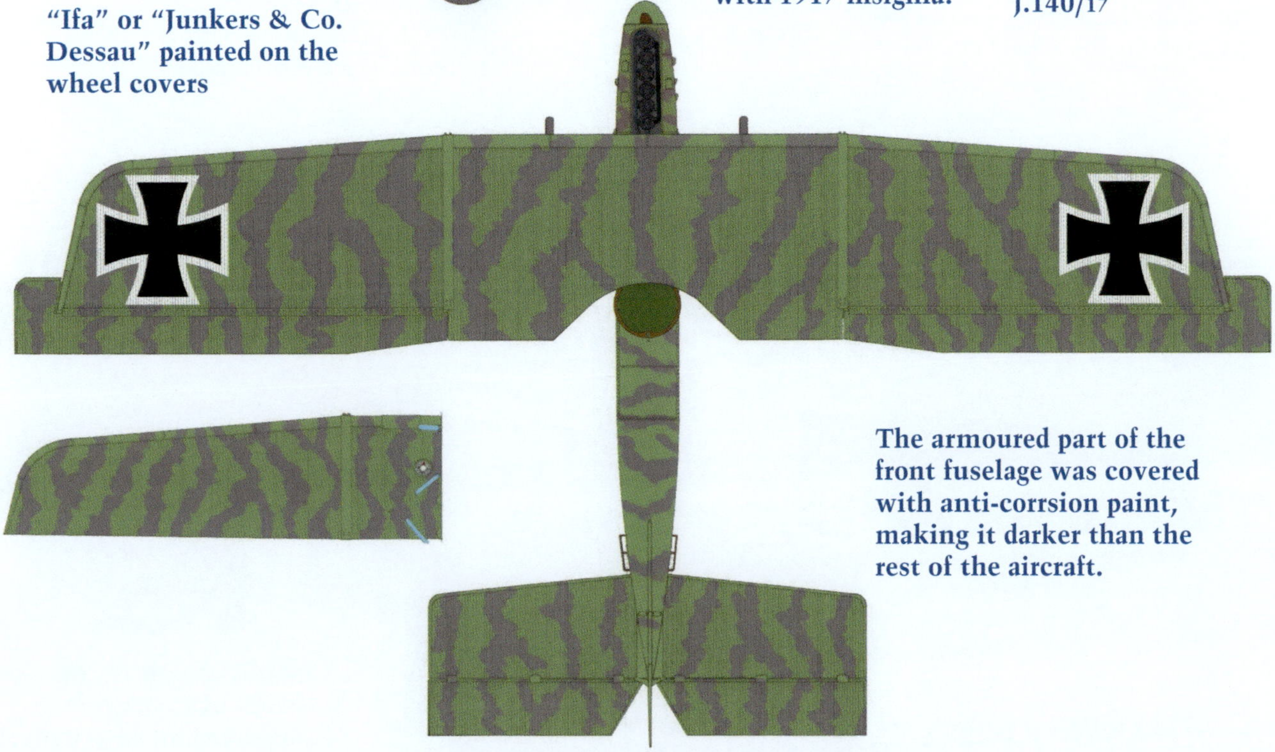

The armoured part of the front fuselage was covered with anti-corrsion paint, making it darker than the rest of the aircraft.

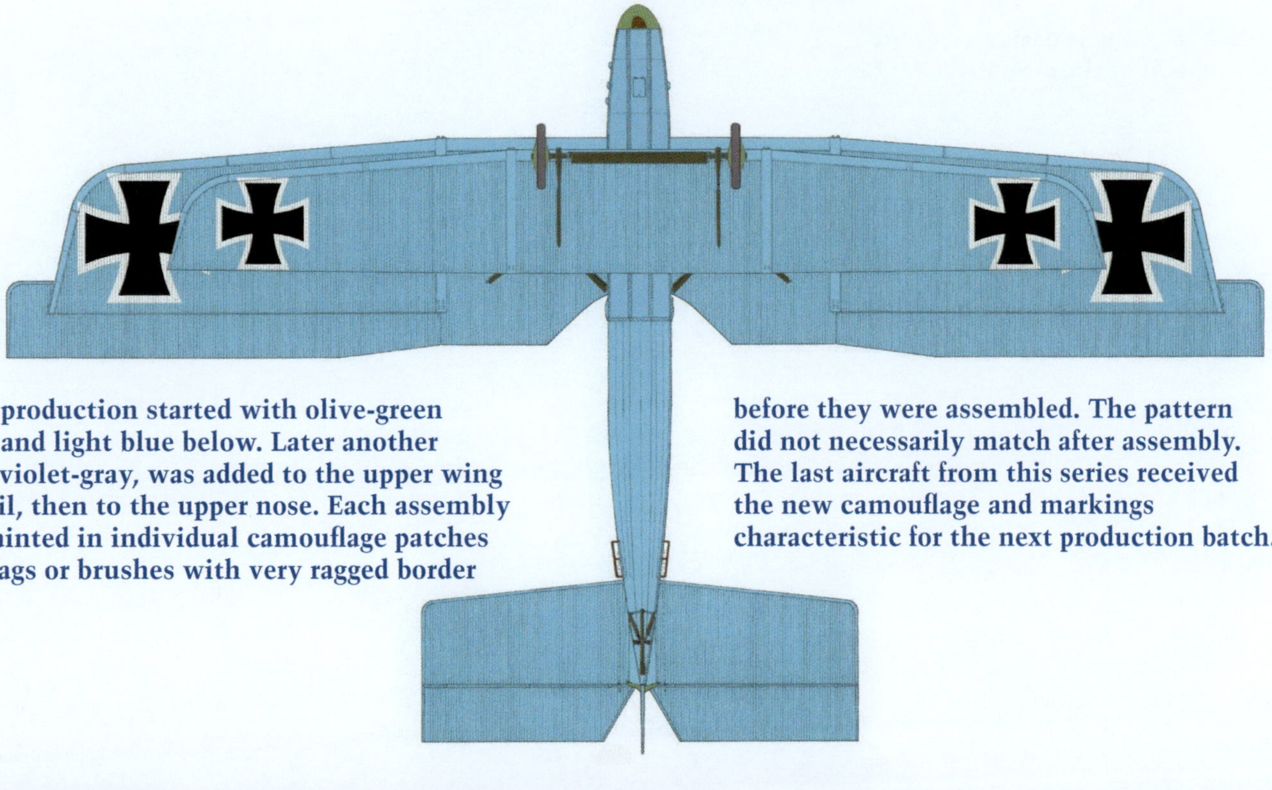

Batch production started with olive-green above and light blue below. Later another color, violet-gray, was added to the upper wing and tail, then to the upper nose. Each assembly was painted in individual camouflage patches with rags or brushes with very ragged border before they were assembled. The pattern did not necessarily match after assembly. The last aircraft from this series received the new camouflage and markings characteristic for the next production batch.

Junkers J.I Factory Colors

© Piotr Mrozowski
Junkers J.I
(Ifa) batch 576/18 to 615/18
April 2018

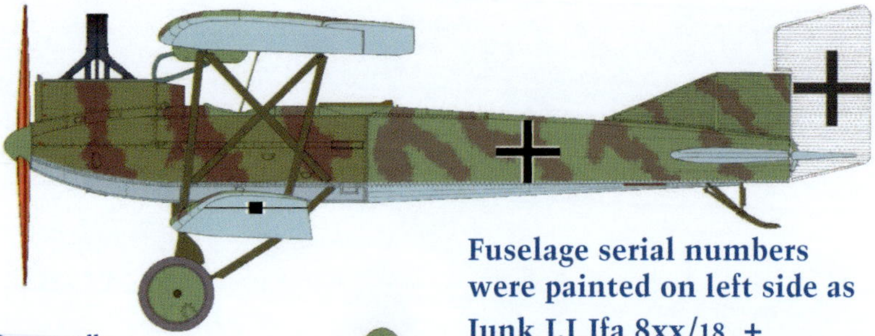

Fuselage serial numbers were painted on left side as Junk J.I Jfa 8xx/18 + with 1918 insignia early in the batch. Later they were painted as Junk J.I + Jfa 8xx/18

"Ifa" or "Junkers & Co. Dessau" painted on the wheel covers

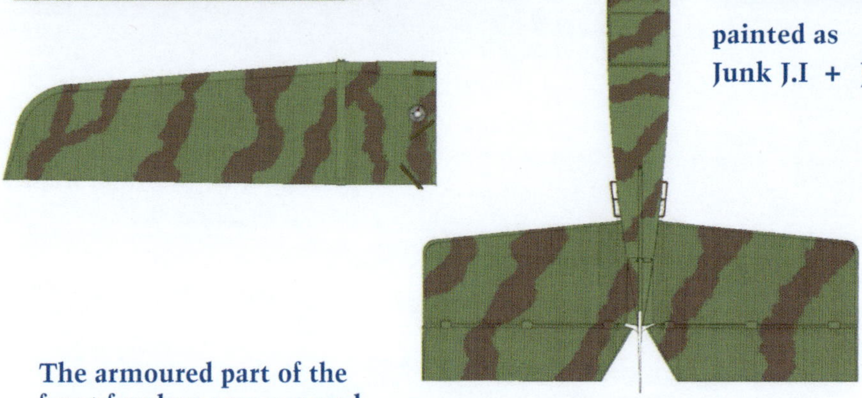

Some aircraft in this batch had slightly extended fin and rudder.

The armoured part of the front fuselage was covered with anti-corrsion paint, making it darker than the rest of the aircraft.

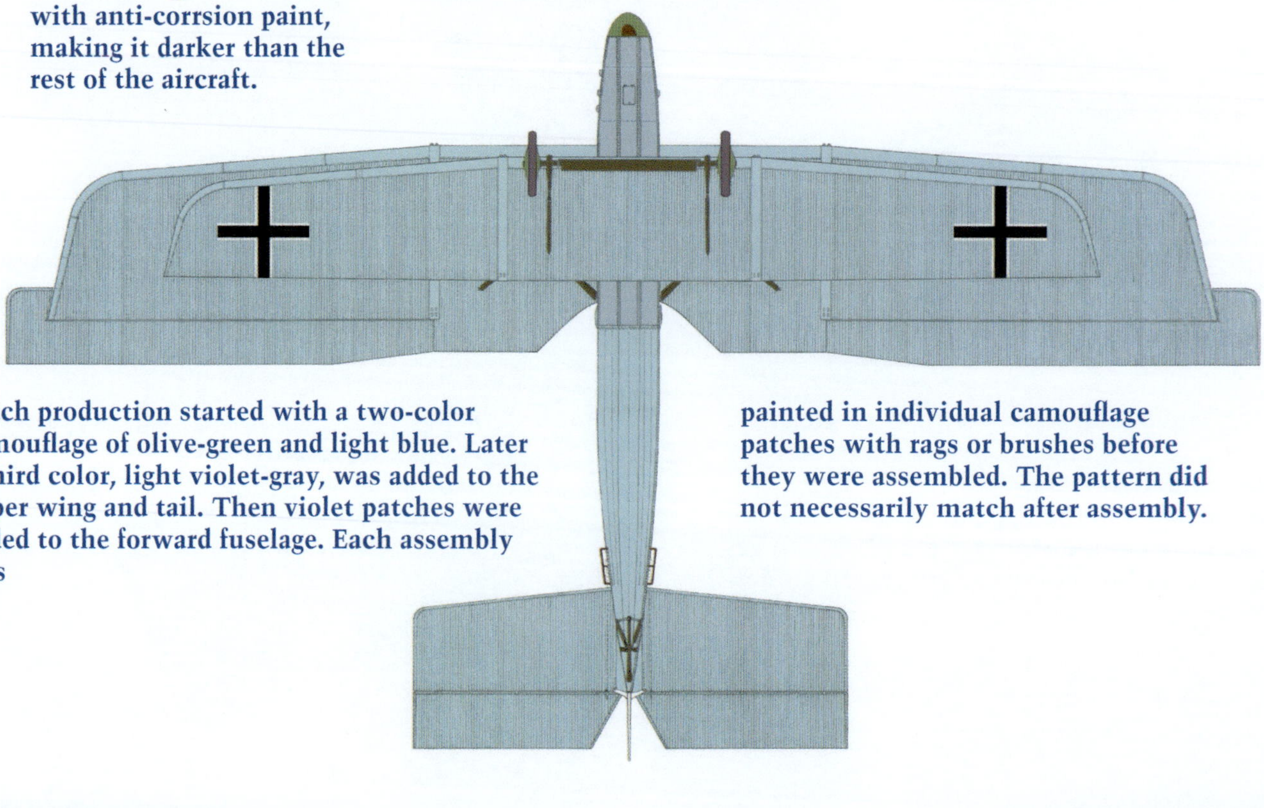

Batch production started with a two-color camouflage of olive-green and light blue. Later a third color, light violet-gray, was added to the upper wing and tail. Then violet patches were added to the forward fuselage. Each assembly was painted in individual camouflage patches with rags or brushes before they were assembled. The pattern did not necessarily match after assembly.

Junkers J.I Factory Colors

© Piotr Mrozowski
Junkers J.I
(Ifa) batch 576/18 to 615/18
April 2018

Fuselage serial numbers were painted (both sides) as Junk J.I + Jfa 5xx/18 with 1918 insignia.

"Ifa" or "Junkers & Co. Dessau" painted on the wheel covers

Some machines in this batch had the rear fuselage sides covered with 4- or 5-colored printed camouflage fabric that was applied as available but not on all machines.

Dark 4-color Day Pattern:
J.I 583/18
J.I 762/18

Dark 5-Color Day Pattern:
J.I 873/17
J.I 586/18 (Canada)

The armoured part of the front fuselage was covered with anti-corrosion paint, making it darker than the rest of the aircraft.

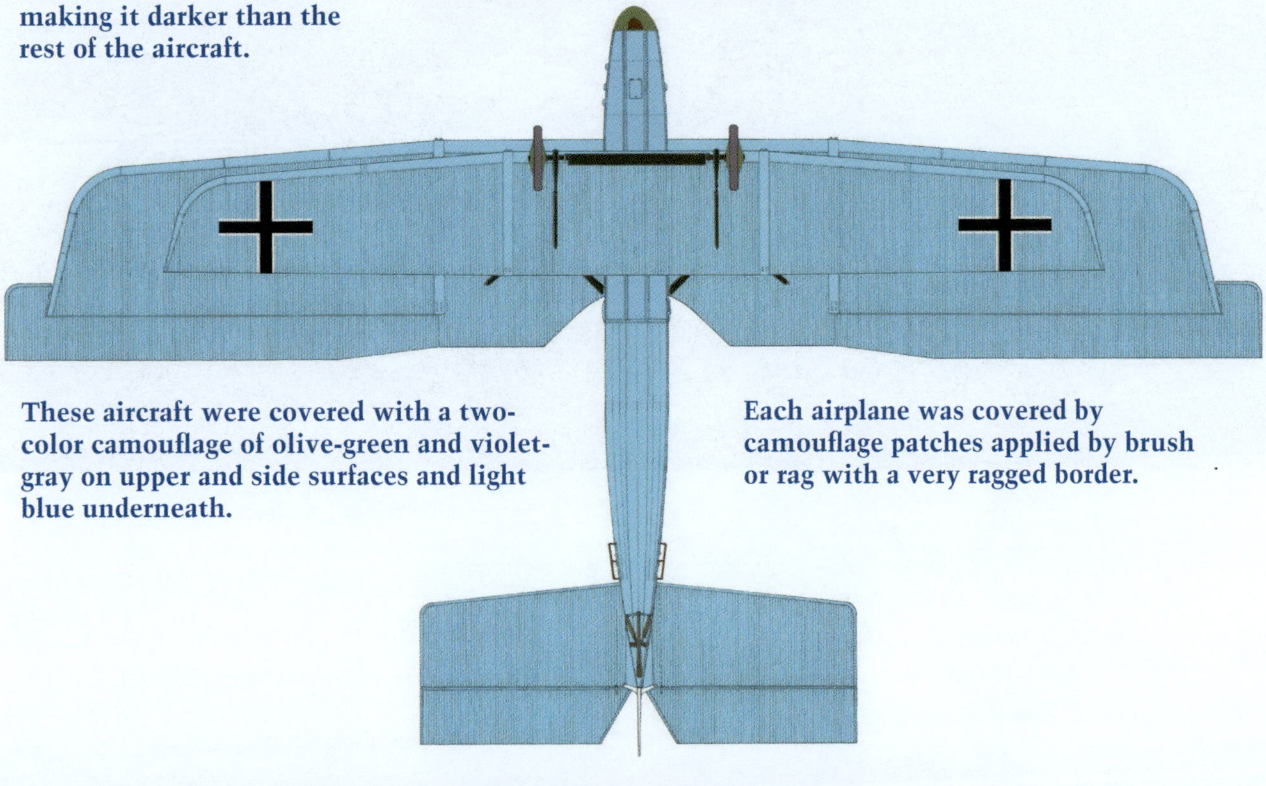

These aircraft were covered with a two-color camouflage of olive-green and violet-gray on upper and side surfaces and light blue underneath.

Each airplane was covered by camouflage patches applied by brush or rag with a very ragged border.

Junkers CL.I Factory Colors

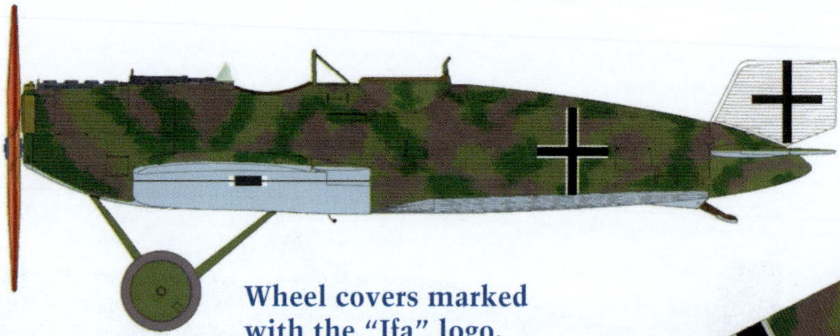

Wheel covers marked with the “Ifa” logo.

© Piotr Mrozowski
Junkers CL.I 1802/18
From 1801/18 to 1802/18
April 2018

Armament: One fixed Spandau firing forward for the pilot and one flexible Parabellum for the gunner.

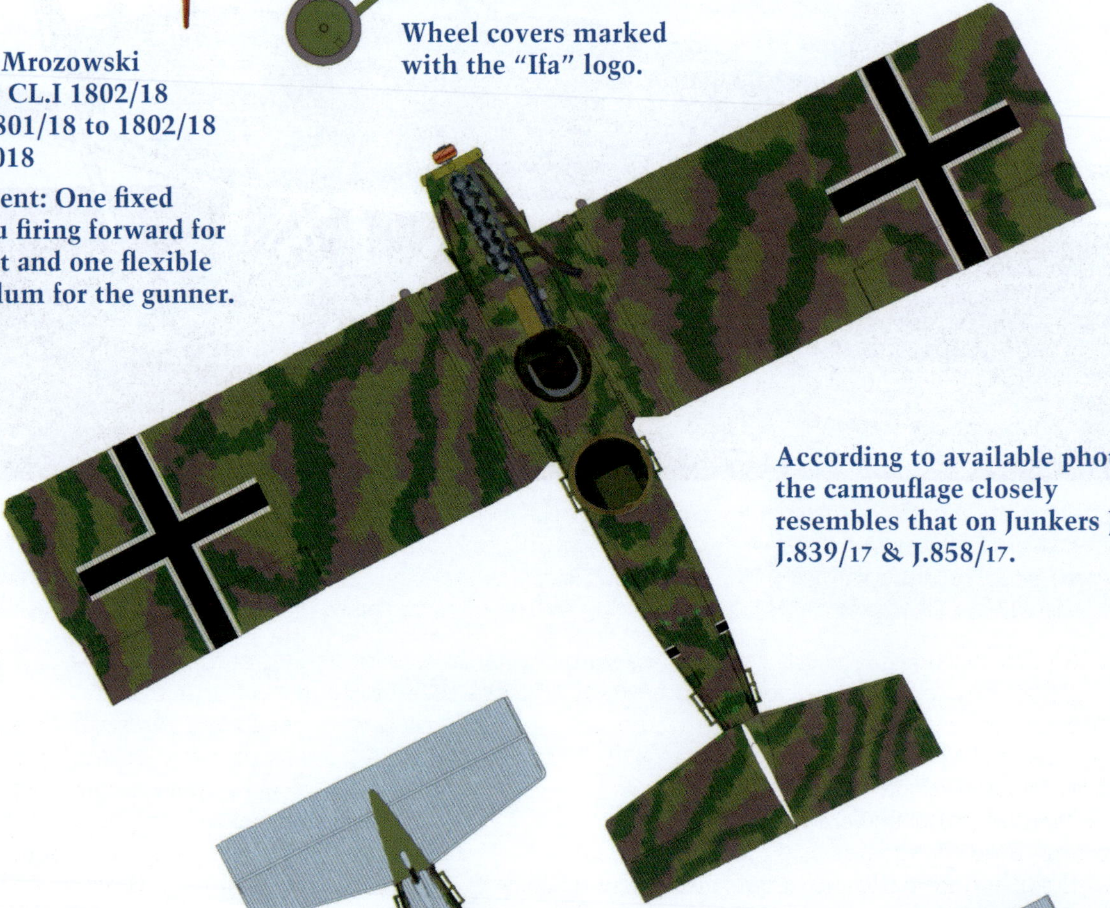

According to available photos the camouflage closely resembles that on Junkers J.I J.839/17 & J.858/17.

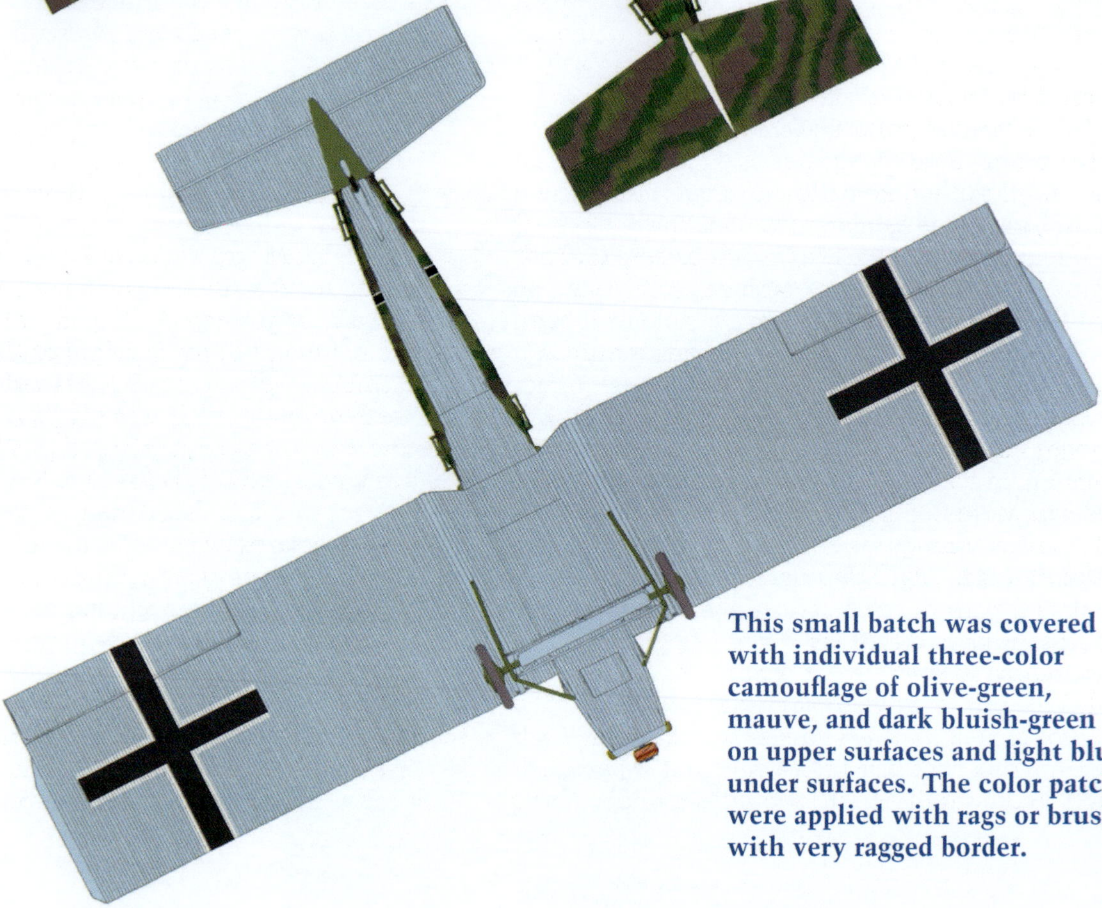

This small batch was covered with individual three-color camouflage of olive-green, mauve, and dark bluish-green on upper surfaces and light blue under surfaces. The color patches were applied with rags or brushes with very ragged border.

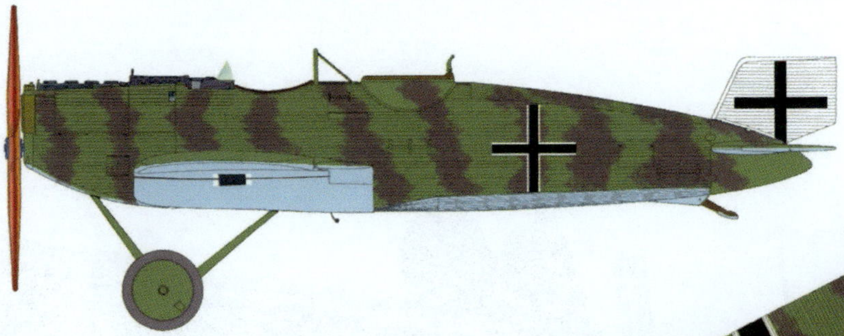

© Piotr Mrozowski
Junkers CL.I 1805/18
From 1803/18 to 1809/18
April 2018

Armament: Two fixed Spandau firing forward for the pilot and one flexible Parabellum for the gunner.

This small batch was covered with individual two-color camouflage of olive-green and mauve on upper surfaces and light blue under surfaces. The color patches were applied with rags or brushes with very ragged border.

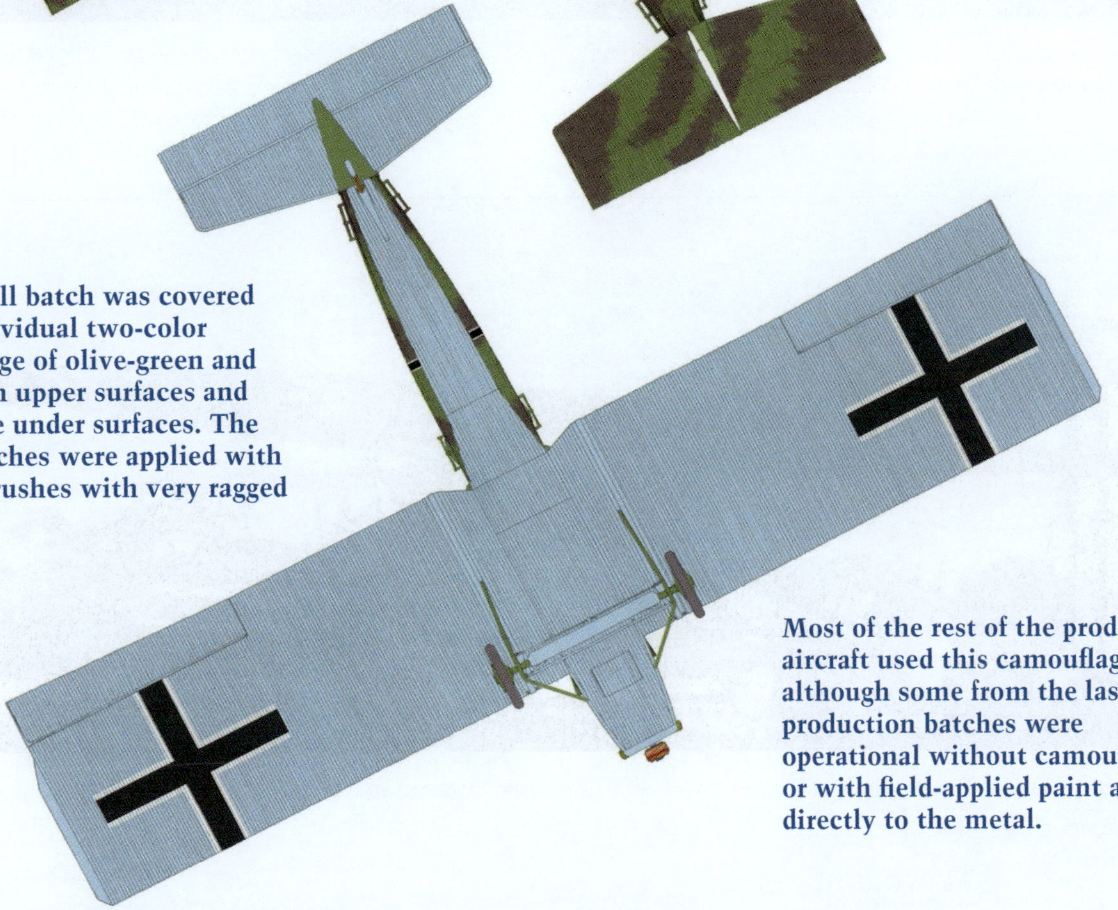

Most of the rest of the production aircraft used this camouflage, although some from the last production batches were operational without camouflage or with field-applied paint applied directly to the metal.

Junkers D.I Factory Colors

© Piotr Mrozowski
Junkers D.I
From D.5180/18 to
D.5189802/18
April 2018

Armament: Two fixed Spandau firing forward for the pilot.

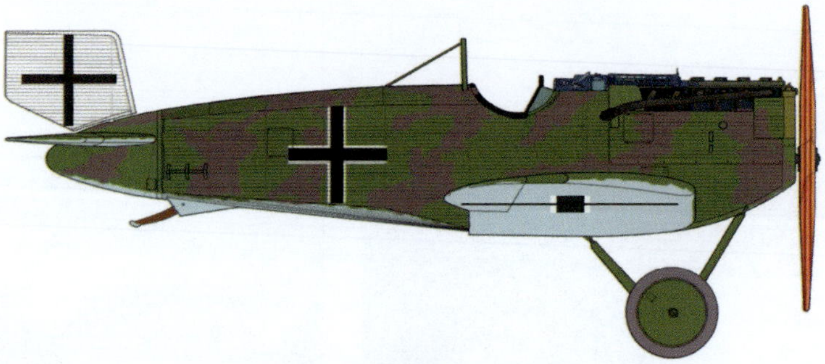

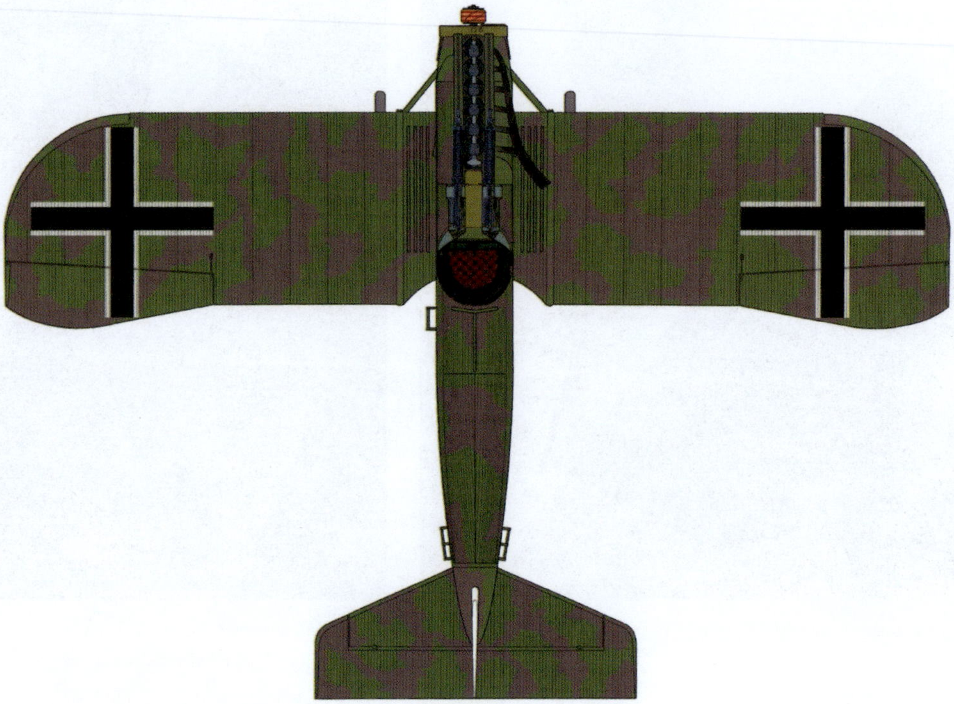

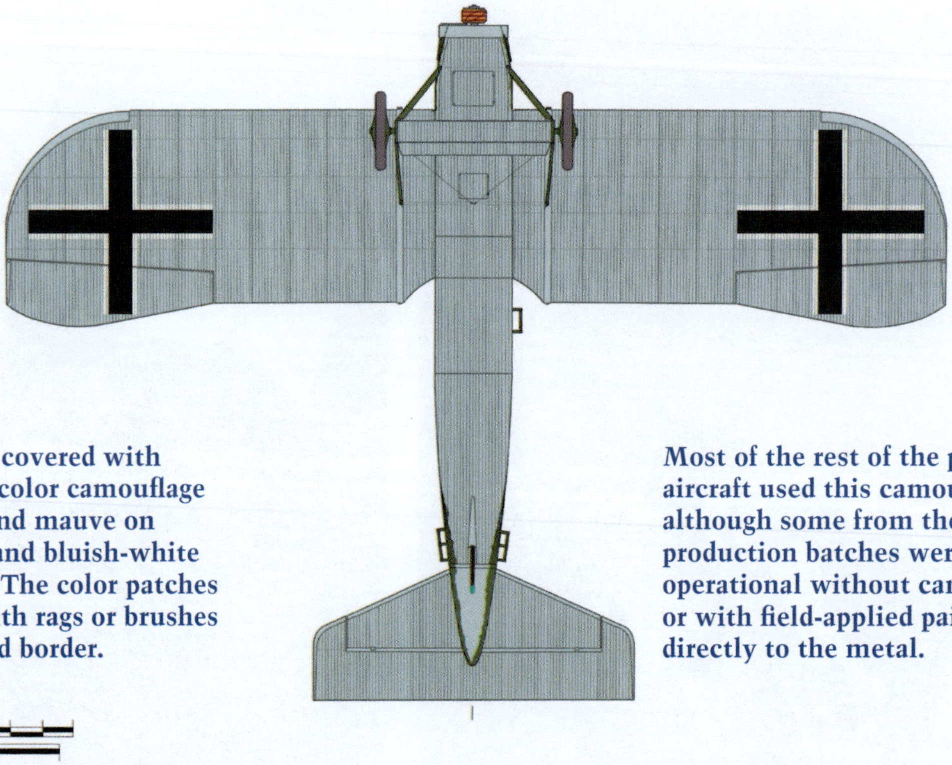

This batch was covered with individual two-color camouflage of olive-green and mauve on upper surfaces and bluish-white under surfaces. The color patches were applied with rags or brushes with very ragged border.

Most of the rest of the production aircraft used this camouflage, although some from the last production batches were operational without camouflage or with field-applied paint applied directly to the metal.

Above: J.138/17 is in the two-colour scheme. Note the stencils on the nose at the catches that allow the clam shell engine cowling doors to open. Under this it reads JFa over Farb. No 148, over [Junk.I]. Note how the lower surface colour extends onto the upper fuselage. The port lower wing is missing. (AHT AL0776-134)

Above: The camouflage on J.858/17 appears darker than usual. Late style narrow crosses in all positions. LVG biplanes in background.

This Page: Unfortunately, the story behind this crash of J.143/17 is not known, nor whether the crew escaped. The mixed markings on this machine are interesting in that the lower surfaces of the upper wing have the interim cross, while the curved cross is still on the upper wing where it would have been difficult to repaint into the new style. The lower wing had the curved cross as the white outline is still visible. There is no outline to that applied under the upper wing. The rear fuselage markings do not continue under the fuselage. (Piotr)

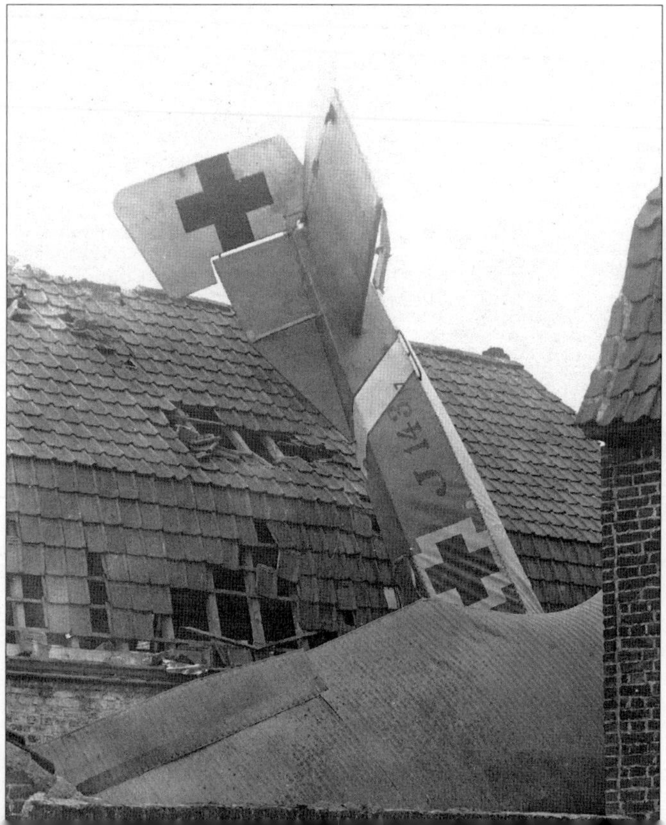

This Page & Following Page, Top: The result of a hard landing? The armoured front section of J.839/17 is intact as is the rear fuselage except where it gave way in the accident. Note the lack of a cross on the underside of the upper wing. This machine has the corrugated fin. (AHT AL194-005 to 008)

Above: This painting was from a postcard that was widely sold during the war. The dull colour of the J.I would be more in keeping with the areas it operated in on the Western Front, but the colours of the early J.I biplanes is unknown. Note that the J.I is accompanied by Junkers J 1 monoplanes with their early curved cross markings.

suggested as green however a Junkers advertisement showed the aircraft as wearing brown. Given the assigned task of the machine this would be a logical colour.

The British report on the J.I biplane was compiled from the wrecks of two machines. It was reproduced in *Flight* commencing with the 26 February 1920, issue. Under "Colouring" it described the camouflage as follows:-

The machine is painted in matt colours. The upper surface of the planes has irregular masses of the usual green and mauve tints, while the underside is painted a bluish-white colour. The struts are green, as is the armoured portion of the fuselage.

A weight legend was painted on the fuselage.

G/3 Bd3/31. This Junkers J.I was reported as 181/17, and was "salved near La Vacquerie during recent operations.... The planes are camouflaged in mauve and green on the top surfaces, and painted white underneath." The machine was built on 5 August 1918, and had a weight legend on the fuselage.[2]

The remnants of paint on J.586/18, residing in the Canadian National Aviation Museum, show that the lower surfaces were a light sand-yellow colour, while the upper surfaces were mauve and green.

In conclusion the results of seven years research by Wingnut Wings since the release for their original Junkers J.I aircraft kit sums up the knowledge of Junkers colour schemes to date:-

Period reports indicate that the Junkers J.I was painted in pale green on the upper surfaces, with darker green struts and undercarriage. The undersides were painted a very pale blue. Many

Above & Below: An abandoned D.I found post-war. This and the following photographs are thought to have been taken at Hombeek, Belgium. There appear to be bullet holes in the fuselage corrugated sheets. The tailplane is a light colour (white). There is no evidence of a serial on the fuselage indicating that it may have been overpainted. (SDTB)

Above & Below: This D.I appears to be in fine condition except for the lack of tyres. Note that the fuselage again appears to have been overpainted a single solid colour and the rudder, elevators and tailplane appears to be white. The wings are in the two-colour scheme. This is possibly the machine acquired by the US. The Fokker D.VII in the background has been poorly treated by souvenir hunters with the fuselage stripped of fabric. (SDTB)

Above, Below, & Following Page: This appears to be the same machine in these four photographs and it was photographed at the same location as the above machine, Hombeek in Belgium. The wings show the standard camouflage pattern with the fuselage overpainted and a two-colour band painted around behind the cockpit. On this machine the tailplane appears to be the same colour as the fuselage. Note the access door on the port side of the fuselage to the rear of the national marking. There are at least four Fokker D.VII fighters in the background. (SDTB)

aircraft had mauve camouflage applied to the upper surfaces in a wide variety of patterns. The armoured steel front portion appears to have sometimes been painted dark green like the struts or possibly left in red oxide primer (appearing very dark in period photos). At some stage the undersides were painted in a pale sand colour, possibly applied at the unit, before being adopted as standard at the factory for later production aircraft, many of which had their fabric surfaces covered in pre-printed lozenge camouflaged material.[3]

J 9 (Military D.I)

A D.I machine was found at Evere aerodrome near Brussels and was the subject of a Ministry of Munitions report on the type. The report was reproduced by *Flight* commencing in their 1 April 1920, issue. Under the heading "Painting" the following was recorded:-

The body is painted a chocolate-brown colour, except underneath, where a white pigment has been applied. The wings are painted a pale green with irregular patches of light mauve on top, and white underneath. The tail planes and elevator are white above and below.

Close examination revealed the fact that under the layer of chocolate paint the body was a layer of pale green colour, and a similar colour could be seen on the tail planes wherever the white had peeled off. The chocolate and white were all flat, unvaried colour. Careful scrutiny of the fuselage *side revealed the fact that on the top of the green colour on the starboard side, the inscription "JUNK.D.I." had been painted - the slightly raised edges of the letters could just be traced. This had been obliterated by the chocolate paint.*

The fuselage showed evidence of being hit by several bursts of machine gun fire but whether this occurred while in flight or after it was abandoned is not clear. Photographs included with the report show a machine on its belly without a rudder. Late war narrow crosses were applied. Four D.I monoplanes in various condition were obtained in Belgium after the German retreat.

J 10 (Military CL.I)

No documentation has been found describing J 10 colour schemes. From photographs, it appears that they were finished similar to the later production J 4 (Military J.I) biplanes in green and mauve upper surfaces over light blue lower surfaces, as described above.

J 11 (Navy CS.I floatplane)

The J 11 (Cs.I) examined by the British at Warnemünde showed no paint or varnish upon the sheet metal.[4]

End Notes Chapter 13

1. Memorandum for Maj Bane. Subject: *Preliminary Report on Visit to Junkers Plant at Dessau, Germany.* 1st E.E. Aldrin, USAS. Lt 01/10/22. Copy in P.M. Grosz Collection Box 482.
2. The serial is incorrect. This machine was also quoted as a J.II in another document. TNA MUN4/5010. "Report on Junker Two-Seater.30.10.1918". This machine was the subject of an US Intelligence report that gave the colours as green and purple. Another example where a person's perspective of a colour is different. "Summary of Intelligence, AEF" for October 1918. Reprinted in *Cross & Cockade (US)*, Vol.3 No.3, P.271. According to the report the German pilots did not like the J.I and called it the "*Nöbel-Waggon*,"as it was too heavy and unwieldly to use.
3. Email from Richard Alexander, Wingnut Wings, 22.05.2017.
4. *Report on the German Naval Air Service – Seaplanes and Airships*, Air Ministry, No date, but post-Armistice.

Below: The Japanese hand coloured photographs and sold them as postcards. The J.I 762/18 has undergone this process. The lozenge fabric is well shown but the colours are not authentic.

Afterword

Above & Facing Page: The massive Junkers G.38 was the closest to a flying wing that Junkers could achieve given the technology of the time. The JG1 flying wing project had been closed down by the Allies after the end of World War I. The G.38 had a wing with a span of 44 m and a chord of 10 m, and an aerofoil shape that was high enough to allow passengers to sit in the wing at the root where it joined the fuselage. The inner engines had four bladed airscrews whilst the outer pair had twin bladed airscrews. The oil coolers may be seen under the engine. They could be lowered in flight.

Construction was the usual Junkers all-metal pattern with multi-spar wings and the airframe covered with corrugated Duralumin. The machine could carry 30 passengers; eleven in the fuselage, with two seats in the glazed nose, and the rest in the wings.

One G.38, D-APIS, was impressed on the outbreak of World War 2, and was destroyed by the RAF at Tattoi airfield in Greece.

Japan built six bomber versions of the G.38 as the Ki-20. Japan was the only other country to be interested in operating the G.38.

During the war years there was tremendous growth in aviation. Handley-Page in the UK had built to the limit of wood and wire construction with the V/1500 four engine bomber. In France, the wooden monocoque fuselage had a resurgence as exemplified by the Nieuport 29 C.1 fighter. Only in Germany was there advances in applied aerodynamics and only in Germany was the all-metal aeroplane developed and this was due to the direction of Professor Junkers. In addition to Peter M. Grosz and Harry Woodman's praise of Junkers, Charles Gibbs-Smith in his *The Aeroplane – An Historical Survey,* attributes the development of the all-metal monoplane as the most far-reaching innovation of its day. It was to be decades before the concept was to be followed by other aircraft building countries.

At the end of the war the Junker-Fokker merge was dissolved with Junkers regaining full control. Junkers took over the Junkers-Fokker facility at Dessau and founded the *Junkers Flugzeugwerke AG.* Professor Junkers had a prolific life with some 1,000 plus patents being granted to him in the fields of aerodynamics, thermodynamics and internal

combustion engines. His successful business career meant that initially he had the funds to pursue his theories carefully and scientifically. Unlike Fokker who could have his workmen turn out a new prototype in a short time to prove or disprove a concept in the field, the all-metal aircraft required more time and a careful background of research before committing to cutting metal. It was a completely new field and it was Junkers bold visionary commitment that saw it through to success.

Although duralumin was openly published in the German technical press before the war the Allies did not utilise it. Herald Penrose in his magnificent history of British aviation noted that when an example of the Junkers deep cantilever wing was loaded to destruction at the Royal Aircraft Establishment, neither Frank Barnwell from Bristol where they were working on the M.R.1 all-metal biplane, nor Robert Bruce from Westland were interested enough to witness the tests.[1] When the results of the Junkers experiments were available in captured airframes, even *Flight* misidentified the key alloy as magnesium rather than copper. It was not until Junkers began to prove his post-war civil aircraft that interest in the material began in Britain.[2] The British Air Publication 1107, *A Manual of Rigging for Aircraft,* was published in 1925 and included the following comments on Junkers construction: -

The principle of construction used in the German Junker machines includes the use of the fuselage covering as a factor in the strength of the body. A number of cross bulkheads are built up of channel section duralumin strips which take the place of longerons. To this framework is riveted the covering which is corrugated so as to withstand bending stresses in the direction of its length.[3]

This entry was illustrated by drawings of the Junkers D.I. By this time the RAF was interested in metal construction.

Luckily situated in that part of Germany not occupied by the victorious Allies, Junkers was able to continue to work forward building all-metal passenger aircraft. Despite the action of the Inter Allied Aircraft Control Commission he was successful and his aircraft grew renown for long-distance flights and developed a reputation for

Junkers Metal Aircraft Delivered to the German Army Administration Up to 31 March 1919[1] 1. Type D.I (*Kampfeindecker*) with 160-hp Mercedes Engine			
Date	**Company**	**No. Delivered**	**Type**
1918			
May	Jfa	..1	D.I
Aug	Jfa	..2	Junk.D.I
Oct	Jfa	..5	Junk.D.I
Nov	Jfa	..7	Junk.D.I
Dec	Jfa	..1	Junk.D.I
1919			
Jan	*Jfa*	..2	Junk.D.I
	Jco	12	Junk.D.I
Feb	*Jfa*	3	Junk.D.I
	Jco	7	Junk.D.I
Total		**40**	

1. Document dated 07.04.1919. Copy via Bruno Schmäling.

ruggedness in some of the worse areas to operate aircraft in the following years, particularly in South America and New Guinea. Junkers was a benevolent employer. He offered his workers a guaranteed yearly wage, did not fire them during slack periods but kept them on. The Junkers companies suffered financial difficulties in 1931 and it was proposed to pressure Junkers to leave the company, however he owned most of the patents that supplied the wealth of the enterprises. Removed in 1934 from control of his factory by the Nazis, whom he opposed, his patents were expropriated and he was placed under house arrest. Two years later on 3 February 1936, Hugo Junkers died on his 77th birthday. The rest of his patents were taken over from his wife for a fraction of their worth. The Third Reich regime retained the Junkers name to capitalise on the reputation of the rugged Junkers aircraft. It is unfortunate that the Junkers name became synonymous with terror when the Ju.87 *Stuka* dive bomber, with its siren wailing, led the *Blitzkrieg* of the German Army in World War II.

Junkers was a socialist pacifist and was always interested in civil aviation. The five-seat civil transport that became the F.13, drawing on the lessons learnt from building the J 8 and J 10, first flew in 1919 and became the most widely used passenger transport of the 1920s.[4] The rugged tri-motor Junkers Ju.52 that served as a transport in airlines around the world before World War II and was produced in France and Spain after that conflict, was the last serial produced aircraft that used the corrugated sheet method of construction. Although used as the main *Luftwaffe* transport during the war its civil use would be the legacy that Professor Hugo Junkers would have wanted.

Peter M Grosz summed up the most remarkable aspect of the Junkers World War I story – that is that Junkers and *Idflieg* managed to create an entirely new industry while suffering the blockade of the British in a war of attrition. The war was to see many new technological breakthroughs in the art of war – the use of poison gas, the tank – but none would have the effect that metal aircraft construction would have on military and civilian life in the century that followed.

The German J type *Infanterie* armoured aircraft of World War I that entered production were, with the exception of the Junker J.I, conversions of existing types. The British also adopted this approach with their Sopwith Salamander that was a conversion of the Snipe and the Sopwith Buffalo that was developed from the earlier Bulldog. The French Salmson 4 was lightly armoured and 12 were constructed before the Armistice and remained in service until 1920. The US Le Pere LUSAG-11 was in development when the Armistice was signed and never entered production. The type disappeared

Junkers Metal Aircraft Delivered to the German Army Administration Up to 31 March 1919
2. Type J (Gepanzerter Infanterie-Doppeldecker)

Date	Company	No. Delivered
1917		
Feb/Jun	*Jco*	3*
May	*Jco*	2
Aug	*Jfa*	2
Oct	*Jfa*	3
Nov	*Jfa*	3
Dec	*Jfa*	8
1918		
Jan	*Jfa*	7
Feb	*Jfa*	9
Mar	*Jfa*	13
Apr	*Jfa*	6
May	*Jfa*	17
June	*Jfa*	20
July	*Jfa*	19
Aug	*Jfa*	23
Sept	*Jfa*	25
Oct	*Jfa*	24
Nov	*Jfa*	21
Dec	*Jfa*	16
1919		
Jan	*Jfa*	6
Total		**227**

* Test machines.

during the years between the two world wars and was not to be seen again, but the armoured cockpit concept for low-level attack aircraft re-emerged as a tank buster in the form of the Henschel Hs 129 and Ilyshin Il-2 *Sturmovik* of World War II fame. After the Korean war the Ilyshin faded from Eastern bloc inventories. It was to be 1972 before the concept was taken up again with the Fairchild Republic A-10 Thunderbolt II twin jet ground attack aircraft taking to the air.

Junkers Metal Aircraft Delivered to the German Army Administration Up to 31 March 1919
3. Type CL.I (Leichtes Schlachtflugzeug)

Date	Company	No. Delivered
1918		
Jan	*Jfa*	1
Mar	*Jfa*	1
June	*Jfa*	1
Sept	*Jfa*	1
Oct	*Jfa*	4
Nov	*Jfa*	6
Dec	*Jfa*	4
1919		
Jan	*Jfa*	6
Feb	*Jfa*	9
Mar	*Jfa*	11
Jan	*Jfa*	6
Total		**44**

Junkers Metal Aircraft Delivered to the German Army Administration Up to 31 March 1919
4. Type Marine (Wasserflugzeug)

Date	Company	No. Delivered
1918		
Oct	*Jfo*	1
Nov	*Jfo*	1
Dec	*Jfo*	1
Total		**3**

Summary

1. Type D.I	40
2. Type J.I	227
3. Type CL-I	44
4. Type CLS-I	3
Total	**314**

Note: The D table included the J 1 and six J 2 monoplanes to give a total of **321** metal aircraft. These have been omitted from the above tables.

Appendix 1: Junkers Military Aircraft Post-Armistice

The *Liste der Luftfahrzeuge Und Motoren Nach Typen,* (Report on Aircraft and Engines) dated 16.01.1920, noted the following Junkers aircraft amongst the aircraft recorded in various sections:

1. Airworthy airframes and engines:
14 Junk J.I (200 hp Benz) listed with 218 C Types.
1 Junk D.I (Merc 160) listed with 67 D Types.

2. Airworthy airframes without engines:
2 Junk J.I listed with 67 C Types.

3. Repairable airframes with engines:
1 Junk CL.I (160 Mercedes) and 1 Junk Ifel[6] (200 Benz) listed with 201 C Types.

Under the section *Material der Fliegerstaaffeln der Sicherheitswehren* (Equipment of the Security of the Security Defence Forces) were recorded the following:-

I. Airworthy airframes with engines:-
1 Junk CL.I (160 Mercedes III) listed with 122 C Types.

III. Recoverable airframes with engine:-
2 Junk J.I (160 Merc D.III) listed with 44 C Types. (N types are also included)

IV. Recoverable airframes with engine:-
1 Junk Cl (160 Mercedes D.III) with 15 C Types.

Under the section *Flugzeuge und Motoren des Reichs-Verwertungsamtes (RVA)* (Aircraft and Engines of the RVA) were recorded:-
(a). In store:-
I. Aircraft with engines:-
8 Junk CL.I listed with 387 C Types.

V. Without engines:-
3 Junk CL.I and 3 Junk J.I listed with 1301 C Types.

An addendum recorded an extra 1 Junk J.I (Jfa) (200 Benz) and 1 Junk D.I (185 BMW) for the RVA.

Under the section *Flugzeuge und Motoren im Eigentum der Fabriken* (Aircraft and Engines owned by the manufacturer) were recorded:-
1 Junk CL.1 and 1 Junk D.I.

In the text mention is made of Junkers problems with *Idflieg* in getting acceptance of his methods of construction. From the few documents we have, it can be seen that there was a campaign against Junkers and his methods.

The following letter was written by Junkers to Major Seitz on 30 July 1918.

Re: Manufacture of Wooden Aircraft

To the enclosed letter I would like to make the following observation: I leave it at that to what extent the manipulations of our competitors are implicated in blowing out the flame of life of the inconvenient competition from metal aircraft. The suggestion to go over to aircraft manufacturing using wood is based on two reasons:

1. **Scarcity of material**
This problem should once for all be thoroughly clarified. According to my information there is, at the present time, only a shortage of drawn tubes. It can definitely be counted on that this shortage will be removed in the foreseeable future, either by tube substitutes or by increased production of the tubes. Duraluminium sheet metal is still being delivered in sufficient quantities and, according to reports, no shortage is to be expected.

2. **The longer time frame required for the production of new types made of metal compared to wood.**
This drawback will be compensated by the substantial other advantages of metal construction.

If, according to the suggestion of Mr Bauer, we should use metal aircraft manufacture in parallel to wooden aircraft manufacture, then the development of metal aircraft manufacture would suffer. The present difficult situation would be still more difficult by the division of personnel and other resources.

Therefore, I cannot approve of Mr Bauer's suggestions but should, of course, adjust my view in line with circumstances in the case where my assumptions would prove to be incorrect.

Signed H. Junkers

Appendix 2: The Junkers Company Post-War

The total number of employees of the company was 510 on 21 June 1919. In the aircraft manufacturing division the J 13, the aircraft that was to be the famous F 13, had been completed and had successfully made two test flights.[7] The J 13 II was almost complete. "Of the D-type machines here, two have been completed for the air transport services possible mail transport and have been moved to the airfield. The wings for the 5 remaining D-type machines are being built." The seaplane bought back from the Navy was being modified to a civilian passenger transport. The rear of the fuselage would be modified to conform with that of the first prototype which was at Wilhelmshaven. This most probably would have been *Marine Nummer* 7503.

Eight workers had been hired to dismantle the 43 J-type machines purchased back from the Army, "a job that will take some 40 days." What they were to do with the armoured plate is not stated.

The aircraft manufacturing division of the company urgently needed more jobs. It was suggested that if the testing of the J 13 continued to be successful, then six J 13 airliners be laid down. "To what extent we will be allowed to build aeroplanes after the signing of the Peace Treaty, is to be awaited. At the present moment, we have not received any information in this matter form the Government." The other work of the Junkers factories, making iron furniture, windows, cabinets, tables, etc., was uncertain. The major factories were not committing to building due to the uncertain political situation. The management could see work running out for their workers in the various divisions.[8]

The intent of the Peace Treaty was to eliminate the German aviation industry. Britain and France did not want any competition in the post-war era and they could see the advances made by the German aeronautical industry and made every effort to supress German aviation both civil and military.[9]

The following report by the US Attaché's Report of 26 April 1921, shows the situation of the Junker's factory at that time.

The US Naval Observer in Berlin sent a message to Washington on 17 December 1920, wherein he noted that the President of the IAACC reported that 11 Junkers all-metal aeroplanes had been ordered seized by the Commission but were being shipped to the USA, (Shipment scheduled to leave Hamburg on 16 December 1920), and that this shipment was being made without the authority of the Commission and requesting that the aircraft be seized on arrival in the US.[10] The machines were not shipped but returned to the Junkers factory at Dessau "where they were now being overhauled as a result of their treatment while awaiting shipment at the port of Hamburg."

The German Government had issued an export licence but the IACC seized the shipment and had "opened most of the boxes and had allowed the equipment to lie around in the open, exposed to inclement weather and to loss through theft, The Junker Company deciding that the shipment should not be allowed to go to the United States in this condition, and therefore asked to have the aeroplanes returned to their factory for full inspection and overhaul."[11]

As a result of this seizure, the activities of the Junkers company were

somewhat curbed. Despite the tacit consent of the German Government to commercial aircraft construction, that company has feared the possible action that the Council of Ambassadors might take and has proceeded with only enough construction work to keep their factory force nominally busy. 500 men are employed in all, but most of this number is engaged in the construction of water heaters and other commercial metal contrivances.

Great difficult is experienced in obtaining motors for the regular 4 – 5 passenger single-motor type (that would be the monoplane that became the F.14. Author's note). *The factory has only five or six of such motors available, which must be used successively in various planes for tests as each new plane is completed. Neither the 200 H.P. Benz, nor the 180 H.P. B.M.W. motors can be purchased now in Germany, nor are they being built, so Junkers had had to go outside Germany for motors. Tests are now being made with a Sidley-Puma English motor.*

Above: The prototype of the F.13. This machine portrayed Junkers ideas that were developed in WWI in a civil transport. (via L Andersson)

Below: An F.13 reproduction built by the volunteers at the Technikmuseum "Hugo Junkers", Dessau.

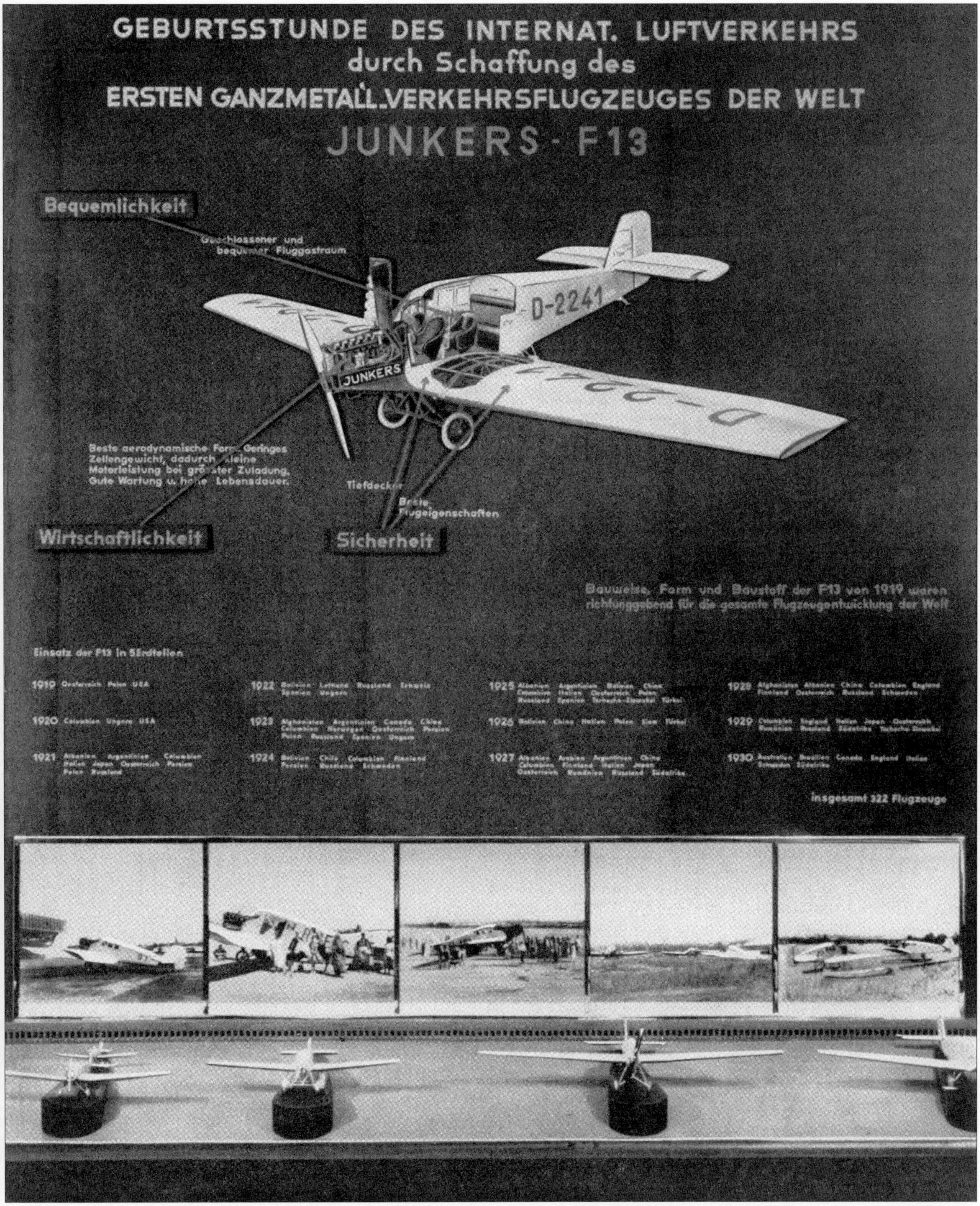
GEBURTSSTUNDE DES INTERNAT. LUFTVERKEHRS
durch Schaffung des
ERSTEN GANZMETALL-VERKEHRSFLUGZEUGES DER WELT
JUNKERS-F13
Bequemlichkeit
Geschlossener und bequemer Fluggastraum
D-2241
JUNKERS
Beste aerodynamische Form. Geringes Zellengewicht, dadurch kleine Motorleistung bei größter Zuladung. Gute Wartung u. hohe Lebensdauer.
Tiefdecker
Beste Flugeigenschaften
Wirtschaftlichkeit
Sicherheit
Bauweise, Form und Baustoff der F13 von 1919 waren richtunggebend für die gesamte Flugzeugentwicklung der Welt
Einsatz der F13 in 5Erdteilen
insgesamt 322 Flugzeuge

Appendix 3

Junkers (Jco) & Junkers-Fokker (Jfa) Army Orders to June 1918								
Order Date	**Type**		**Qty**	**Serial No**	**Mfg**	***Idflieg* No.**	**Junk No.**	**Comments**
1915								
30 Jun		J 1	1		Jco	A7L 96/7.15	1	
31 Jan	E.I	J 2	6	E.250–255/16	Jco	B.66471/15	2	Also B.66645/15.
1916								
03 Nov	J.I	J 4	3	J.425–427/17	Jco	B.310779/16	3	J.425 Load test. J.426 & J.427 flight testing.
26 Dec	CL.I		3	E.701–703/16	Jfa	B.311166/16		Specified only as test aircraft.
1917								
14 Mar	J.I	J 4	50	J.100–149/17	Jco	B.371522/17	5	
17 Nov	R.I		2	R.57–58/17	Jfa	B.1183887/17		
1918								
17 Jan	J.I	J 4	100	J.800–899/17	Jfa	B.376127/17	24	
25 Feb	CL.I	J 10	10	CL.1800–1809/18	Jfa			
26 Mar		J 7	1	D.2266/18	Jfa			Accepted as 'model' aircraft.
01 May	D.I	J 9	10	D.3110–3119/18	Jfa			
20 Jun	J.I	J 4	40	J.576–615/18	Jfa			
25 Jun	D.I	J 9	10	D.5170–5179/18	Jfa			
25 Jun	D.I	J 9	10	D.5180–5189/18	Jco			D.5180/18 static test example.
July	J.I	J 4	100		LiHo			Not approved by Junkers.
July	D.I	J 9	50		Brand			
Source: P.M. Grosz Collection.								

Appendix 4: Junkers Patents

Junkers quickly gained patents in Germany, Sweden, Denmark, Norway, England, France and the USA following the end of the war. His control over his method of construction saw him sue Fokker for patent infringement and winning. His refusal to let John Larsen in the US modify the F.13 to suit US conditions led to the estrangement of Larsen and the collapse of the agreement. The Nazi Party gained control of Junkers valuable patents and name prior to and after his death. It must be remembered that Junkers was not only the holder of aeronautical patents but made improvements in heating, diesel and aircraft engines. A better appreciation of Junkers many activities is underway in the Technikmuseum "Hugo Junkers" in Dessau, Germany, where exhibits cover all of Junkers wide ranging expertise.

Patent-001: This device was invented to enable rivet connections in the walls of hollow bodies, and more especially tubular bodies such as the long metal tubes used in the construction of aircraft whose interior is not easily accessible.
Patent-002 & 003: These diagrams show drawings from a 1918 series of patents covering the monoplane with self-supporting surfaces devoid of all external stay wires or the like.
Patent-004: The various parts of the airframe were subject to separate patents. The upper diagram relates to the wing spars. The middle diagram relates to the tubular structure of the body of the aircraft. The lower diagram shows a proposal to bury the

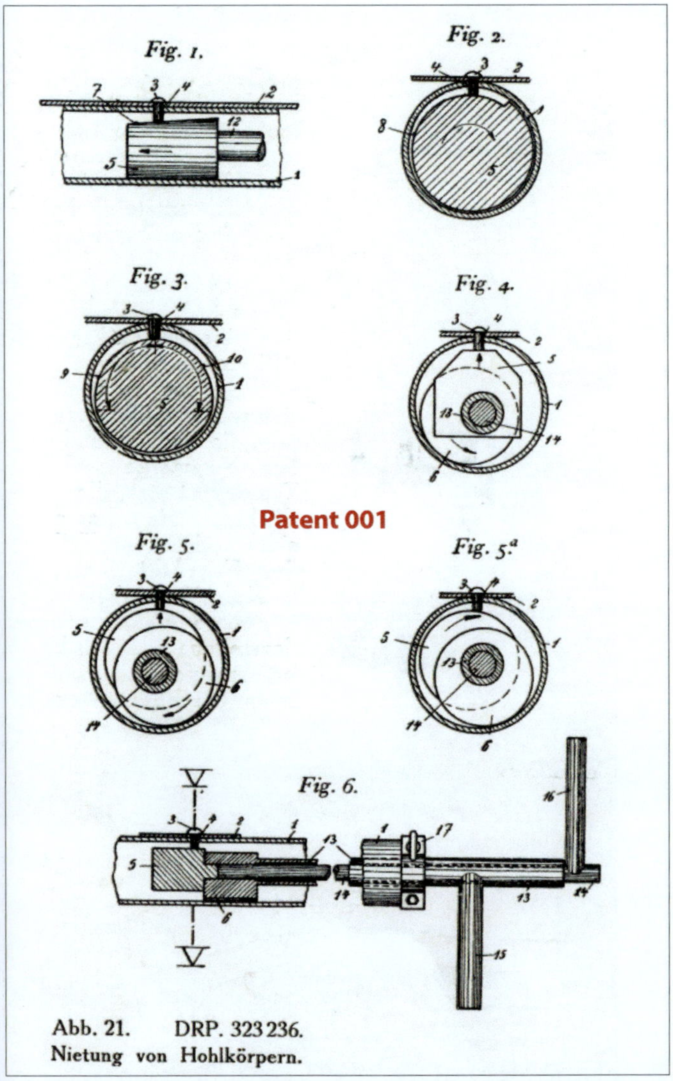

Abb. 21. DRP. 323 236.
Nietung von Hohlkörpern.

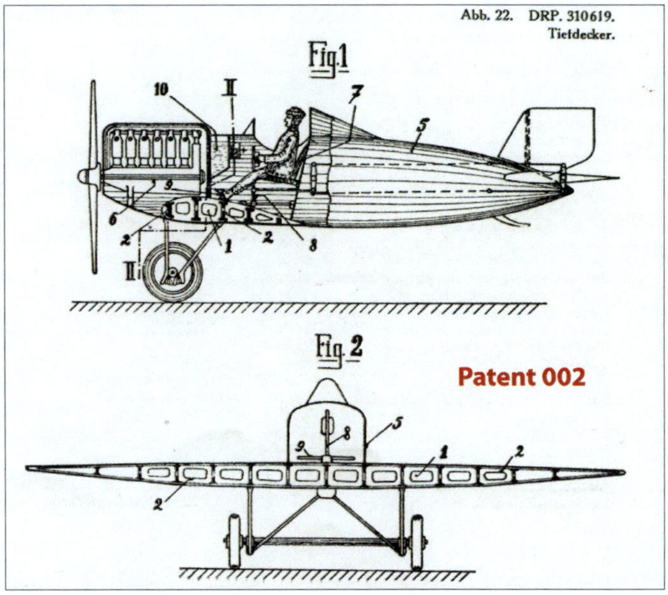

Abb. 22. DRP. 310619.
Tiefdecker.

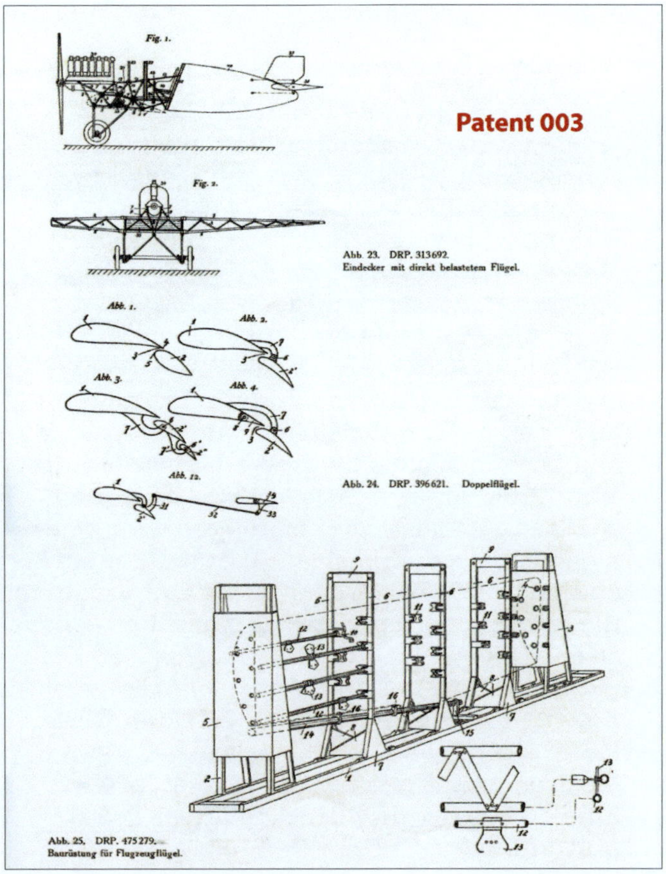

engine in the thick wing of Junkers usual design.

Patent-005: Junkers was granted US Patent 1,564,354 on 8 December 1925 for an Armoured Aeroplane.

The patent noted that aeroplanes having their bodies protected by armoured plate were produced by covering the body structure with armour plates. Junkers construction allowed the armour plates themselves to transmit the forces arising during the operation of the aircraft.

The numbers on the drawings refer to:
1 & 2. Side wall.
3. Central bottom plate.
4 & 5. Oblique bottom plates.
6. Front wall.
7. Rear wall.
8 & 9. Cross frames – motor mounts.
10. Frame supporting instrument panel.
11. Door hinges.
12. Hinged door enclosing motor.
20. Lower wing.
21. Upper wing.
22 to 26. Supporting struts.
30. Front portion of body.
31. Rear portion of body.
32. Rudder.
33. Horizontal tailplane.
34. Tailskid.

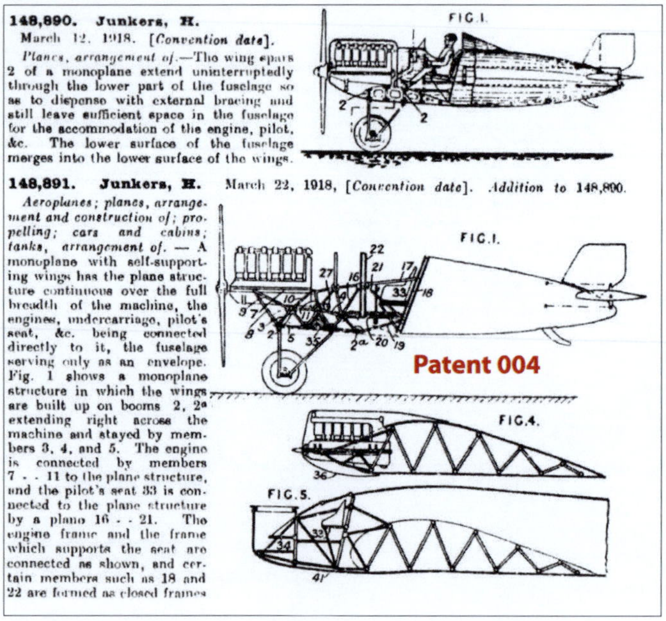

148,890. Junkers, H.
March 12, 1918. [*Convention date*].
Planes, arrangement of.—The wing spars 2 of a monoplane extend uninterruptedly through the lower part of the fuselage so as to dispense with external bracing and still leave sufficient space in the fuselage for the accommodation of the engine, pilot, &c. The lower surface of the fuselage merges into the lower surface of the wings.

148,891. Junkers, H. March 22, 1918, [*Convention date*]. *Addition to* 148,890.
Aeroplanes; planes, arrangement and construction of; propelling; cars and cabins; tanks, arrangement of. — A monoplane with self-supporting wings has the plane structure continuous over the full breadth of the machine, the engines, undercarriage, pilot's seat, &c. being connected directly to it, the fuselage serving only as an envelope. Fig. 1 shows a monoplane structure in which the wings are built up on booms 2, 2a extending right across the machine and stayed by members 3, 4, and 5. The engine is connected by members 7 - - 11 to the plane structure, and the pilot's seat 33 is connected to the plane structure by a plane 16 - - 21. The engine frame and the frame which supports the seat are connected as shown, and certain members such as 18 and 22 are formed as closed frames

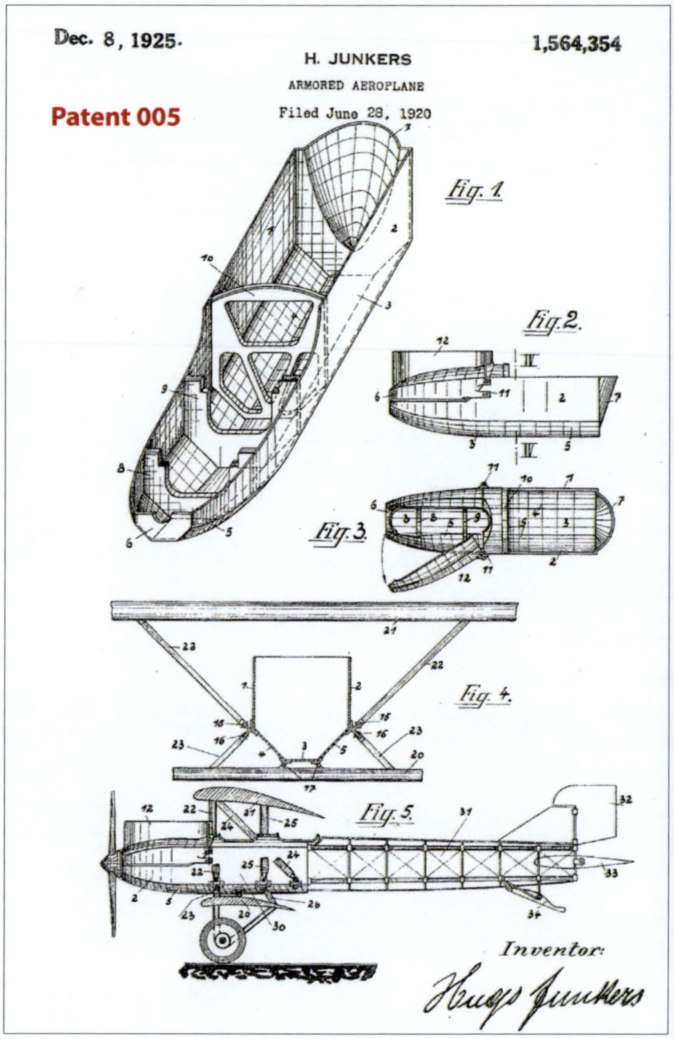

End Notes Afterword & Appendices

1. The Bristol M.R.1 had to initially fly with wooden wings as problems with the metal wings meant that they were not ready in time. The metal wings were of metal construction with fabric covering. See also Owers, C.A. *British Aircraft of WWI Vol.1. Experimental Fighters Pt.1,* Aeronaut Books, USA, 2017.
2. In response to Professor Junkers paper to the RAeS in January 1923, Major F.M. Green stated that "we had less faith (in Duralumin) … and that, as a matter of fact, our constructors had been forbidden by the Air Ministry to use Duralumin for any parts likely to be highly stressed. As most parts of an aeroplane were highly stressed, this meant that to all intents and purposes we were not using Duralumin in the construction, preferring to use high-tensile steel." *Flight,* 11.01.1923. P.24.
3. Air Publication 1107, *A Manual of Rigging for Aircraft,* Air Ministry, HMSO, UK, March1925. P.35
4. The French called the F.13 "the craft of the future." Morrow Jr, J.H. *German Air Power in World War I,* University of Nebraska Press, USA, 1982. P158. & 164.
5. Document dated 07.04.1919. Copy via Bruno Schmäling.
6. Note the use of the "Ifel" instead of the "J".
7. For the story of the F 13 see Andersson, L; Endres, E; Mulder, R & Ott, G. *The World's First All Metal Airliner - Junkers F 13,* EAM Books, 2012.
8. "Manufacturing Report". 25.06.1919. Copy via L Andersson.
9. These matters are covered in more detail by Andersson and Sanger.
10. Office Naval Intelligence to Operations (Aviation), Subject: "Eleven 'Junkers' Aeroplanes Shipped to the United States over Protest of Aeronautical Inter-Allied Commission of Control." 31 December 1921. Copy in P.M. Grosz Collection Box 483.
11. Letter from (Attaché?), Germany to (USN?) Aviation, 14.02.1921. P.M. Grosz Collection Box 483.

Bibliography

Anderson, L & Sanger, R. *Retribution and Recovery – German Aircraft and Aviation 1919 to 1922,* Air Britain, UK, 2014.

Byers, R.W.E. *Power and Initiative in Twentieth Century Germany, The Case of Hugo Junkers,* PhD Dissertation for Doctor of Philosophy, University of Georgia, 2002.

Byers, R. "An Unhappy Marriage: The Junkers-Fokker Merger", *Journal of Historical Biography 3,* Spring 2008.

Biddle, C.J. *The Way of the Eagle,* Scribners' sons, NY, 1919.

Cowin, H. *The Junkers Monoplanes,* Profile Publications No.187, UK, 1967.

Cowin, H. "Junkers' Early Giants." *Air Pictorial,* July 1981. P.274.

Bowers, P.M. "Professor YOOnkers' Tin Donkeys." *Air Progress,* Spring 1961, P.64.

Casari, R. *U.S. Army Aviation Serial Numbers and Orders 1908-1923 Reconstructed.* Military Aircraft Publications, USA, 1995.

Die Junkers Lehrfchau, Junkers Flugzeug-und-Motoren Aktiengesellschaft, Dessau.

Duiven, R & Abbott, D-S. *Schlacht-Flieger!,* Schiffer, USA, 2006.

Gentilli, R. "WWI German Aeroplanes to Italy", *Windsock International,* Vol.13, No.1, P.18.

Grey, P & Thetford, O. *German Aircraft of the First World War,* Putnam, UK, 1962, P.156.

Grosz, P.M. *Junkers J.I,* Windsock Datafile No.39, Albatros Productions, UK, 1993.

Grosz, P.M. & Terry, G. "The Way to the World's First All Metal Fighter," *Air Enthusiast No.25,* August 1984.

Grosz, P. *Junkers D.I,* Windsock Datafile No.33, Albatros Productions, UK, 1992.

Herris, J. *Germany's Armoured Warplanes of WWI,* Aeronaut Books, USA, 2012.

Herris, J. *Germany's Fighter Competitions of 1918,* Aeronaut Books, USA, 2013.

Herris, J. *German Monoplane Fighters of WWI,* Aeronaut Books, USA, 2014.

Hucker, R. "Junkers' Tin Donkeys." *Air Classics,* Vol.15 No.5, May 1979. P24.

Hundertmark, M & Stenile, H. *Phoenix aus der Asche* Die *Deutsche Luftfahrt Sammlung Berlin,* Siberstreif, Verlag GmbH, Berlin, 1985.

Jane's Fighting Aircraft of World War I, Studio Editions, UK, 1990.

Junkers, Prof H. "Metal Aeroplane Construction," *The Journal of the Royal Aeronautical Society,* Vol.27, 1923, P.406.

Leaman, P. "The Fokker-Junkers Seaplanes," *Cross & Cockade International,* Vol.46/2, 2015, P.104.

Meier, H.J. "Ein Langstrecken-Nachtbomber von Junkers," *Luftfahrt International,* 1/80, P.25.

Meier, H.J. "Zweimotoriger Junkers-Tiedecker (Projekt 1918)", *Luftfahrt International,* 1/80, P.25.

Miertsch, W. *Vom Lilienthalgleiter zur fliegenden Annelise,* Anhaltische Verlagsgellschafat mbH, Germany, 1919.

Neuman, G.P. *Die Deutschen Luftstreitkrafte im Weltriege,* E.S. Mittler & Sohn, Berlin, 1920.

Penrose, H. *British Aviation. The Great War and Armistice.* Putnam, UK, 1969.

Rabe, H-G. "A Forgotten Pour le Mérit Flyer – Leutenant Wilhelm Paul Schreiber." *Cross & Cockade* USA, Vol.15, No.2, Summer 1974. P.179.

Reis, K. *The Moles – Underground Activity 1919-1935, Vol.1.* Dieter Hofflann, Germany, 1970.

Ricco, P, Courrier, P & Soumille, J-C. *Les Avions Allemands Aux Couleurs Francaises,* Tome 2, Aicdoc, France, 1997.

Servaites, J. "The Junkers Monoplanes and Metal Shaping Techniques." *Over the Front,* USA, Vol.20, No.1, Spring 2005. P.18.

Stair, I.R. "Junkers D.I." *Aero Modeller,* June 1968.

Wagner, W. *Hugo Junkers. Pionier der Luftfahrt - seine Flugzeuge,* Bernhard & Graefe, Germany, 1996.

Weyl, A.R. *Fokker: The Creative Years,* Putnam, UK, 1965.

Woodman, H. "The Tin Donkeys of Dessau," *Airfix Magazine,*

Woodman, H. *Junkers Monoplanes at War,* Windsock Datafile No. 131, Albatros productions, UK, 2008.

www.geocities.ws/hjunkers/ju_who.htm. "Junkers – Who is Who?"

http://geocities/c0m/hjunkers/ju_J4_al.htm. (Referenced 15.08.2003)

Ganzmetallflugzeug J1u.J2 Stahlbauweise. Förderverein Technikmuseum, Hugo Junkers. Copy from Junkers Museum, Dessau.

Junkers J.I. Wingnut Wings, New Zealand. (Kit instruction booklet).

Liste der Luftfahrzeuge Und Motoren Nach Typen, Berlin, 1920.

"Metal Aeroplanes – R sum of Professor Junkers' Paper read before R.Ae.S." *Flight,* 11.01.1923. P.24.

Panzer Doppeldecker Typ JUNK JI, Junkers-Fokker-Werke A.G., Dessau, Germany.

Report on Junker Two-seater. (RAF G/3Bde/31).

Copy in TNA MUN 4/5010.
"Report on the Junker Armoured Two-seater Biplane J.I." Ministry of Munitions Report republished in *Flight* from 26.02.1920.
"The Junker Single-Seat All-Metal Monoplane Type D.I." Ministry of Munitions. Reprinted in *Flight* from 1 April 1920.
Files and documents from The British National Archives (TNA); the USA National Archives (NARA); the Peter M Grosz Collection at the Deutsches Technikmuseum, Berlin; and the Technikmuseum "Hugo Junkers", Dessau.

Left: Junkers J.I on display at the Berlin museum between the wars was cut away to show the structure. This machine had the corrugated metal covering of the rear fuselage.

Junkers J 4 (Military J.I) British G/3Bde/31 Photos

These photographs were taken of G.3Bde/31, a J.I found abandoned by British troops near La Vacqurie. It was badly damaged but, with another badly damaged example obtained by the French, the British prepared a report on the type.

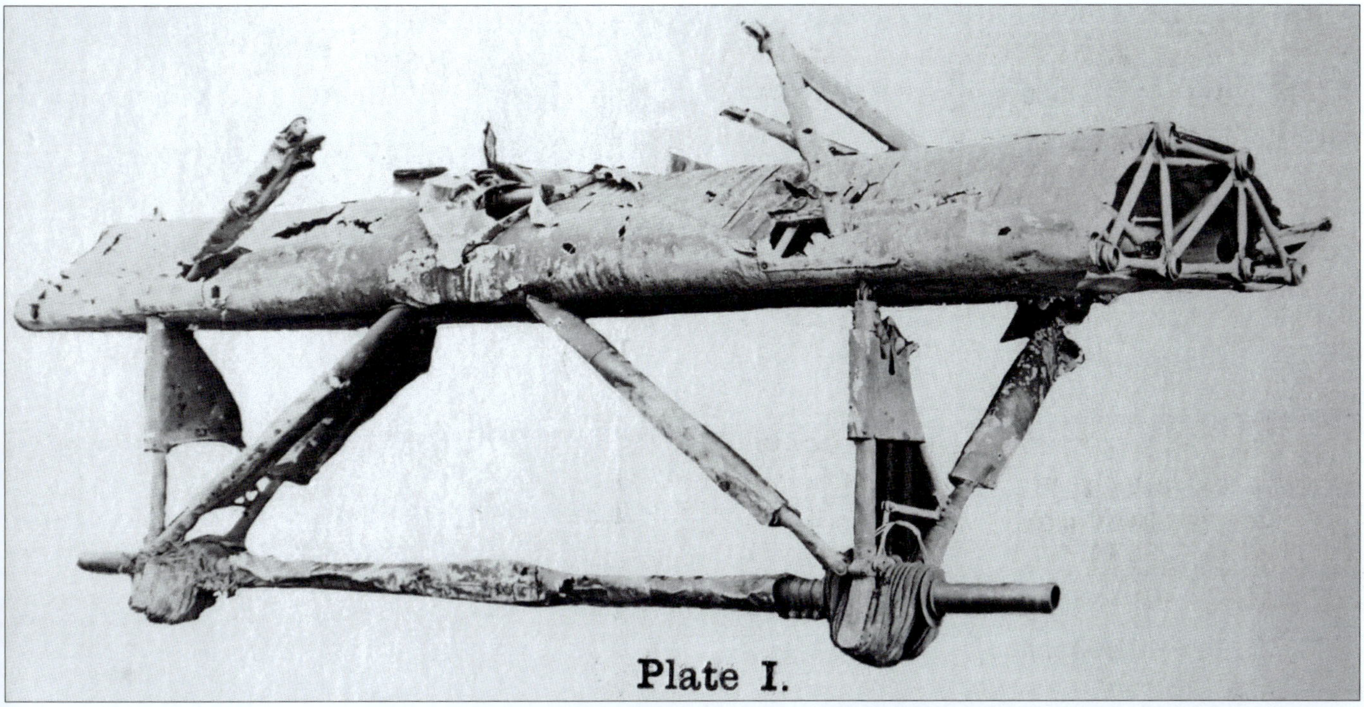

This Page: The lower centre section and undercarriage unit. The compass mount is seen in the left lower wing. Note the different types of corrugated aluminum skin.

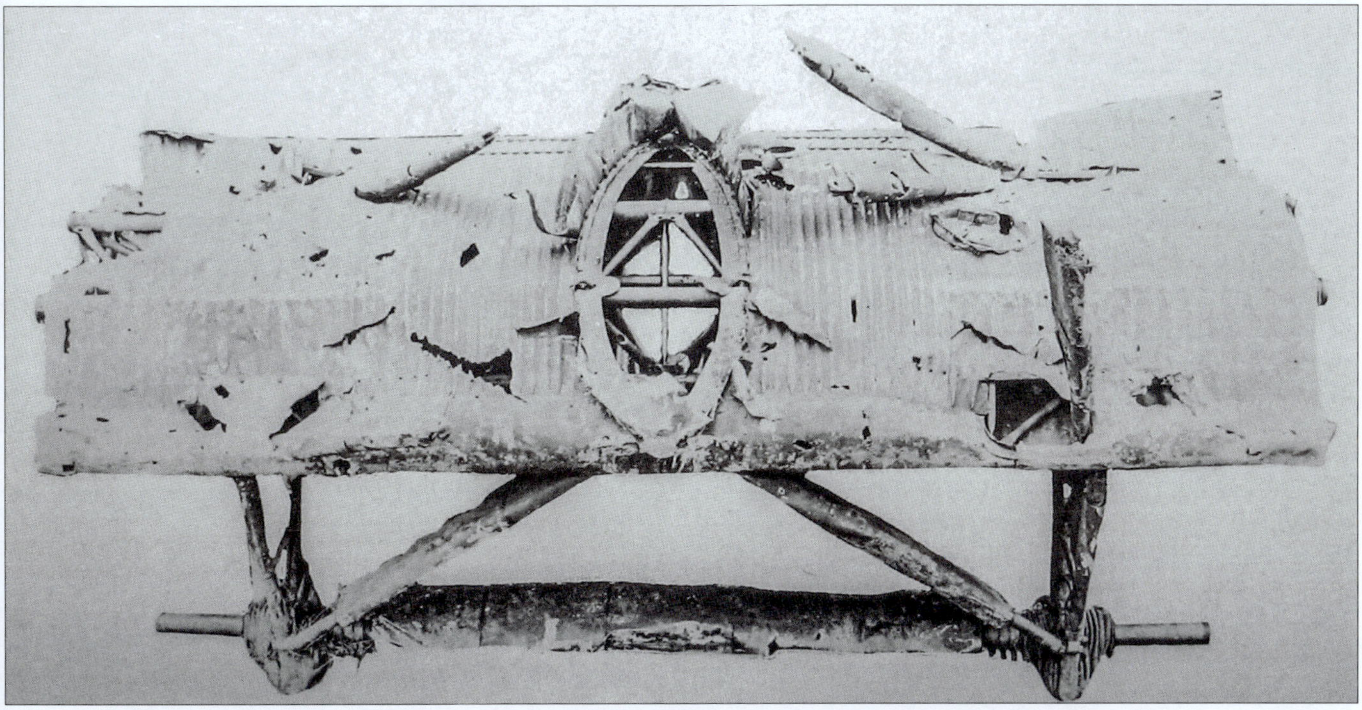

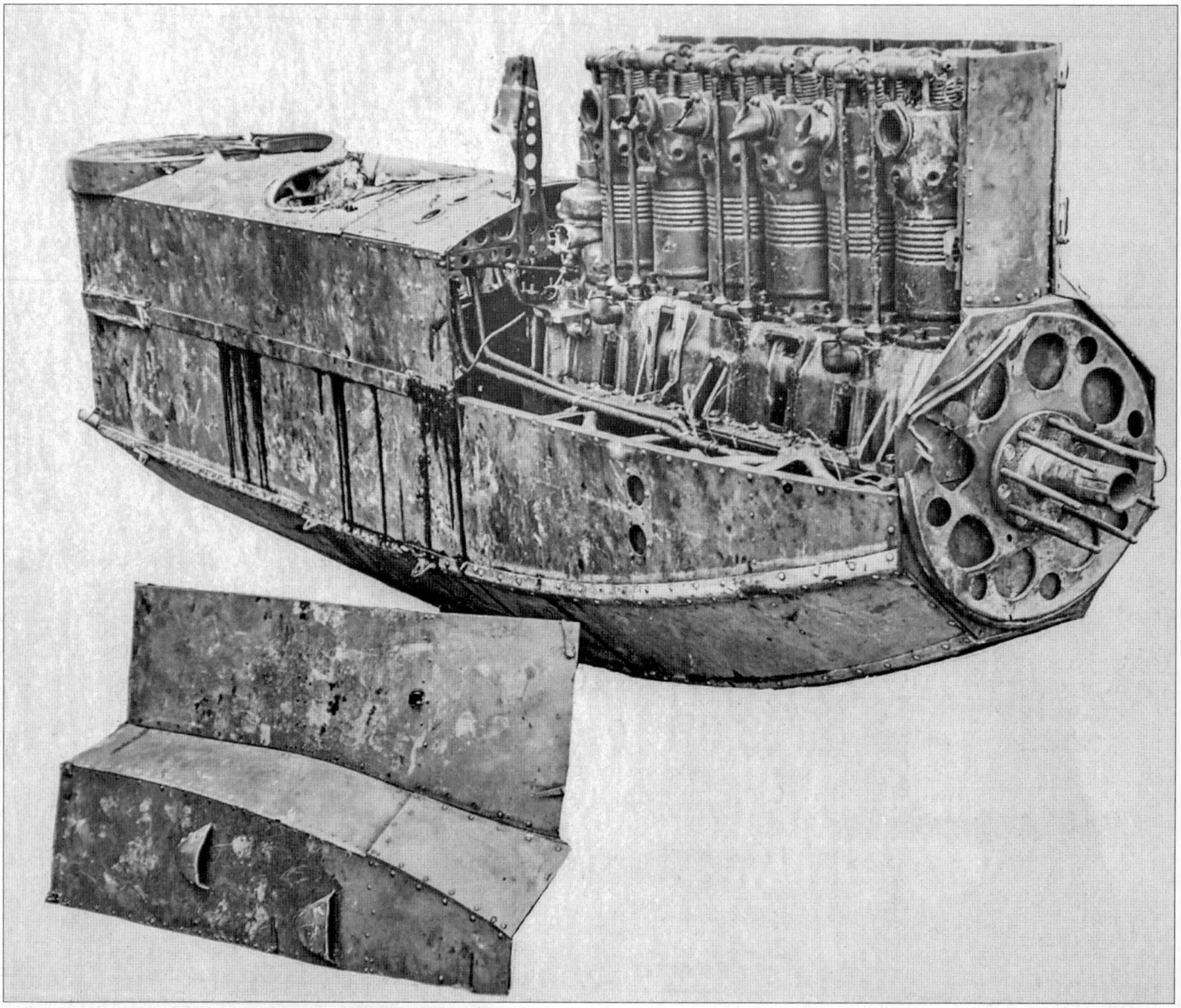

Above: Note the stencils to the forward fuselage: *Leergewicht* (Empty weight)1590 & below that *Nutezast* (Useful load) 383.5kg. The number 181 is thought to be the machine's *werke nummer*. Although badly damaged it appears that the camouflage colours have been applied by hand.

Right & Facing Page, Top: The armoured shell containing the engine, pilot and gunner. The armour plates were riveted together and formed part of the structure.

Below: Upper wing panels showing the tubular spars and smaller duralumin tube braces. The camouflage scheme appears to be of two colours.

Bottom: View of the wing showing the internal construction.

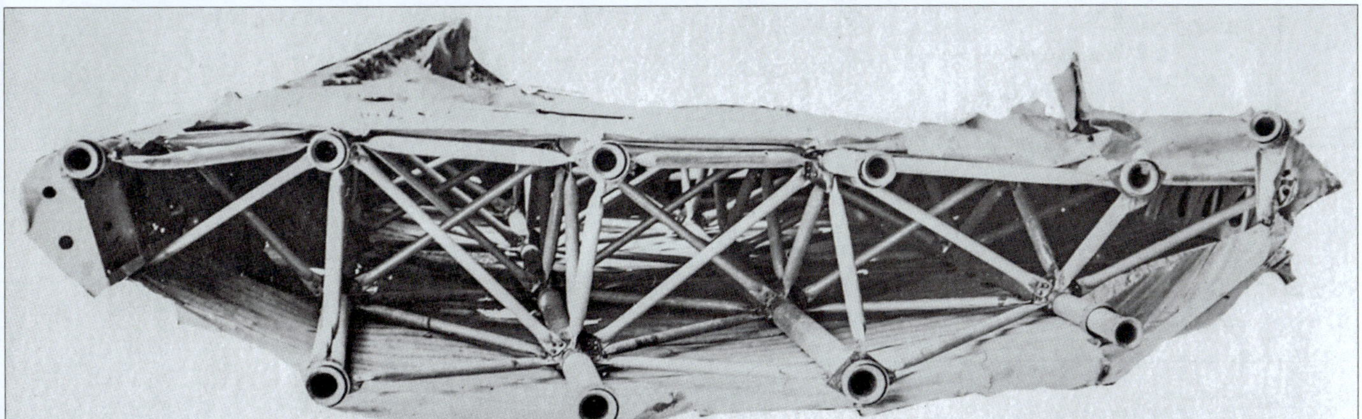

Instruction Manual for JUNK. J.I. Armoured Biplane

Junkers-Fokker–Werke A.G. Dessau

Advantages of the Junkers Type of Metal Aeroplane with Unbraced Wings

Strength
In spite of the absence of struts and bracing wires, a high degree of safety is obtained with the Junkers construction.

The results of the loading test carried out by the P.U.W. der Fligertruppen (Testing section and workshop of the Air Service), gave a margin of safety 30 per cent. higher than the required value (5.8 factory of safety)

Bullet-Proof Qualities
The wing structure does not include any member which, if damaged might endanger the safety of the whole. The liability of this machine to damage of any kind caused by projectiles is therefore extraordinarily low.

Safety Against Fire
These machines, including rudder and fins, being almost entirely constructed of non-inflammable material are impervious to incendiary bullets or fires started in the carburettor.

Speed
The unbraced wings and narrow fuselage without struts and bracing wires, which all add to the head resistance of the machine, enable the highest possible percentage of the engine power to be applied to increase speed and climb.

Field of Vision
The absence of struts and bracing wires, and the favourable arrangement of the wings, enable a very good view to be obtained.

Availability for Service
The machine requires no rigging, and therefore no truing up is necessary. No distortion occurs after a long period of exposure to the weather.

Uses and Properties of the Armoured Biplane
The armoured biplane is a machine specially constructed for the requirements of infantry contact work.

Special attention has therefore been paid to the protection of the engine, crew and wireless. The weight of the armouring is 470 kg. and therefore, the climb of this machine is low as compared to a fighter machine, and it requires a longer run at starting and landing.

Owing to the aerodynamic qualities of the thick wings, this machine possesses a high speed and an excellent gliding capacity.

As regards the equipment, special attention had been paid to obtain a convenient and simple arrangement of the fittings.

Preference is given to the W/T apparatus over the armament.

Armouring
The armouring consists of a casing (open only at the top) of highly tempered special steel 5 mm thick, made by the well-known "*Panzerwerke*" of

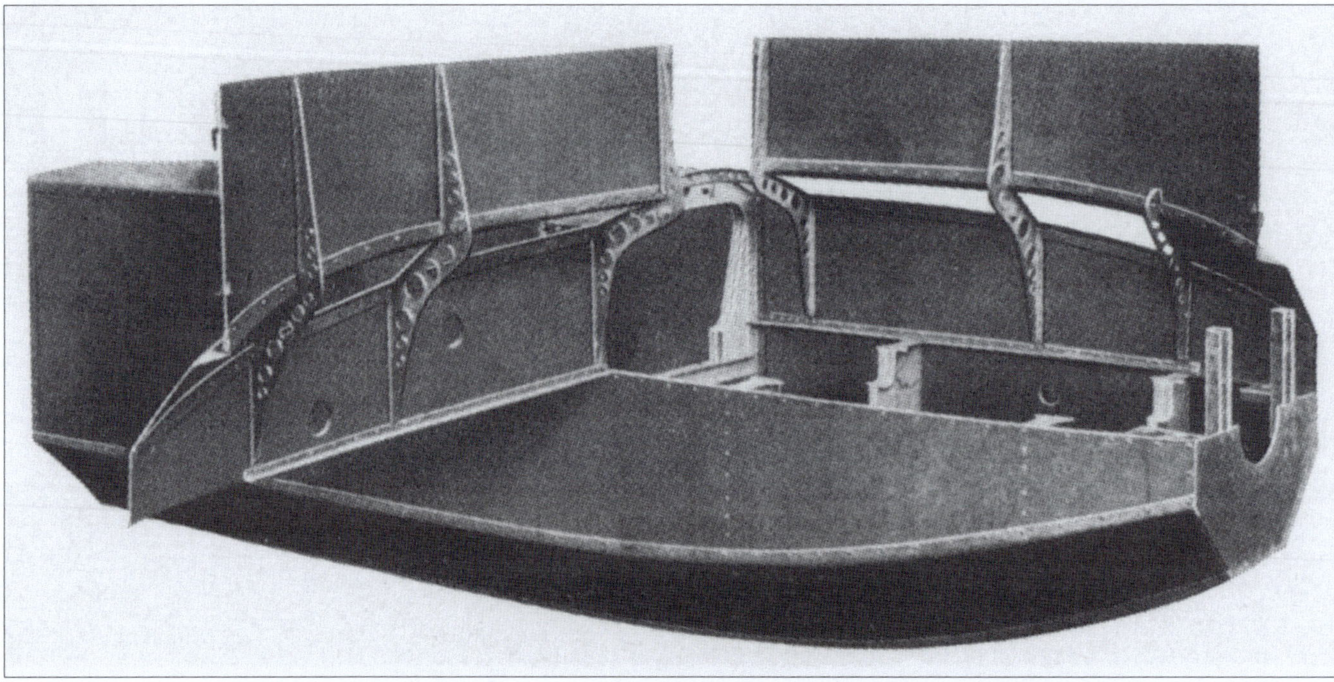

Dillingen. This armouring is an efficient protection against rifle fire and shrapnel at the closest possible range. The armoured casing weighs 470 kg.

The engine armouring comes up to the top of the engine.

The engine pilot, fuel tanks, W/T apparatus, ammunition and part of the controls are all within the armoured casing.

Any part of the controls outside the armouring are duplicated.

Engine Installation

A 6-cylinder 200 H.P. Benz engine* is used (*see* description of action and fuel supply system issued by the Benz firm of Mannheim).

* *Actually 230 H.P.*

Fitting

The fitting is so carried out that he engine can be uncovered on all sides, in spite of extensive armouring of the upper part, by means of hinged panels, easily opened. The bolts on the front panel eliminate any possibility of an accidental opening. The positions of the bolts are shown by coloured signs. Hinged panels, easily and quickly opened, are provided for inspection of the carburettor and oil pump.

The supply of air to the carburettor and crank case is carried out by means of special wind traps and supply lines.

Fuel Supply System

The fuel supply system ensures the greatest possible reliability.

The necessary controls are reduced to a single cock 1 fitted as shown on the diagram, and petrol is pumped into the gravity tank by means of the hand pump until the petrol gauge shows that the gravity tank is full.

The engine is then started, the control cock being put at position 2. When the petrol gauge registers a pressure of about 3/10 of an atmosphere (the pressure can be regulated by means of the adjusting screw of the relief valve), the control cock is put at position 3. In the case of fire in the carburettor, and when at rest, control cock I should be in position 4.

In case of a breakdown of the engine pump, the gravity tank is switched in by putting the control cock at position 2. As the gravity tank contains about 30 litres, the machine can fly on it for at least half-hour at half throttle.

Refilling of the gravity tank is carried out either through the excess pressure of the engine pump or by means of the hand-pump, the control cock being at position1.

Should the gravity petrol tank become quite empty owing to a breakdown of the engine pump, it is still possible to supply the engine with fuel by continuous use of the hand pump, the control cock being placed in position 3.

The main petrol tank is divided into two separate compartments by means of a vertical patrician, so that the whole tank does not empty should one of the compartments be damaged.

In such cases, it is possible to cut out the damaged compartment of the tank, by means of the three way cock on the right side of the fuselage, so that fuel is only taken up from the undamaged compartment (see diagram of petrol supply system).

Two drain cocks are fitted near the bottom of the rear wall of the double tank by which the main tank can be emptied rapidly.

The gravity tank is emptied by the drain cock in the bottom of the petrol filter.

Proeller

The machine carried out its flight test with a propeller constructed by the *Axial-Propellerwerke* of Berlin. According to the latest experiments a propeller 2.94 m in diameter and with a pitch of 1.90 m revolving at 1,380 to 1,400 r.p.m. on the test bench has been found suitable.

Radiator

These machines are fitted with a jet radiator of the Junkers type, with a hood open back and front which decreases the head-resistance of the radiator.

The adjustable sections of the hood are regulated by means of an adjusting screw fitted at the side, according to the temperature of the surrounding atmosphere

During the hot months, a maximum opening of the hood should be given, but during the cold weather the opening should be proportional to the temperature. The amount of the opening should be the same back and front.

The opening of the hood should be so regulated that the temperature of the cooling water does not exceed 75 deg to 80 deg. The action of the

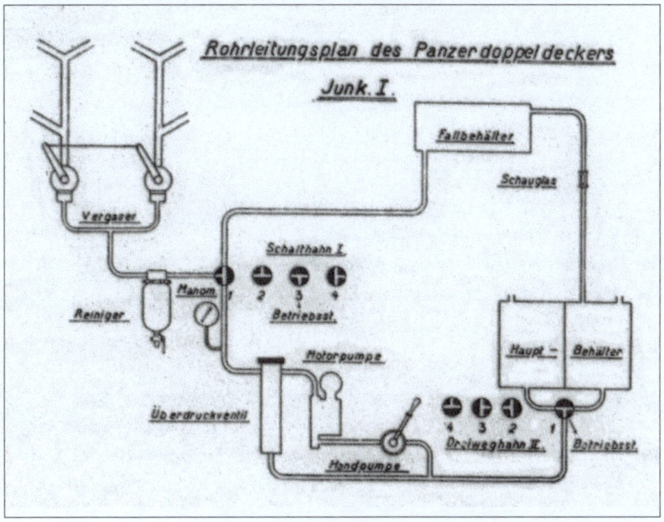

Gebrauchsanweisung Nr.............
zum Flugzeug Nr.............

Panzer=
Doppeldecker
Typ
JUNK J I
Mil.-Nr.............

Junkers-Fokker-Werke A.G.
DESSAU

Abdruck und Weitergabe auf Grund der
Militärstrafgesetze in jeder Form verboten

radiator can be ascertained at all times by means of a thermometer fitted in the cooling system. Care should be taken that after each preliminary run before starting, the water tank is refilled, as not till this has been done can it be safely assumed that the whole water system is completely filled.

Control System
The controls are primarily worked by the control column, the action of which is transmitted to the main control shaft by means of a system of rods to which the controlling surfaces answer very easily. The rudders and ailerons are partly balanced. An adjustable double compensating spring takes up the weight of the elevator in such a way that when at rest the tension on the control column is about 2.5 kg.

The control column should have only slight play in its central position. This is rendered necessary by the type of control system used. The ailerons and elevators are constructed of metal and are therefore fire-proof. Should the fuselage covering be burnt away the machine can still be controlled.

W/T
Special care has been taken to fit the W/T apparatus so that it can be worked conveniently. *Telefunken* apparatus for both sending and receiving (specification 99) is fitted to this machine. The dynamo is easily accessible and adjustable. It is part armoured. The length of aerial is fixed at 37 m for the *Telefunken* sender and at 38 m for the *Huth* sender.

Armament
A "Parabellum" machine gun is fitted in the observer's cockpit on a rotary turret. Three ammunition drums are fitted to the right and left of the observer's seat and easily accessible. Two more drums are fitted under the seat. One thousand rounds can be carried altogether. *(Author's note: No MG for the pilot and no mention of downward firing guns).*

Cameras
From series No.101/17 upwards, these machines are provided with the necessary fittings for cinematograph cameras, hand camera, and magazines.

The first bay of the fuselage behind the armour is made easily accessible from above and below by means of sliding or removable panels in the sheet metal armouring. The cinematograph camera is suspended from underneath. The dynamo should be fitted on the cabane to the left of the fuselage. Switch, regulating resistance, and voltmeter should be screwed to the plywood lining of the left side of the fuselage, in place of the front map carrier, so as to be easily accessible to the observer.

The conductors are led to the engine outside the armouring, through holes provided for the purpose. A bag for the hand camera is strapped in the first bay of the fuselage, above the cinematograph camera.

Sheet metal boxes are provided to take the magazines.

Signaling Apparatus
A pocket is provided on either side of the fuselage to carry the supply of the usual lights, each pocket holding 10 lights *(flares)*.

Care and Handling of the Machine

General

When carrying out any work on the machine, the following points should be observed:-

The wings and tail plane are covered with light metal sheeting thick, the strength of which is quite sufficient to bear normal flying stresses, but, like fabric, cannot stand a heavy load over a small area.

Care should therefore be taken not to stand on or lean against these surfaces, and that no heavy article with sharp edges, such as petrol-tins, etc., are placed upon them. Never move the machine by pressing on the struts.

When moving the wings or the whole machine, care should be taken to handle the wings with the palms of both hands as far as possible in the centre of the rivet joint. When storing wings, always lay them on a layer of straw or wood shavings, previously prepared and as level as possible.

The wings very soon become dented if this is not done. These dents are not a source of danger, but a loss of time in incurred by their removal, which requires a certain skill. Moreover, this operation cannot be repeated, and always spoils the look of the machine.

Transport

A fuselage truck 10 m in length, and a truck for the various parts, 7 m in length, are required for transport by rail. The fuselage is loaded as a complete unit but without undercarriage or tail planes. The wings, struts, and tail surfaces are packed separately in wooden crates or cases. The fuselage can also be towed on its undercarriage by a tractor in the usual way.

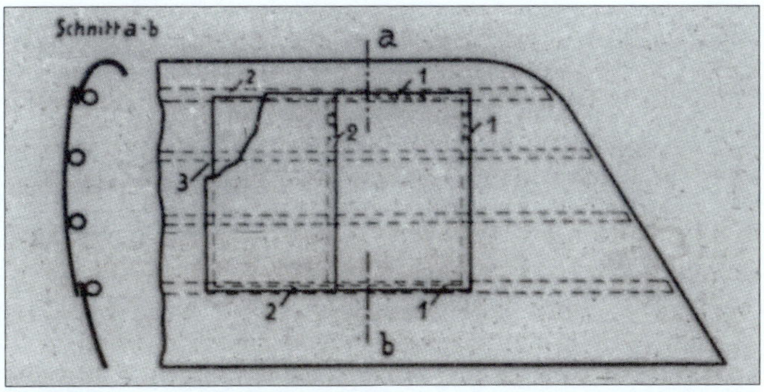

Assembly

Assembly should if possible, take place in a shed with a roof strong enough to bear the weight of the top wing (about 250 kg).

Should this not be possible, the wing can be raised on high wooden trestles. When unpacking the various parts they should be placed in their proper position around the fuselage (see diagram).

The time required for assembling the machine varies with the number of men available. With six to eight men the machine should be ready for flight

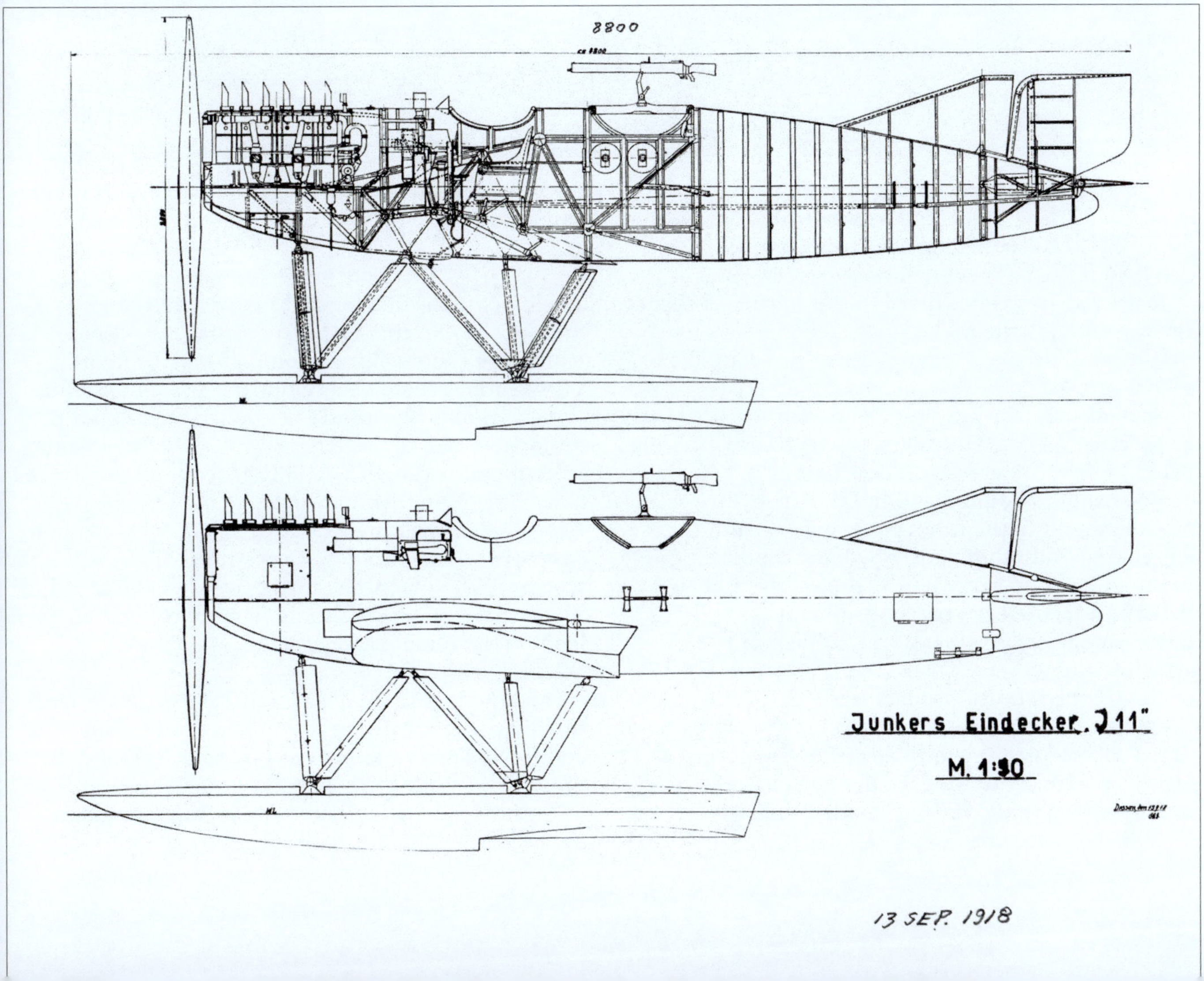

in four to six hours according to the appliances available. The work should be carried out by two groups, four to six men at the wings, and two to three men fitting the tail surfaces.

If the radiator is not fitted to the centre section of the top wing, it should be screwed on and secured first of all. The two top wings must be secured and secured to the centre section simultaneously.

Special spanners are supplied to fit the nuts of the connecting pieces. The aileron control rods are then fitted.

Rope should be slung around the uncovered points of attachment of the tubular framework, and the whole drawn up sufficiently high for the fuselage to be slipped underneath. Whilst the struts are being fitted and secured the two bottom wings are fitted in the same way as the top wing. The points of attachment can then be covered. The pipes of the cooling system must also be fitted.

During this time the second group should have fitted and secured the tailplane (the connecting pieces are similar to those of the wings), followed by the fin, elevator and rudder. Finally, the strut sockets in the bottom wing and fixed tail surfaces should be covered and the control cables inserted and secured.

Dismantling

The machine is dismantled in the reverse order.

Both the erecting and dismantling, the centre of balance of the machine should always be kept in view. Should there be any uncertainty concerning the position of the centre of gravity owing to the removal of one of the large parts, it is advisable to load the tail skid with sand bags to avoid the danger of the machine turning turtle.

When the machine is not in use it is advisable to support the armoured casing on a trestle to take the weight of the machine off the spring of the tail skid. The trestles supplied should be used to remove the load on the undercarriage shock-absorbers.

Maintenance

As already mentioned, no rigging is necessary with this machine. Examine the capping nuts of all connecting pieces at regular intervals to make sure there is no working loose.

The wing covering and tubular frame work are

rust-proof, the object of the coating being merely to render the machine less visible.

Any parts of the control system liable to friction such as pins and bearings, should be lubricated with a few drops of oil during assembly and subsequently at regular intervals. Special instructions are issued for the care of the engine and W.T. apparatus.

In trestling up, the machine must never, as is sometimes done elsewhere, be supported or raised by the wings. Only the trestle supplied may be used for trestling up the machine.

Repairs

Repairs to wings and tail of this machine require totally different materials from those required for ordinary machines.

Extensive repairs are hardly possible at the front or at aviation parks. The most rapid method of repairing damages is by obtaining the required spare parts. Trained mechanics can be had at any time for instruction purposes, when required. A tool-box and a case containing a supply of materials is supplied with each machine, so that small repairs can be carried out quickly on the spot.

A list of contents is given in all the boxes.

The framework mainly consists of longitudinal members in light metal tubing, iron connections, and light metal tubular or Z struts. Damaged longitudinal members can be repaired by cutting away the dented or torn section of tubing near the connection and replacing it by anew section. A previously prepared sleeve is slipped over the join and fastened by means of four rows of rivets.

Damaged struts are entirely replaced and riveted to the connecting piece in the usual way.

Connecting pieces and sleeves are fixed to the tubing by internal riveting, for which a special tool is used.

Repairing Damaged Covering

Damaged parts of the metal covering are cut away as n ear as possible to the lateral seams and longitudinal members. This must only be undertaken when necessary to repair part of the framework (*cf* sketch).

The covering of these surfaces is carried out in the following order according to the sketch above:

1. Fit the new corrugated sheet metal.
2 Rivet seam 1 – 1 in the usual way.
3. Rivet seam 2 – 2.
4. Rivet seam 3 – 3 in the usual way.
5. Rivet seam 4 – 4 by hollow riveting.

Hollow riveting by means of a special apparatus is used whenever it is impossible to use a holding-up device, as in ordinary riveting.

Repairing Damage to Tail Surfaces.

Repairs to the metal covered tail surfaces are carried out as above. In cases of extensive damage, it is advisable to order a new part. Fabric covered surfaces are repaired in the usual way. Small slits in the sheet metal can easily be closed by means of fabric and a rubber solution or "Syndetikon."[1]

Repairing Damage to Undercarriage and Skid

Damaged undercarriages and skids are difficult to repair, and new parts should be fitted.

The machine can be propped up by means of trestles under the armoured casing.

It should be noted that the trestle under the bottom wing is only for safety against gusts of wind. Under no circumstances must the weight of the machine be borne by trestles under the wings.

1. Invented in Germany by Otto Ring in 1878, Syndetikon all-purpose glue is still manufactured. After Otto's death in 1937 the company was run by female relatives until after WWII when it was obtained by Hein Ruck and moved to Hamburg. In 1994 the technology was bought by Bettonville, NV of Belgium. It is sold in a 19th Century style tube.

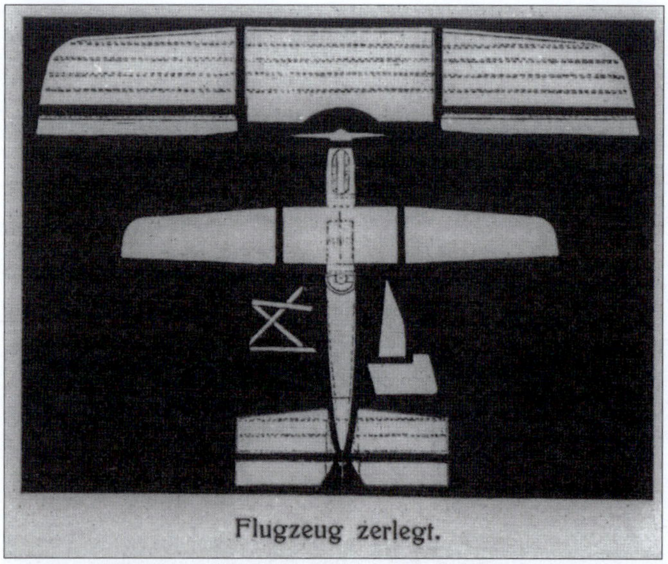

In the case of extreme damage to the undercarriage, a beam should be passed under the fuselage in front, and it necessary behind the bottom wing, and the machine gradually raised by inserting legs under these beams.

Spare Parts

The following spare parts are supplied with every machine: 1 axle, 2 undercarriage wheels without tyres, 1 skid with spring, 1 complete set of interplane struts, 1 spare propeller, 1 tail skid, 2 trestles for trestling up, 1 lifting jack, 1 case containing repairing material (light sheet metal corrugated and plain, light metal tubes of the required diameter), 1 tool-box (hollow riveting apparatus, necessary material for riveting, supply of the most necessary split pins, rivets and screws).

The apparatus for internal riveting can be obtained from the aviation park.

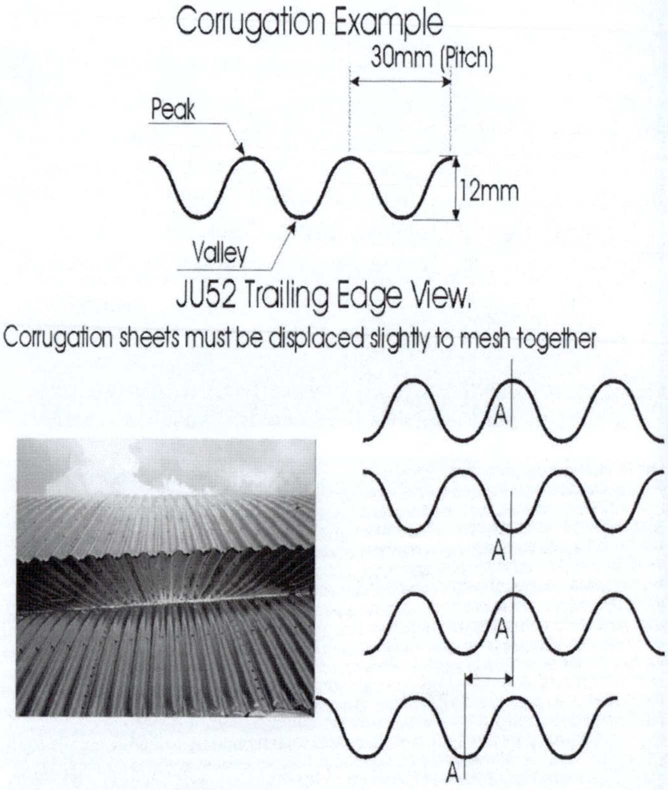

Above: This photo and sketch details the corrugated wing skin and how the skins were joined at the trailing edge of the wings. The photo is of the postwar Ju-52, but the construction of the WWI aircraft was nearly identical.

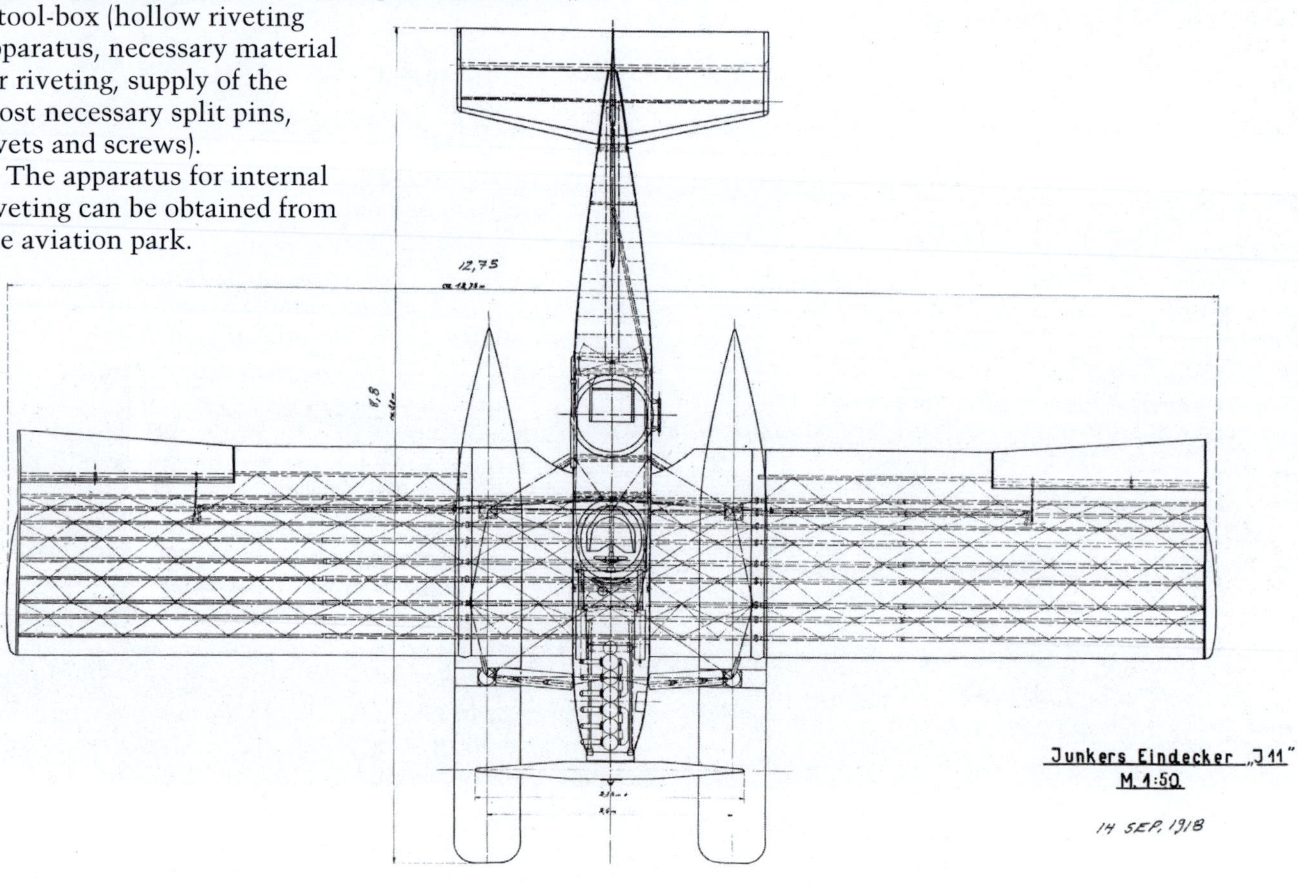

Photos from the Junkers D.I Report

J.I.
583

Junkers J.I J 143/17 in early scheme with modified crosses to the intermediate thick style. The intermediate type cross was applied over the underwing cross and was newly applied to the underside of the top wing. At the time of its demise the crosses on the top of the upper wing were still the early curved variety.

Allied Examples of Armoured and Metal Aircraft Construction

Above & Below: Wooden mock-up of the armoured shell protecting the pilot, engine, fuel tanks, etc., of the US LUSAGH-11 ground attack aircraft. It was designed due to the Allies pressing for a type to mirror the success of the German armoured aircraft.

Facing Page, Bottom: The domed top of the crew's compartment was removed when this photograph of the LUSAGH-11 was taken at McCook Field. Note the McCook Field No., P-89, on the rudder. The LUSAGH-11 was one of the ugliest aircraft of the Great War. For the full story of this aircraft see Casari, R., *American Military Aircraft 1908–1919*, Aeronaut Books, USA, 2014.

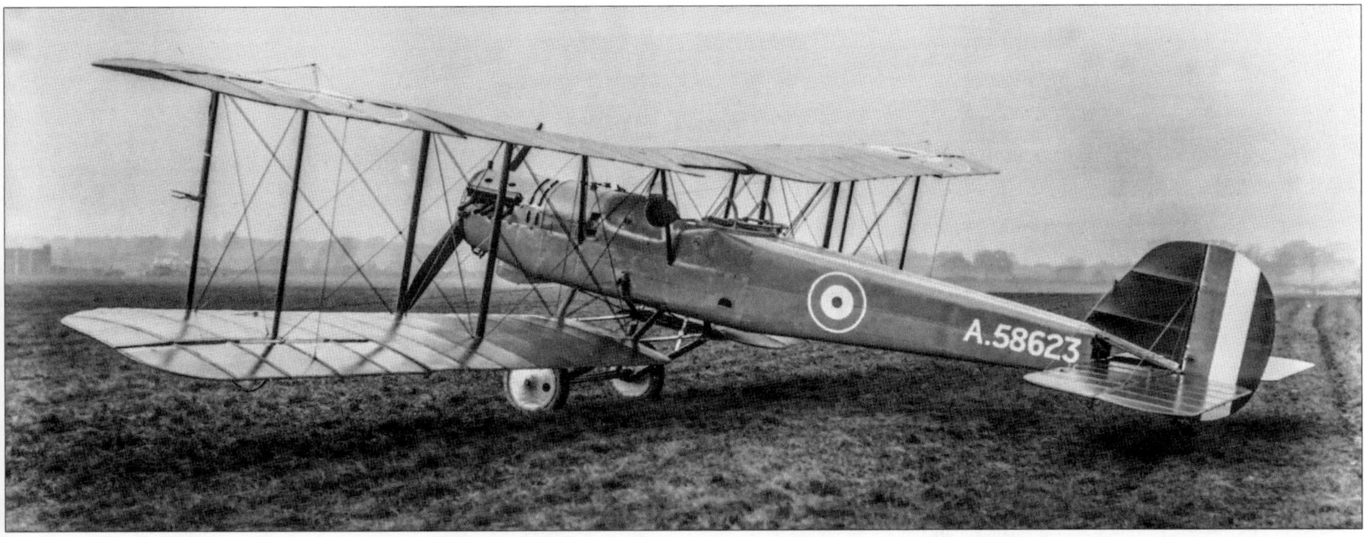

Above: Bristol M.R.1 was an attempt to build an all-metal aircraft with a monocoque fuselage but fabric covered metal wings. The wings failed to meet their strength requirements and the machine was first flown with wooden wings. For the full story of this machine see *British Aircraft of WWI, Vol.1, Experimental Fighters Part 1*, in this Centennial series.

Right: The Sopwith Salamander was a conversion of the Snipe fighter with armoured plates forming a shell for the cockpit. Its performance was such that if it had entered service it would not have been a success and an easy prey for enemy fighters.

Junkers J 9 (D.I)

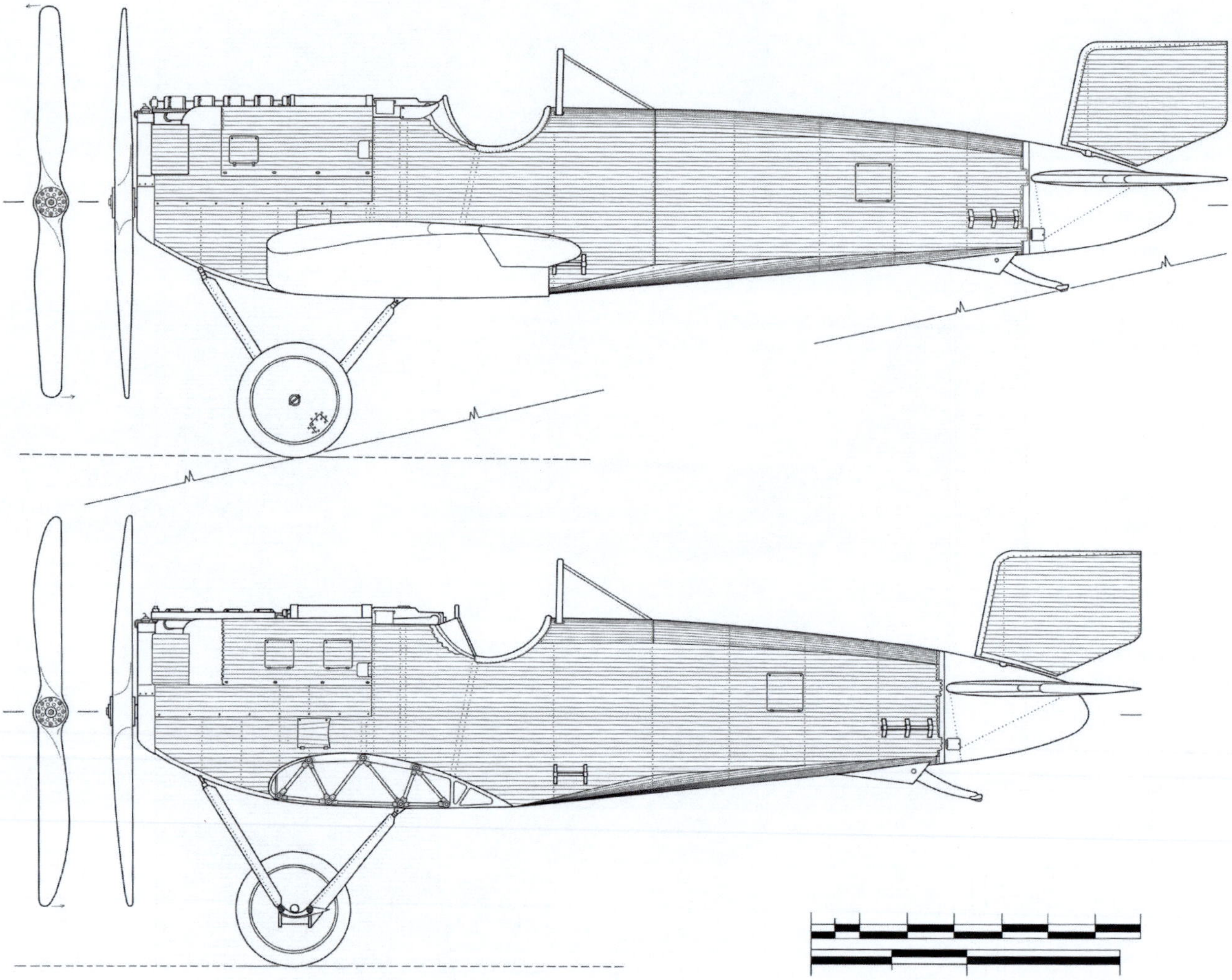

Junkers J 9 (D.I)

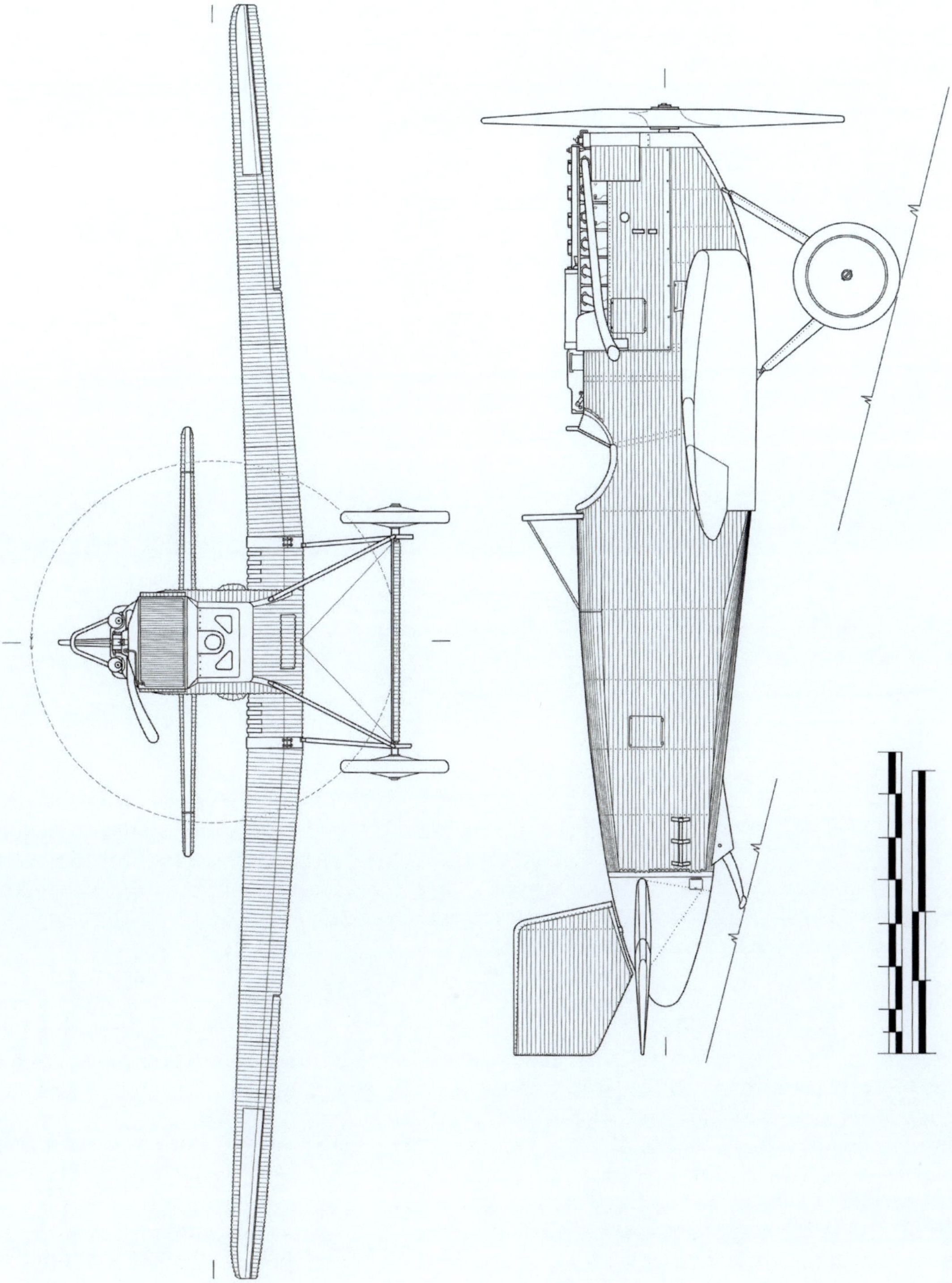

Junkers J 9 (D.I)

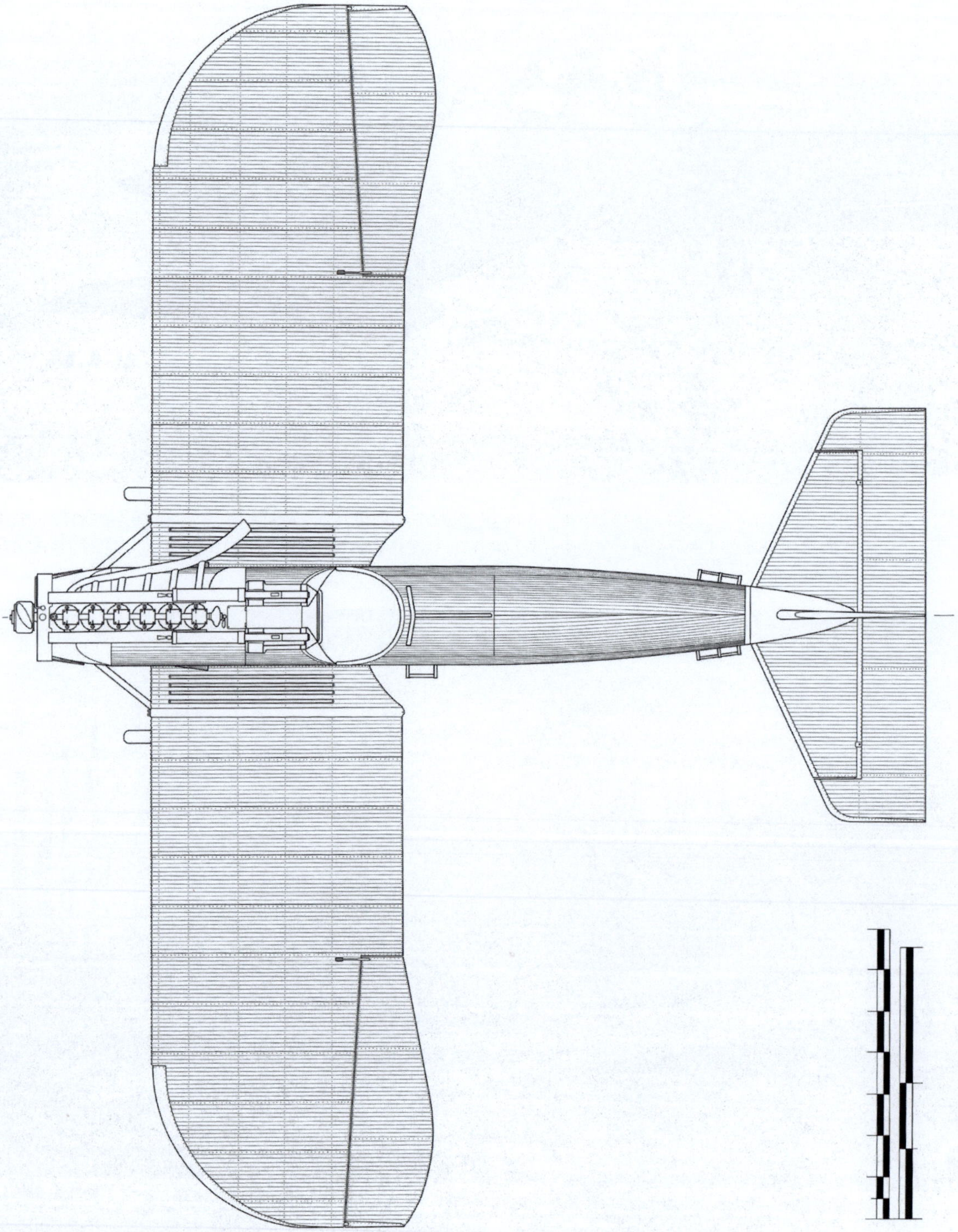

Junkers J 9 (D.I)

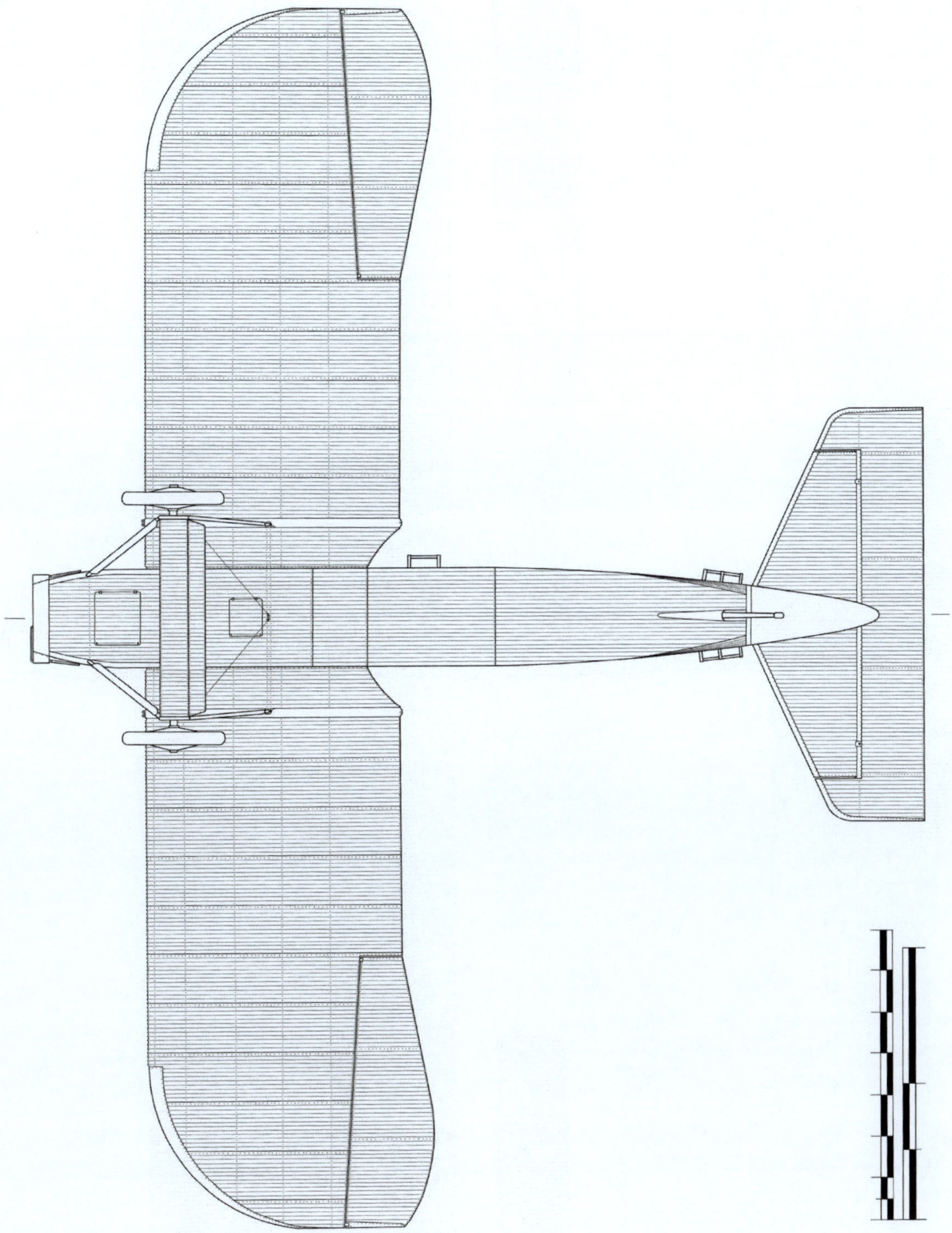

Junkers J 10 (CL.I)

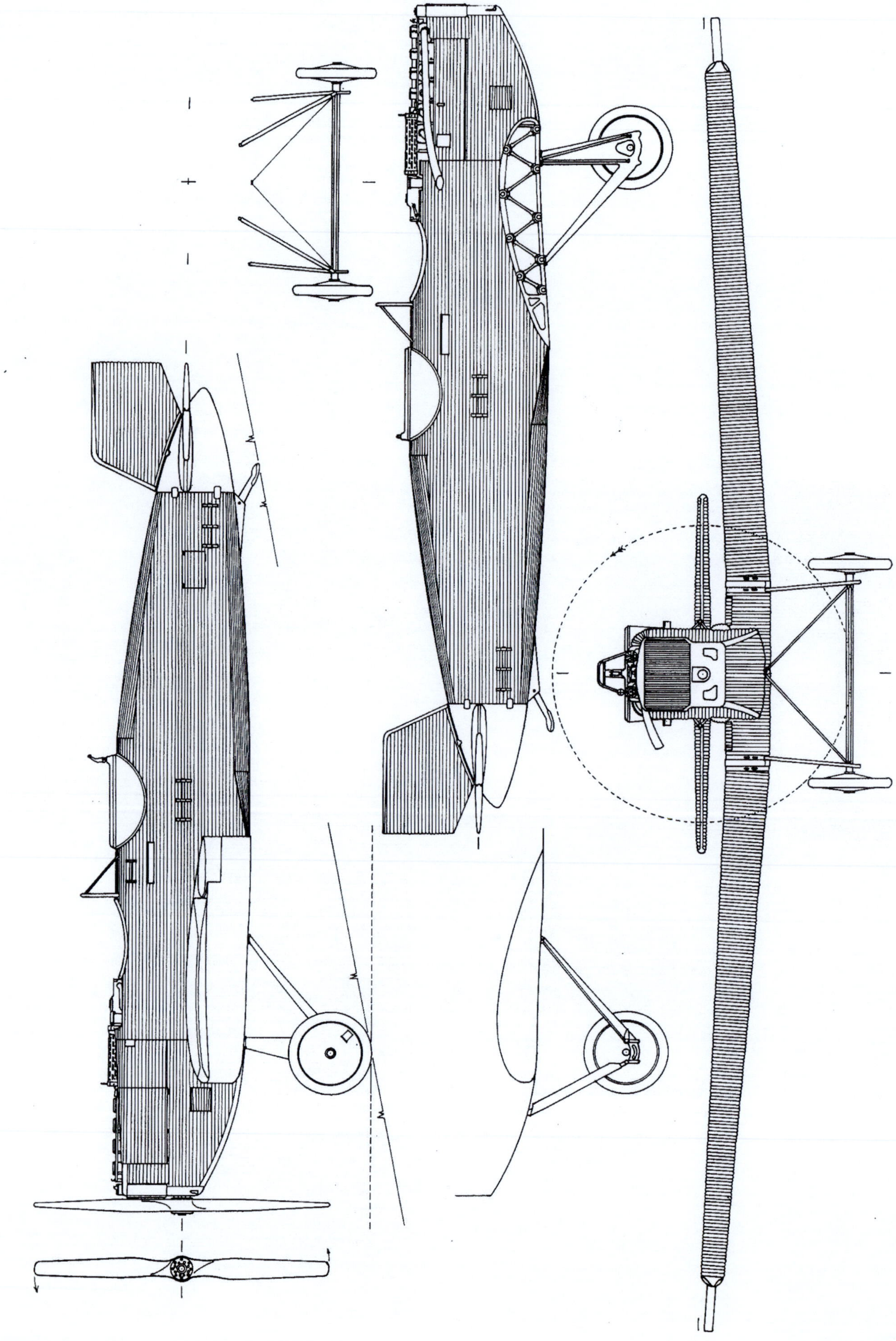

Junkers J 10 (CL.I)

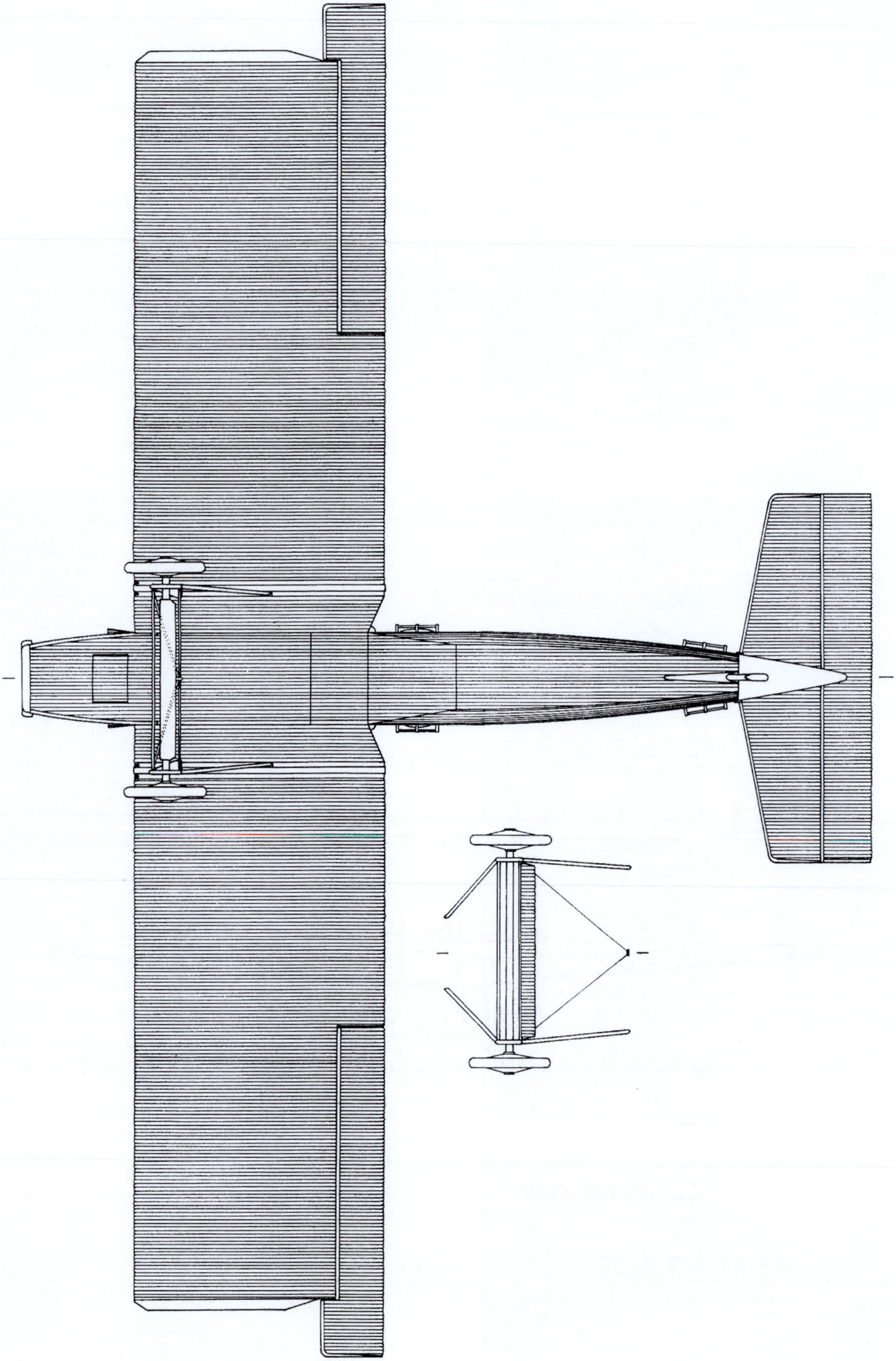

Junkers J 11 (Cs.I)

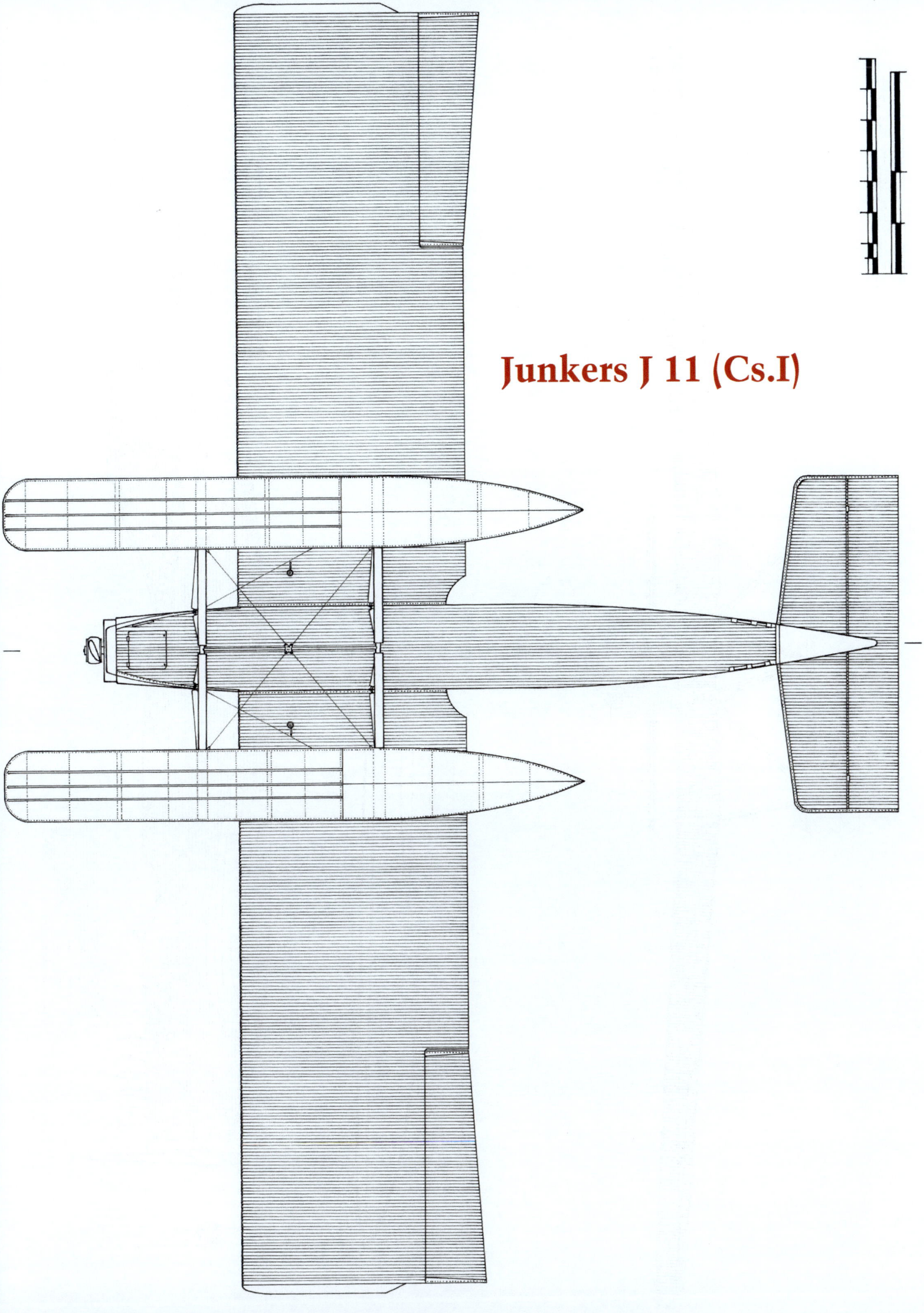

Junkers J 11 (Cs.I)

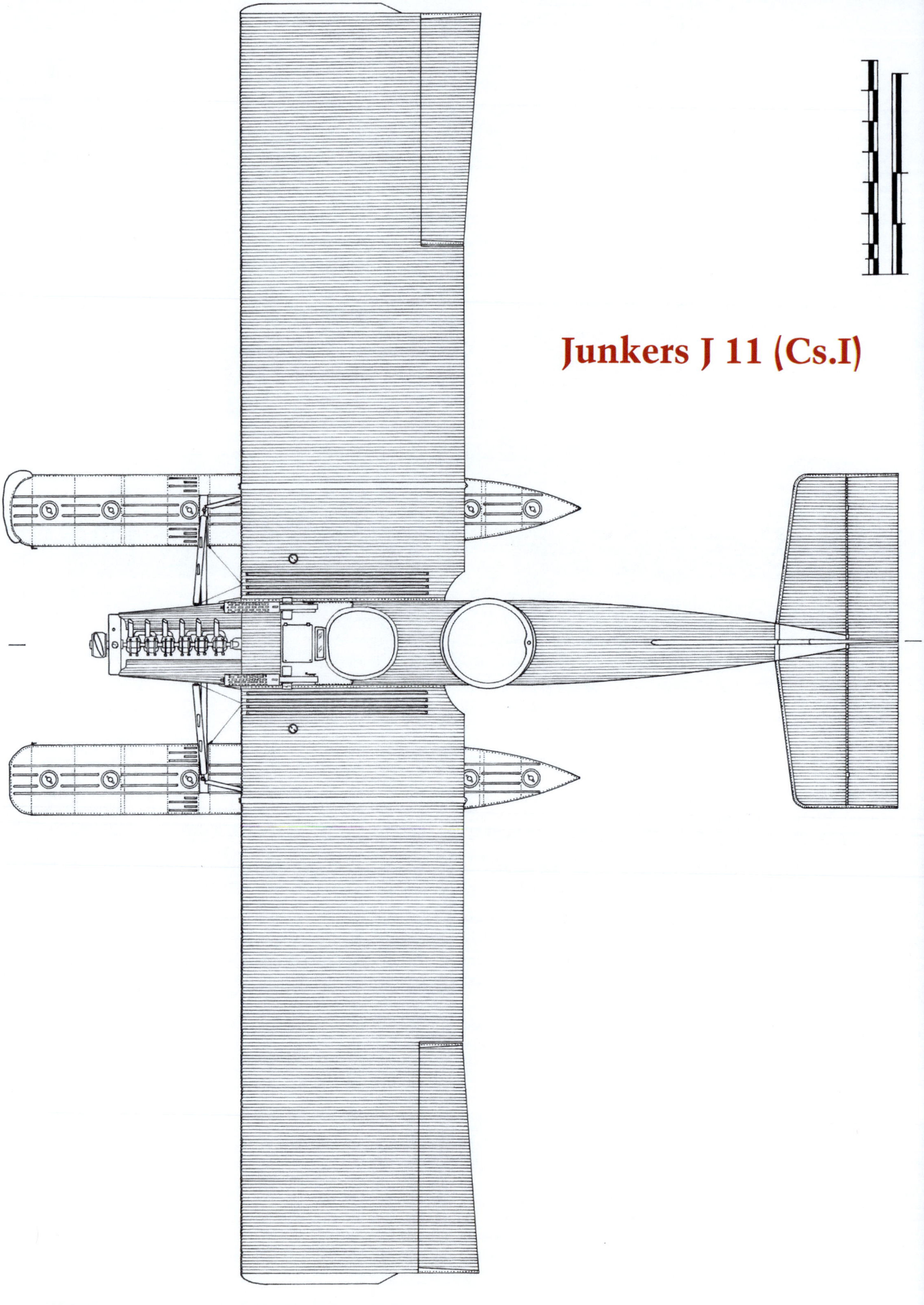

Junkers J 11 (Cs.I)

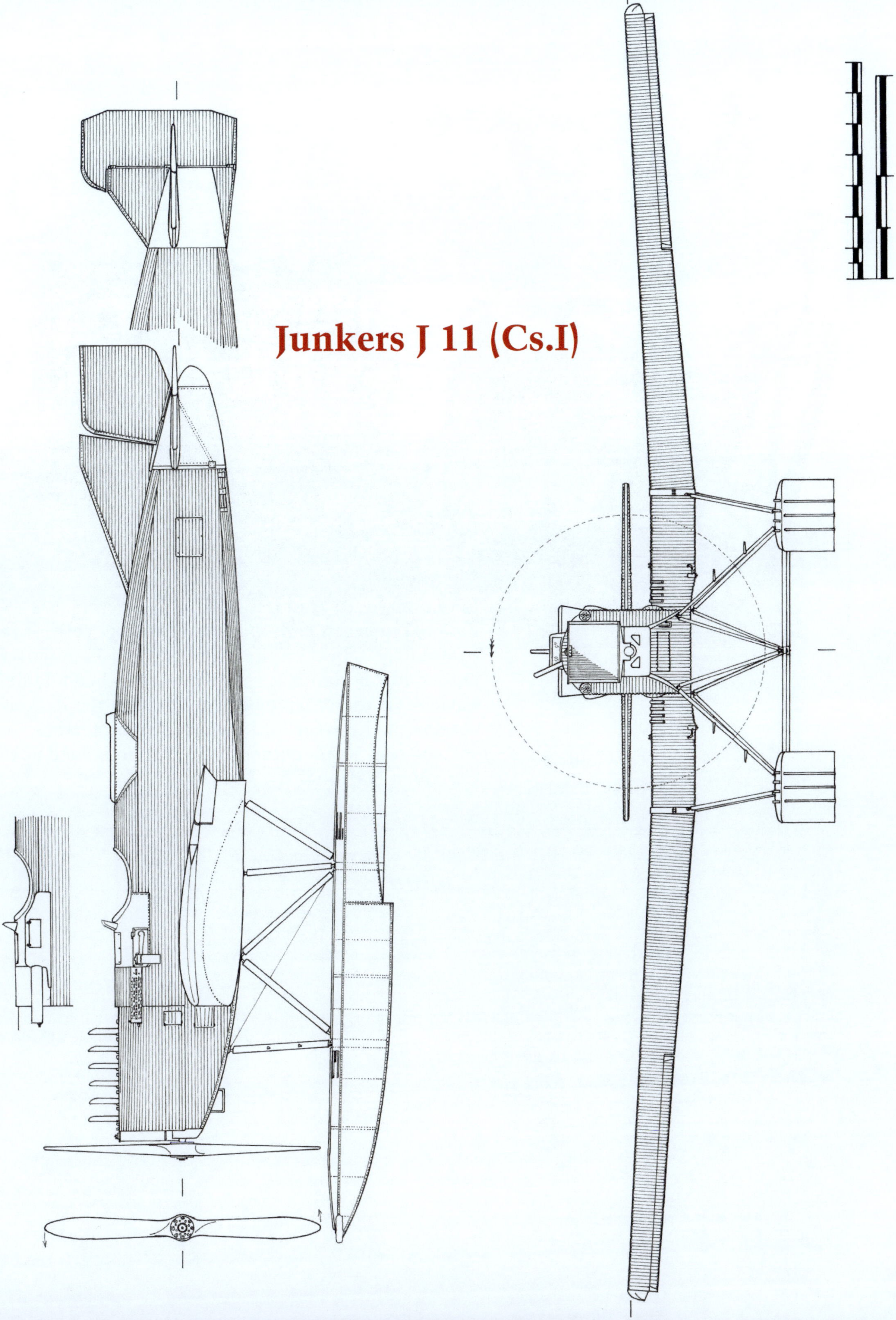

Junkers J.I 586/18

Like many late production J.I, this aircraft was finished in green and mauve camouflage with lozenge camouflage fabric on the rear fuselage. The lighter 'underside' 5-colour lozenge fabric has been depicted however it many have been covered in the darker version of the 5-colour lozenge. The underside surface was 'sand' colored. Aircraft preserved at the Canadian National Air Museum.

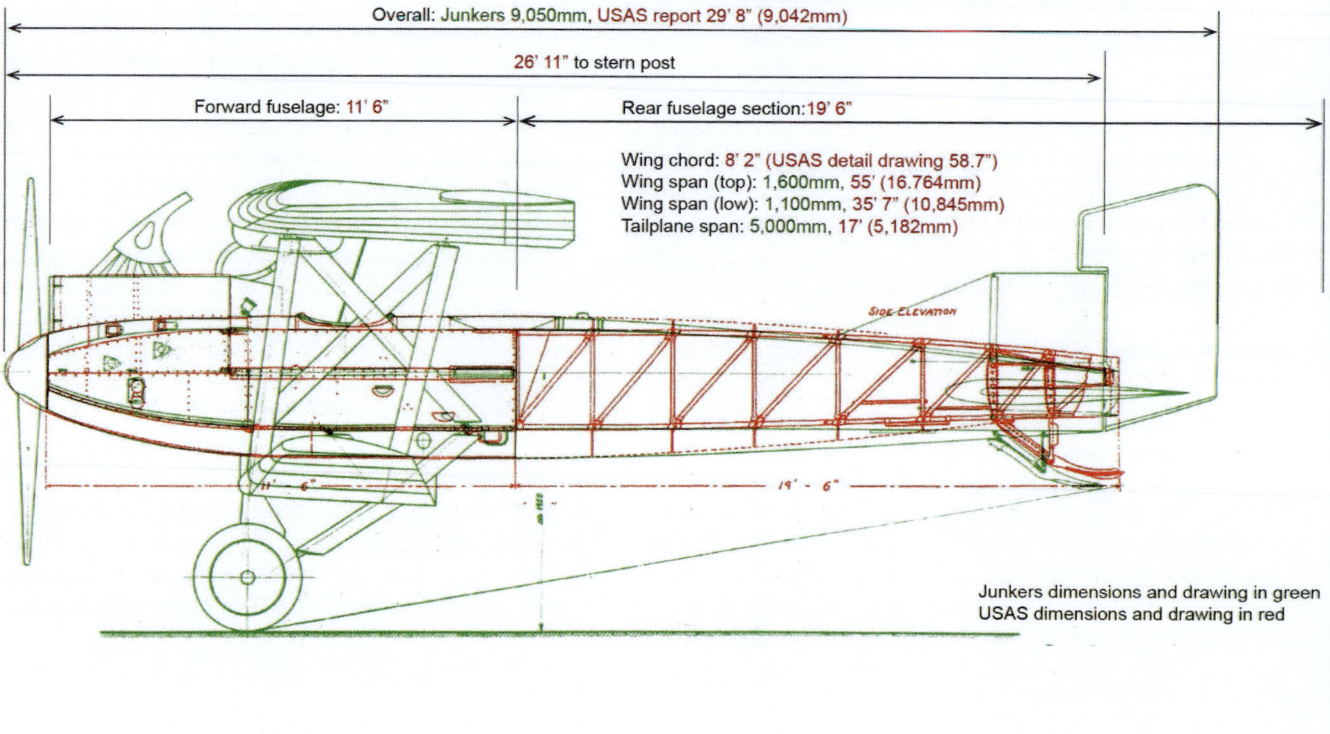

Printed in Great Britain
by Amazon

54576019R00112